Managing Reference Data in Enterprise Databases

Binding Corporate Data to the Wider World

The Morgan Kaufmann Series in Data Management Systems

Series Editor: Jim Gray, Microsoft Research

Managing Reference Data in Enterprise Databases: Binding Corporate Data to the Wider World
Malcolm Chisholm

Information Visualization in Data Mining and Knowledge Discovery
Edited by Usama Fayyad, Georges G. Grinstein, and Andreas Wierse

Data Mining: Concepts and Techniques
Jiawei Han and Micheline Kamber

Understanding SQL and Java Together: A Guide to SQLJ, JDBC, and Related Technologies
Jim Melton and Andrew Eisenberg

Database: Principles, Programming, and Performance, Second Edition
Patrick and Elizabeth O'Neil

The Object Data Standard: ODMG 3.0
Edited by R. G. G. Cattell et al.

Data on the Web: From Relations to Semistructured Data and XML
Serge Abiteboul, Peter Buneman, and Dan Suciu

Data Mining: Practical Machine Learning Tools and Techniques with Java Implementations
Ian H. Witten and Eibe Frank

Joe Celko's SQL for Smarties: Advanced SQL Programming, Second Edition
Joe Celko

Joe Celko's Data and Databases: Concepts in Practice
Joe Celko

Developing Time-Oriented Database Applications in SQL
Richard T. Snodgrass

Web Farming for the Data Warehouse
Richard D. Hackathorn

Database Modeling & Design, Third Edition
Toby J. Teorey

Management of Heterogeneous and Autonomous Database Systems
Edited by Ahmed Elmagarmid, Marek Rusinkiewicz, and Amit Sheth

Object-Relational DBMSs: Tracking the Next Great Wave, Second Edition
Michael Stonebraker and Paul Brown with Dorothy Moore

A Complete Guide to DB2 Universal Database
Don Chamberlin

Universal Database Management: A Guide to Object/Relational Technology
Cynthia Maro Saracco

Readings in Database Systems, Third Edition
Edited by Michael Stonebraker and Joseph M. Hellerstein

Understanding SQL's Stored Procedures: A Complete Guide to SQL/PSM
Jim Melton

Principles of Multimedia Database Systems
V. S. Subrahmanian

Principles of Database Query Processing for Advanced Applications
Clement T. Yu and Weiyi Meng

Advanced Database Systems
Carlo Zaniolo, Stefano Ceri, Christos Faloutsos, Richard T. Snodgrass, V. S. Subrahmanian, and Roberto Zicari

Principles of Transaction Processing
Philip A. Bernstein and Eric Newcomer

Using the New DB2: IBM's Object-Relational Database System
Don Chamberlin

Distributed Algorithms
Nancy A. Lynch

Active Database Systems: Triggers and Rules for Advanced Database Processing
Edited by Jennifer Widom and Stefano Ceri

Migrating Legacy Systems: Gateways, Interfaces, & the Incremental Approach
Michael L. Brodie and Michael Stonebraker

Atomic Transactions
Nancy Lynch, Michael Merritt, William Weihl, and Alan Fekete

Query Processing for Advanced Database Systems
Edited by Johann Christoph Freytag, David Maier, and Gottfried Vossen

Transaction Processing: Concepts and Techniques
Jim Gray and Andreas Reuter

Understanding the New SQL: A Complete Guide
Jim Melton and Alan R. Simon

Building an Object-Oriented Database System: The Story of O_2
Edited by François Bancilhon, Claude Delobel, and Paris Kanellakis

Database Transaction Models for Advanced Applications
Edited by Ahmed K. Elmagarmid

A Guide to Developing Client/Server SQL Applications
Setrag Khoshafian, Arvola Chan, Anna Wong, and Harry K. T. Wong

The Benchmark Handbook for Database and Transaction Processing Systems, Second Edition
Edited by Jim Gray

Camelot and Avalon: A Distributed Transaction Facility
Edited by Jeffrey L. Eppinger, Lily B. Mummert, and Alfred Z. Spector

Readings in Object-Oriented Database Systems
Edited by Stanley B. Zdonik and David Maier

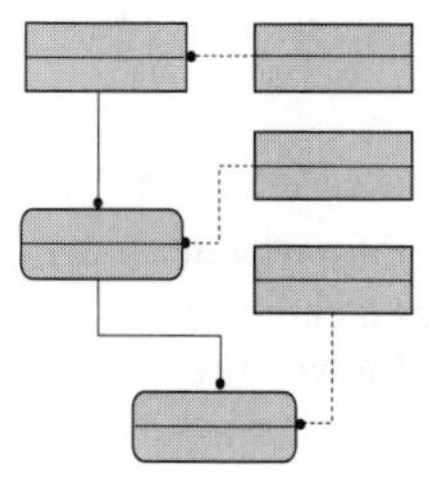

Managing Reference Data in Enterprise Databases

Binding Corporate Data to the Wider World

Malcolm Chisholm

MORGAN KAUFMANN PUBLISHERS

AN IMPRINT OF ACADEMIC PRESS

A Harcourt Science and Technology Company

SAN FRANCISCO SAN DIEGO NEW YORK BOSTON
LONDON SYDNEY TOKYO

Executive Editor	Diane Cerra
Senior Production Editor	Elisabeth Beller
Assistant Editor	Belinda Breyer
Cover Design	Ross Carron Design
Cover Image	© Stone/Art Wolfe
Production, Text Design, Composition, and Copyedit	Leyba Associates
Proofreader	Beverly Godwin
Technical Illustration	Technologies 'N Typography
Indexer	Barbara Kohl
Printer	Courier Corporation

ACADEMIC PRESS
A Harcourt Science and Technology Company
525 B Street, Suite 1900, San Diego, CA 92101-4495, USA
http://www.academicpress.com

Academic Press
Harcourt Place, 32 Jamestown Road, London, NW1 7BY, United Kingdom
http://www.academic press.com

Morgan Kaufmann Publishers
340 Pine Street, Sixth Floor, San Francisco, CA 94104-3205, USA
http://www.mkp.com

Printed in the United States of America

05 04 03 02 01 5 4 3 2 1

Library of Congress Cataloging-in-Publication Data

Chisholm, Malcolm, 1953–
Managing reference data in enterprise databases / Malcolm Chisholm.
p. cm.
Includes bibliographical references and index.
ISBN 1-55860-697-1
1. Database management. 2. Business—Data processing. I. Title.

QA76.9.D3 C45 2001
005.75'8—dc21 00-043560

This book is printed on acid-free paper.

To my wife, Rina, and our children, Kenneth, Neil, Mark, and Christopher,
for all the inspiration over the years.

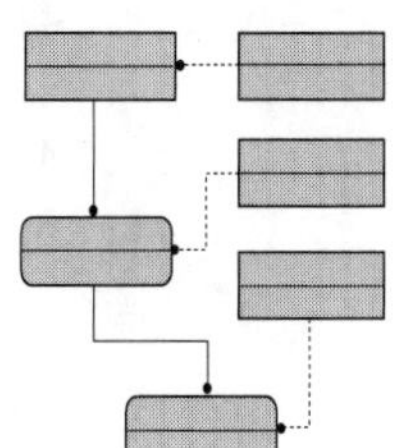

Contents

Acknowledgments

I am grateful to all my former employers who gave me the opportunity, sometimes involuntarily, to work with reference data. My first task as a junior programmer with Tube Investments at Walsall, England, was to look after many sets of little decks of punched cards called "constants." These card decks, I was informed, contained important information that was used in many mainframe jobs. I could never quite understand why a junior programmer had to look after them if they were so important, and why the information was on punched cards and not in magnetic media. Only later did I realize that I was dealing with a special class of data that really was important, but not very popular—reference data.

In most of my subsequent career I somehow stayed involved with reference data. Eventually, when I led the effort to create a corporate data model at the United Nations Development Programme, I knew enough to try to tackle reference data as a separate subject. I was given the latitude by my boss, Mr. Bob Abbott, to directly tie reference data management to the data model in our ERWin CASE tool. The fact that we could generate a reference data management system directly from a data modeling tool proved the validity of the approach.

In addition to those from my work experience, many other people have assisted with the material in this book. I am especially grateful to Anna Wadsworth of BSI for information on ISO. Diane Cerra of Morgan Kaufmann guided the development of the manuscript and arranged for reviews that greatly improved its quality. I am also grateful to Paddy Hood and Marc de Supervielle for reading the manuscript and providing their perspectives on reference data.

Most of all I am grateful to my wife and children for their patience during the time it has taken me to complete the manuscript. Reference data is not a family-oriented topic, but without their support this book would not have been possible.

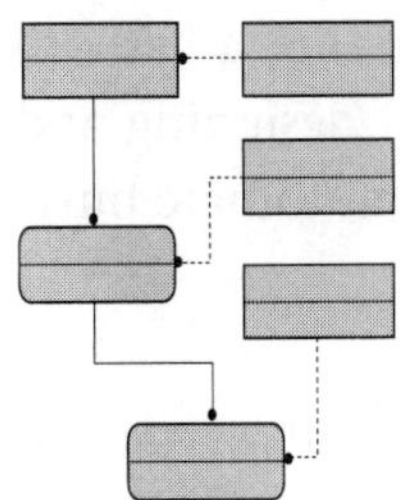

Introduction

It is no exaggeration to say that reference data is something that can be found in the database of nearly every computerized information system ever created. What is more, most information technology (IT) personnel would readily agree with this statement. Yet very few of these same IT personnel regard reference data as a distinct and important component of their systems, and in fact it is generally regarded as rather unexciting. Because of these attitudes, reference data usually ends up being neglected, even though its universal presence is a strong hint that it should be taken seriously.

Reference data is actually a mixed bag of things but is a recognizable concept even to those with little experience in the field of information systems and even to many users of information systems. A definition of reference data is given in Chapter 1, but broadly speaking it is data that is rarely updated, is retrieved often, and is not generated as part of any of the transactions that the operational systems of an enterprise are designed to handle. It can go by other names, like *lookup tables* and *constants*, and is not generally regarded by managers, analysts, and developers as something very special—and may even be viewed as a necessary nuisance which is to be gotten out of the way as quickly and easily as possible when building a system. Developers can then get down to the real business of designing and building the complex components that users need to automate business processes or deliver information on demand.

It is strange that reference data has been shown such little respect, because it has certain characteristics that predispose it to cause problems big enough to affect people's careers. Chief among these is the fact that its scope is so wide that it is typically used across many transactions that impact a database, frequently across many of the databases of an enterprise, and sometimes even beyond. Thus, if something goes wrong with it, the effects can be widespread.

On the other hand, reference data is usually contained in database tables that have a small number of columns and not many rows. This gives the impression of simplicity. Indeed, a screen to update such a table may only have a couple of fields on it—something that can perhaps be programmed in a very short time by the most junior member of a development team. So is reference data worthy of anything more than a passing thought?

This book will argue that reference data is not really simple for several reasons, including the fact that even a few reference data tables with a few rows add up to a multitude of dimensions in which the rest of the data in the database may need to be analyzed. It will also be argued that designers need to plan to use reference data at an enterprise-wide level, even within the constraints of decades-old accumulations of legacy systems and the need to get projects done quickly. And then there is the danger that reference data presents: if anything does go wrong, the effects can be widespread, and perhaps catastrophic.

Audience

The emphasis throughout this book is on how an enterprise can manage reference data. Good management of reference data is made a lot easier by good design approaches to system components that maintain and use reference data. Often these components are quite distinct (e.g., databases and programs on a variety of platforms), which means that managing reference data involves a number of disciplines within the world of information systems.

One audience for this book is anyone involved in creating and managing an enterprise's information architecture. Reference data is such an important shared resource in the overall architecture that it deserves to be addressed in its own right.

Another equally important audience is anyone engaged in building or implementing individual information systems. This includes business analysts, systems analysts, data analysts, and programmers. The book offers practical advice on a variety of issues concerned with reference data. It needs to be understood that different situations call for different designs, so different options are described and explored in terms of the requirements that may constrain a designer. However, there are some practices that are simply wrong, and some that are always right, and this book is judgmental.

While there are two audiences, it is important for each to understand the other's perspective. The strategic viewpoint of the information systems architect needs to be informed by an understanding of the special characteristics of reference data, which can only be appreciated by understanding how reference data behaves within the context of a single database or information system. Likewise, those working at the tactical level of building an individual system or database must understand the importance of the bigger picture of reference data within the enterprise as a whole.

It is also hoped that this book will serve a secondary audience of those professionals who are trying to develop conceptual frameworks and approaches that assist in the management of the increasingly diverse types of data and metadata found in modern information systems. Reference data is a common theme in these diverse database components, and it has many unique characteristics and behavior that merit a special focus.

Organization

The book begins with a general discussion of reference data. Much of the book is concerned with the representation of data in databases—after all, reference data is data. This means that data modeling has been used to represent database designs, and the IDEF1X methodology was the one chosen for this purpose, although there are several other excellent options. As not everyone may be familiar with this notation, it is reviewed in Chapter 2. Readers familiar with this subject matter will probably not find it necessary to go through this chapter in detail.

Chapters 3 through 8 explore the characteristics and behavior of reference data. These chapters provide a framework for understanding reference data, but at the same time there is a strong emphasis on practical aspects that can be useful in a variety of information systems disciplines. Chapters 9 through 14 concentrate on the many different ways in which reference data needs to be managed at a tactical level. Chapters 15 through 19 address the needs of managing reference data at the level of the enterprise's overall information systems architecture. Lastly, there are appendices containing some examples of standard types of reference data and matrices that help an organization evaluate the way in which it is managing reference data.

Visit Our Web Site

This book is, of course, a current snapshot of the world of reference data. For more up-to-date information, access to standard reference data, and access to tools for managing reference data, visit the book's Web site at *www.mkp.com/chisholm* and the companion site at *www.refdataportal.com*, which is maintained by the author and his colleagues.

CHAPTER 1

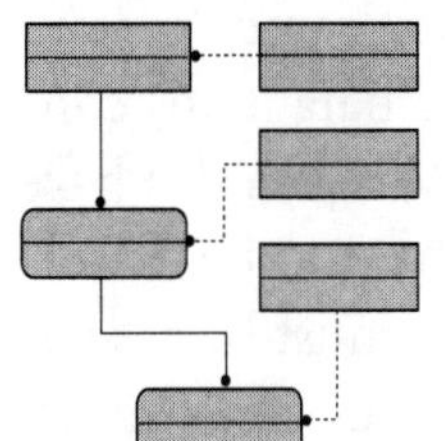

What Is Reference Data?

THE TERM *reference data* is employed widely by information systems professionals but does not seem to have a formal definition. Unfortunately, reference data can mean different things to different people, and so the issue of a definition is very important. This chapter reviews the different ways in which the term is understood and provides a definition used for the remainder of the book.

The term *reference data* has been in use for a long time, and it was commonly used when what are known today as legacy systems were very new. Many of these systems were built before relational databases were prevalent, and they were usually built to automate record-keeping processes (usually for financial records) within business organizations. Each of these systems tended to be built as an island, but it was recognized that each required certain data that was not actually maintained by the system in question. Thus at the level of an individual information system, the term reference data came to mean data that was maintained outside the system, but which needed to be read by the system. This was reference data: it was "maintained" (created, changed, and deleted) outside of systems that "read" it (copied or otherwise used it in processing, but never created, changed, or deleted it).

In those early days, many items of reference data came to have domain values (the set of valid values that exist for a data item) consisting of codes, something that is still true today. While codes have certain advantages, such as saving disk space, they have to be associated with descriptions; for example, the code "USA" must be associated with the description "United States of America." Thus much reference data came to consist of codes and corresponding descriptions. Since programs had to check the validity of codes and retrieve descriptions for outputs, reference data was often called *lookups* or *lookup tables*, terms that have persisted to this day. However, as will be shown later in this book, not all reference data consists of tables made up of codes and descriptions.

A Definition of Reference Data

Although reference data appeared early in the evolution of information systems, it has always tended to be simple in form. Typically it has comprised small sets of data—usually tables consisting of codes and descriptions, and sometimes a few other columns. Perhaps because of this structural simplicity reference data has tended to be overlooked, and it is not possible to find a precise definition of it in the literature. However, examples of reference data do have something in common. Country codes, currency codes, and industry codes are examples of data that is commonly understood to be reference data. Status codes and type codes are examples of more general types of data, which are also generally accepted as reference data. What these examples have in common is that they are used to group other kinds of data in a database, often in ways that can be used to relate an enterprise's data to the outside world.

This book defines reference data in the following way:

> *Reference data is any kind of data that is used solely to categorize other data found in a database, or solely for relating data in a database to information beyond the boundaries of the enterprise.*

Thus reference data really does not drive, or play a primary role in, the transactions that are processed within an enterprise. It exists mainly for the purpose of categorizing—that is, grouping or classifying—the transactional data. Additionally, it can "connect" the enterprise's data to information maintained by other enterprises and organizations. This definition helps in understanding why information systems typically read reference data. It also helps to understand why reference data is so often maintained by organizations distinct from the enterprises that use it, as are, for example, ISO Country and Currency codes.

The term reference data is rather unfortunate for this class of data, as it comes from a database or systems viewpoint, not an enterprise perspective. Something like *classification data* might be more descriptive. Nevertheless, reference data is the term that has been used for many years, and it is used here also.

The definition provided above is the basis for a thorough exploration of the nature of reference data in Chapters 3 and 4. However, there are other types of data that are sometimes called reference data but do not fit this definition, and they need to be briefly reviewed.

Common Data

The notion that reference data is any data a particular information system is not responsible for maintaining, but which it must use, is still quite prevalent. This is especially true for systems development staff, who tend to see things from the perspective of the system they are currently working on. This definition includes a great deal more data than the definition used for this book, since it takes an information system, not an enterprise, viewpoint.

Within an enterprise there may be many information systems that have to obtain data from other systems, for example, by file interfaces or directly reading other databases. Such data requirements may just be an accident of the way the information systems have been designed, or they may be central data that the enterprise needs to run its business. Information on customers and products are typical examples of the latter. Many businesses have created systems architectures that capture information about customer and products in a number of systems. This redundancy of data and independent maintenance functionality gives rise to many data quality problems, such as different information about the same customer being recorded in different databases. Enterprises now realize that they need to change their systems architecture so that this kind of information is maintained in only one place but is available throughout the enterprise.

Customer and product information exemplify data that a business uses to structure its transactions. For example, a transaction can occur when a customer buys a product. One customer can buy many products, and one product can be sold to many customers. Each instance of this activity represents one transaction. This kind of data differs from reference data, as defined in this book, because it is used directly as transactional data in an enterprise, whereas reference data is usually used to categorize transactional data. *Common data* is a better term for this class of data, which can be defined separately from reference data as follows:

> *Common data is data that is utilized by many information systems of an enterprise and should ideally be shared among them. From the perspective of an individual information system, common data is any data that the system requires but which is actively maintained (i.e., created, modified, and deleted) by other information system(s) in the enterprise.*

This definition implies that common data can include reference data, and this is the view within many organizations. However, common data differs from reference data in that it also includes the much more voluminous data used to structure the enterprise's transactions. An enterprise may have millions of customers (common data) living in a handful of countries (reference data). This makes the issues surrounding the management of common data quite different from those pertaining to reference data; for instance, security may be a special concern with common data but not with reference data.

Many organizations seek to tame their common data without necessarily recognizing the distinct nature of reference data. The result can be inconsistencies within strategic projects that are addressing this very important issue. We shall return to this theme in Chapter 19 where the special management requirements of reference data are contrasted with the needs of common data.

External Data

There is another kind of data, called *external data,* that shares one of the traits often found in reference data—the fact that it has its origin outside the enterprise. As organizations become more and more interested in using the information they collect as a strategic resource, they often purchase or otherwise acquire data from providers or other external sources. They import this data to augment their databases (usually data warehouses or marts) so they can perform more and/or better analyses. Such data can be information on competitors, lists of potential customers, demographic data, and so on. External data can be defined as follows:

> *External data is data created outside the enterprise, but which is imported into the enterprise's information systems.*

Just as with common data, this definition can include some kinds of reference data, and again, this is how many enterprises view external data. However, the bulk of external data usually consists of transaction data, and it is very different from reference data. Managing external data is an important issue for many organizations, with many special challenges such as data cleansing, format changes over time, and sudden changes in data granularity. These challenges are different from what is involved in managing reference data, and the two are compared in Chapter 19.

Reference Data in the Literature

The term *reference data* can be found in a number of books and articles about information systems. Sometimes there are specific definitions of the term (see, for example, [En99]), but more often it is assumed that the reader understands what is meant. In the latter case, it is often actually common data rather than reference data that is being discussed, though even this is not always clear. Therefore, the reader needs to weigh what has been written about common data in terms of its applicability to reference data and to the separate class of data used to structure an enterprise's transactions. There should be no doubt of the critical importance of transaction structuring data to every enterprise, but it is quite different from reference data.

Conclusion

We have briefly reviewed the origins of reference data and have arrived at a definition for it. This definition shows how reference data differs from other classes of data that at first glance might appear to be closely related to it. Nevertheless reference data is still a very diverse group of data types, and the real world always throws up examples that less clearly fit the definition. The various kinds of reference data are reviewed in Chapter 3, where subtle differences are carefully examined. However, before we can move to a finer level of detail, it is necessary to understand how database designs can be represented. This is because we will now be dealing with these designs at the level of tables, relationships, attributes, and keys. Chapter 2 provides an overview of the IDEF1X notation used throughout this book to represent database designs. Those readers who are familiar with this notation can skip ahead to Chapter 3, although they too may wish to take a few minutes to go through Chapter 2 and review some basic concepts.

Conclusion

CHAPTER 2

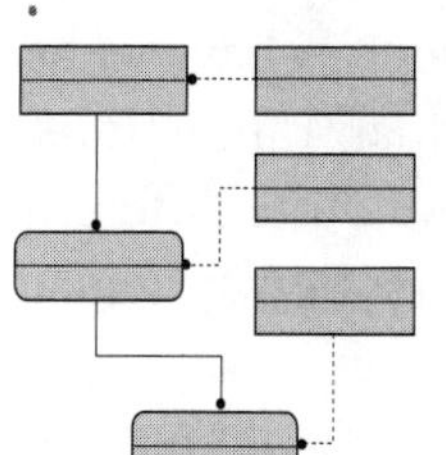

A Few Database Design Concepts

SINCE REFERENCE DATA is *data*, the way databases are designed to hold it is very important. Database design itself is a major field in information technology, and I do not intend to cover it here. However, it is necessary to review some of the methodology that the discussion in the rest of this book uses to describe databases.

Modern database design is based on concepts of relational database theory. In practice this means that each piece of information belongs in only one place in a database, that similar pieces of information are grouped together, and that these groupings may be related by sharing common pieces of information. These items of data are discovered, recorded, and structured into a design by a process called *data modeling*, which is part science and part art. It is part science because there are rules that constrain how a database should be built, and it is part art because it requires extracting complete and correct information about data from business users (not an easy task). Even so, a data modeler may produce a sound database design, only to have other parties—particularly programmers—ask for changes to improve system performance or simply to make their lives easier. Thus, the physically implemented database design may end up being different from the logical database design that better represents the structure of the enterprise's business. In addition, databases that require fast responses to queries have to be designed differently than those that process individual transactions. Hence data warehouses and data marts typically have quite different designs than the databases of more traditional information systems.

The best approaches to data modeling use visual techniques to record database design. There are a number of excellent alternatives available, and the one used in this book is IDEF1X. Again, it is not necessary to get into a detailed discussion of this methodology, but it is important to understand the basics of what it has to offer.

Attributes and Entities

The basic atomic unit of data can be called a number of things. In physical implementations of databases it can be called a *field* or *column*. In a database design, and hence in IDEF1X, it is called an *attribute*, and each attribute must have a unique definition, one different from every other attribute in the database.

Attributes can be grouped together by discovering something they have in common. They form sets, each of which is called an *entity* in a database design and is called a *table* in a physically implemented relational database. A better way of looking at this from a design viewpoint is that an entity is something of interest to the enterprise for which information has to be stored, and the different pieces of information that pertain to an entity are called *attributes*. In data modeling it is usual to first figure out what the entities are, and then the attributes that belong to them, rather than coming up with a list of attributes and trying to group them.

Entities represented in a database design are not individual instances of things, but are the information that describes these things. For instance, a bank may issue several million private label credit cards, but the information used to describe each cardholder's account is identical.

Entities are represented by boxes in IDEF1X, and attributes are lines of text within them. Figure 2.1 gives an IDEF1X example of an entity called `Credit Card Account`, which has the following attributes (of course it could have many more):

- Credit Card Account Number
- Customer Social Security Number
- Date Account Opened
- Credit Limit
- Cash Advance Limit
- Annual Fee

The name of the entity is placed just above the box in IDEF1X. Within the box there is a line that separates the attribute *Credit Card Account Number* from all the other attributes in the entity. This is because *Credit Card Account Number* is the *primary key attribute* of `Credit Card Account`. The primary key of an entity is the attribute or attributes needed to uniquely identify real-world

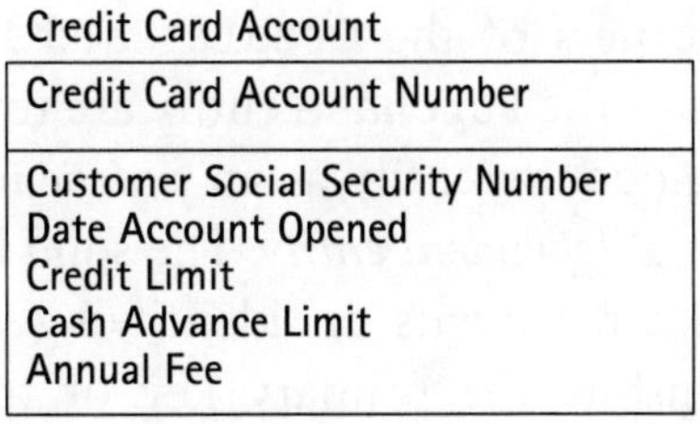

Credit Card Account

Credit Card Account Number
Customer Social Security Number Date Account Opened Credit Limit Cash Advance Limit Annual Fee

Figure 2.1 Credit Card Account entity in IDEF1X.

instances of the entity. Thus every `Credit Card Account` is identified by a *Credit Card Account Number*, which must have a different value for every `Credit Card Account` that exists. In IDEF1X the primary key attributes are shown above the line, and the non-key attributes are listed below it.

Relationships

Entities that have certain attributes in common have a *relationship*. Two kinds of relationship can be described in IDEF1X: an *identifying relationship*, and a *non-identifying relationship*. In both kinds of relationship there is a parent entity and a child entity. The parent entity may be the entity to which the attributes shared with the child primarily belong, or it may be more closely related to the entity in which these attributes primarily belong than the child is. The entity to which the attributes in question primarily belong is the entity in which these attributes are the primary key.

An identifying relationship is one where there is a child entity that cannot exist or be uniquely identified without a parent entity. Figure 2.2 shows the parent `Credit Card Account` entity with a child `Purchase` entity (by convention the singular form rather than the plural is used in entity names). The `Purchase` entity is designed to store basic information about each transaction in which the customer uses the credit card to buy something.

Notice how the corners of the `Credit Card Account` entity are square, while those of the `Purchase` entity are rounded. These mark the `Credit Card Account` entity as an *independent entity*, and the `Purchase` entity as a *dependent entity*. The solid line joining the two boxes in Figure 2.2 represents an identifying relationship. In an identifying relationship, the primary key of the parent entity is migrated into the primary key of the child entity, making the child entity a dependent entity. Thus, *Credit Card Account Number* becomes part of the primary key of `Purchase`. It has "(FK)" placed after it to indicate it is a *foreign key*, that is, it has arrived in `Purchase` as a result of a relationship to another table where it is a primary key.

The "blob" at the end of the relationship line is always on the child side, and so conveys the direction of the relationship.

The relationship has a *verb phrase* that describes the nature of the relationship. In this example it is "finances," so that we can say

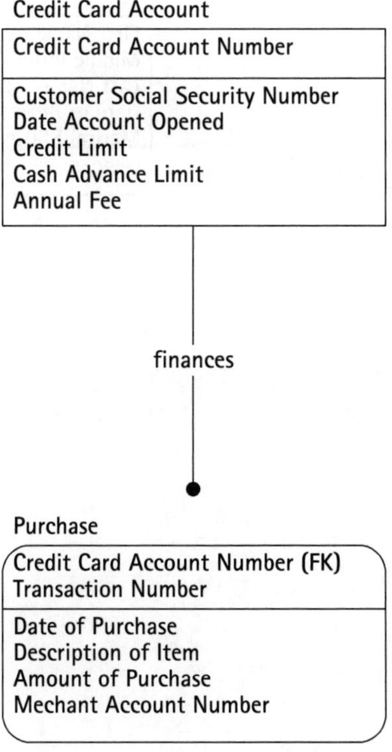

Figure 2.2 An identifying relationship.

"Credit Card Account finances Purchase." This describes the relationship from the viewpoint of the parent entity. It is also possible to describe the relationship from the viewpoint of the child entity, as in "Purchase is financed by Credit Card Account." It is more common to show only the verb phrase describing the parent-to-child view of the relationship on a data model.

It is not easy for data modelers to formulate accurate and precise verb phrases to describe relationships, and they sometimes fall back on more generic statements like "has" and "belongs to," which do not convey the real nature of the relationship being documented.

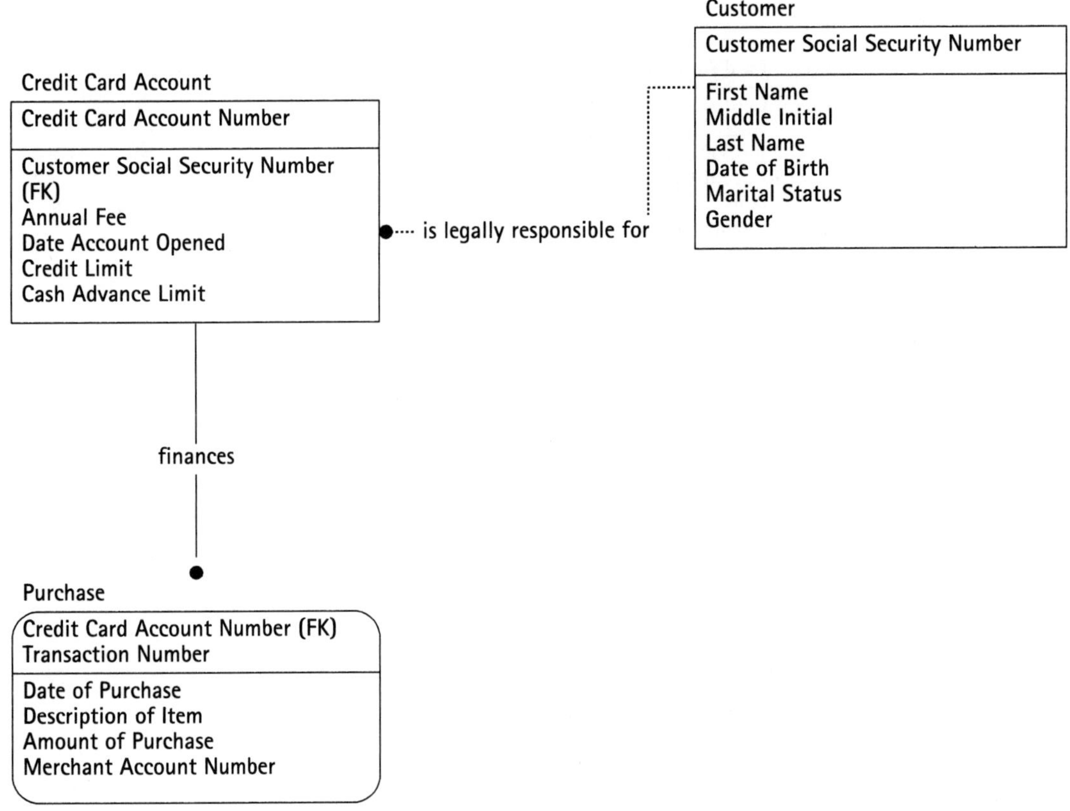

Figure 2.3 A non-identifying relationship.

A non-identifying relationship is similar to an identifying relationship, except that the child entity does not need to be identified by the parent, so the migrated foreign key goes into the non-key child attributes. Figure 2.3 shows a non-identifying relationship between `Customer` and `Credit Card Account`. This time the relationship line between `Customer` and `Order` is dashed instead of solid.

Relationships also have a property called *cardinality.* This specifies the number of instances of entities possible in the relationship. The related property of *optionality* specifies whether the parent, the child, or both must be present in the relationship. In an identifying relationship there must be at least one instance of the parent entity. If there is only a blob at the end of the relationship line, this means that there can be zero or more child entities. Other cardinalities/optionalities that may apply to the child are *one or more, zero or one,* and *exactly* N. These are represented by the letters P, Z, and N, respectively, placed next to the blob. On the parent size there is either *one* or *zero to one.* In the case of *zero to one* the relationship line ends in a diamond on the parent side.

Subtype Relationships

Another important concept implemented in IDEF1X is the subtype relationship. This models a situation where an entity exists as a number of categories, all somewhat different in terms of the non-key attributes they can contain. Figure 2.4 further refines the example in Figure 2.3.

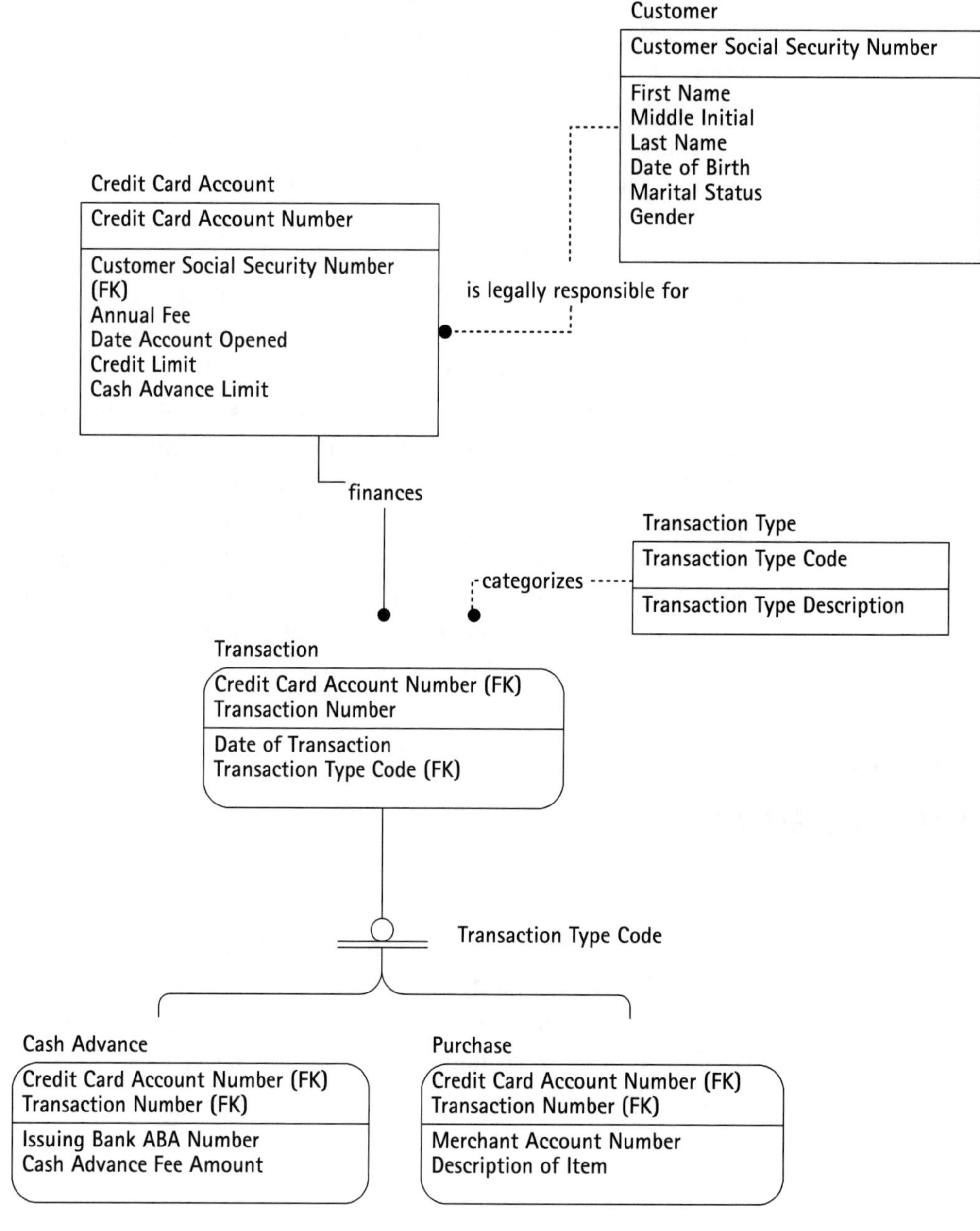

Figure 2.4 A subtype relationship.

A `Credit Card Account` now finances a `Transaction`, which can either be a `Cash Advance` or a `Purchase`. `Transaction` is called the *supertype* and contains the attributes that all *subtypes* (i.e., `Cash Advance` and `Purchase`) have in common. The subtypes have exactly the same primary key attributes as the supertype, and contain non-key attributes that are not shared with other subtypes. Thus `Purchase` has *Merchant Account Number* and *Description of Item*, attributes that apply only to purchases. Likewise, `Cash Advance` has the unique attributes *Issuing Bank ABA Number* and *Cash Advance Fee Amount.*

Figure 2.4 shows the *category* symbol—the circle with the two lines underneath—which indicates we are dealing with a subtype relationship. There has to be an attribute in the supertype to distinguish between the different subtypes. This attribute is called a *category discriminator*, and in Figure 2.4 it is *Transaction Type Code.* It is listed next to the category symbol. This attribute comes from the entity `Transaction Type` where it is the primary key, and this entity is linked to the `Transaction` entity by a non-identifying relationship. In all subtypes there is a similar situation—a category discriminator that comes from a related table.

Conclusion

This brief tour of the IDEF1X has only touched on the basic components of the methodology needed to provide a framework for the discussion of reference data. For those who wish to know more—and there is a great deal more to know—a complete treatment can be found in *Designing Quality Databases with IDEF1X Information Models* by Tom Bruce [Br92]. As noted at the beginning of this chapter, there are other methodologies for representing database designs, and it is not intended to suggest that IDEF1X is better than any other methodology. It is simply the one that is used to represent database designs in this book.

Conclusion

CHAPTER 3

The Diversity of Reference Data

IN CHAPTER 1 we defined reference data as follows:

> *Reference data is any kind of data that is used solely to categorize other data found in a database, or solely for relating data in a database to information beyond the boundaries of the enterprise.*

However, the different kinds of reference data that fall under this definition are actually quite diverse. In this chapter we review them, paying special attention to their unique features. Many of these kinds of reference data will be familiar to professionals involved in systems development, especially database design. Ultimately we shall visit the boundaries of what can be considered reference data. This survey is one step toward gaining an understanding of how to manage reference data, but it also highlights the fact that, within reference data as a general class of data, there are specific subclasses that have their own distinct characteristics and management needs.

Referencing the World beyond the Enterprise with Codes and Descriptions

The use of short codes to represent long descriptive texts in databases is perhaps the most familiar of all the ways in which reference data is implemented. However, it is not often that information systems professionals reflect on what this data represents. There are two interesting facts that stand out about it:

- The things being represented are often completely independent of the enterprise.
- Codes are used to represent these things.

The first of these points is more interesting from a business viewpoint, while the second is more interesting from an implementation perspective. Let us consider the business viewpoint first.

Enterprises process transactions through their information systems which represent the work that the enterprise does. These transactions contain information about things that the enterprise owns or controls, such as products, and things that are external to the enterprise but have some special relationship with it, such as customers. Yet the enterprise exists within the context of a wider world, where geography, currencies, languages, governments, associations of people and organizations, units of measurement, legal constraints, regulatory requirements, generally understood groupings, and the like also exist. The enterprise has no control over such elements, and yet there is a need to analyze the enterprise's data in terms of them. This analysis may be for the enterprise's own understanding of its activities, or it could be for other reasons, such as regulatory reporting.

What is interesting is that the things that are important here are those that lie outside the enterprise. The term *things* implies *entities* to the database designer, and these ultimately translate into tables in a database. An entity is anything about which the enterprise needs to store information. Obviously the most interesting entities to an enterprise are those that are intimately connected to its business, such as its customers, employees, products, orders, and order items. These entities are so interesting to enterprises that many facts are stored about them. Facts about entities are *attributes* to the database designer, and these ultimately translate into columns (also called fields) in a database.

However, the reference data used to group or categorize the enterprise's data is usually only interesting to the enterprise in terms of its use for grouping and categorizing. Hence the enterprise does not want to store many facts about it—indeed the enterprise is usually only interested in the bare minimum of information about reference data. The absolute minimum information that can be stored for any entity is the *primary key* of the entity, which is the attribute or attributes that uniquely identify instances of the entity, and this in turn means the names of these instances. For example, in the case of `Country`, the name of the country would be used; in the case of `Currency`, the name of the currency, and so on.

Unfortunately it is often inconvenient to deal with long names in information systems, and so codes are nearly always used to represent them. Let us look a little more closely at how codes are used.

In general, coded values represent a design solution arising from the need to manage a set of related descriptions (a domain of values) that has to be included in a database. For instance, a global business will have to deal with many countries and will need a list of them. The list could be implemented as a table with a single column consisting solely of proper country names, as in Table 3.1.

Table 3.1 Table of country names.

Afghanistan
Albania
Algeria
Andorra
Angola
Anguilla

No experienced database designer would ever actually do this. Rather, the designer would create a short code to represent each country name, as shown in Table 3.2.

There are a number of benefits to this design:

- The code takes up much less space than the name (description), which can be long (e.g., "Lao People's Democratic Republic"). If many tables need to incorporate country as a column (e.g., all the tables that store addresses), then using the proper descriptive name will use up a lot of space in the database. There may also be restrictions on the length of an index key in certain database platforms, and using long names in compound key expressions could quickly exceed these limits.

Table 3.2 Table of country codes and names.

Code	Description
AFG	Afghanistan
ALB	Albania
AND	Andorra
ANG	Angola
ANL	Anguilla

- If users ever had to type in the name of the country to perform a task against the database, they would quickly get upset. Prior to the more modern graphical user interfaces (GUIs), which have components where users can select items from lists (such as combo boxes and list boxes), it was common for users to type coded values into data entry screens; these codes had to be kept as short as possible to prevent the users from becoming frustrated.

- Typing in long names increases the chances of making spelling mistakes, which a system can be programmed to catch, but which still adds to user frustration.

- Separating code and description makes change easier. If a spelling mistake were found in the description, it would be a tiresome task to comb through the database (and perhaps archived data) to change the description in every table where it occurred. Using a code as a surrogate for a description that exists as one row in one table makes this much more manageable. More often these kinds of changes occur for valid reasons, and not as a result of errors. For example, in our `Country` table the description for "YUG" could have changed from "Yugoslavia" to "Yugoslavia, Former Republic of."

  Change can occur in other ways. Suppose we are faced with a country whose name is much longer than the width of the column will allow. Again it is much easier to increase the column width in one table than in many.

Using codes to represent descriptions is practiced so universally that it is rare to find long texts outside of reference data tables. When it does exist, it tends to be freeform text that is unique to a single instance of a transaction, such as some kind of title or comment.

Very often tables of codes and descriptions contain only two columns: one for the code and the other for the description. As we shall see later, while there can be additional columns, a small number of columns is more typical of reference data tables.

Type Codes

Type codes are special cases of codes and descriptions used to distinguish subtypes in database designs. They are also called category discriminators and were briefly discussed in the section on subtypes in Chapter 2.

Subtypes are used when a database table contains information about a set of categories. In such cases the best design is to separate the unique information about each category into a separate table, and place the information common to all categories in a parent table.

Consider the database design fragment shown in Figure 3.1. It shows the `Employee Position` table for an organization that classifies all its employee positions as either administrative or professional. The correct database design is to create an `Employee Position` table, with a primary key of *Employee Position Id*, and two additional tables: `Administrative Employee Position` and `Professional Employee Position`. The data attributes that are common to all employee positions are placed in the `Employee Position` table; those unique to administrative employee positions are placed in the `Administrative Employee Position` table. Similarly attributes unique to professional employee positions are placed in the `Professional Employee Position` table. All three tables have *Employee Position Id* as the primary key, and `Administrative Employee Position` and `Professional Employee Position` are said to be *subtypes* of `Employee Position`.

A data attribute in the `Employee Position` table is needed to indicate if a given employee position is administrative or professional, and this is supplied by the `Employee Position Type` reference table, which contains two records, as shown in Table 3.3.

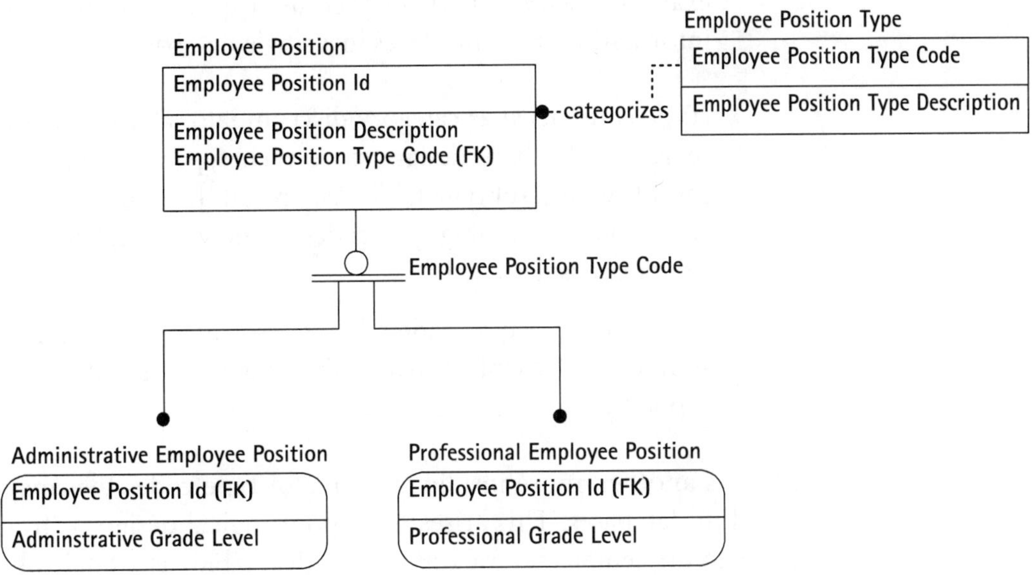

Figure 3.1 The use of Type Codes.

There is something unique about reference data used in this way:

- Type codes used as category discriminators have a relationship with only one table in a database design and cannot exist independently of this table. By contrast, other kinds of reference data may be used in many tables of a database; for

Table 3.3 Employee Position Type table.

Employee Position Type Code	Employee Position Type Description
A	Administrative
P	Professional

example, *Country Code* may be used in address or location information in many places in a single database.

- Type codes used as category discriminators have values that represent database design, since each separate value corresponds with a subtype table. As a result, the data that populates tables containing type codes is known completely when a database is designed.
- Each row in a type code table is associated with a different subtype table. Unfortunately this metadata is not captured explicitly in data modeling tools.

There is another, more insidious source of type codes that may be found in databases. This arises from poor logical design or from a desire to implement several different logical tables as a single physical table. Such denormalization, whether by design or accident, inevitably results in the need to distinguish among different "things" held in a single table. How can this be done? By introducing a type code. Thus in any database design where a type code exists in a table that does not have subtypes, denormalization can be suspected.

Many computerized databases are cursed with tables containing "record type" or something analogous. The consequences of this design are dealt with in more detail in Chapter 12.

One final point about type codes is that the term *type code*, though not a formal term in database design, is nearly always used in the names of attributes that are category discriminators. Sometimes only the word *type* is used, but it is obvious that a code and not a description or something else is meant. Designers seem to have a limited vocabulary when dealing with subtypes, so the words *type* and *type code* can be relied upon to mean that subtypes are nearby, even if they are hidden in denormalized tables.

Status Codes

Another specialized kind of reference data table holds status codes and descriptions. The word *status* is usually used to designate a state of a transaction. This is not always the case, and the term can be applied loosely to other kinds of reference data. Most often, however, status codes track the life cycle of an entity. Unfortunately entity life cycles are not distinctly modeled in IDEF1X notation, nor in many of the other commonly used data modeling methodologies.

A transaction often passes through several distinct states. Consider an order for a product. Table 3.4 illustrates the steps that might be involved.

Each of these steps also describes the status of the order at a particular point in time. Since most transactions consist of a flow of events, it is not surprising that many of them are described by special statuses. These statuses are placed in reference data tables, where the columns consist of a code and a description. Table 3.5 illustrates the values for the *Order Status* that could be used to describe the steps in Table 3.4.

Table 3.4 Steps in processing an order transaction.

Sequence	Transaction Step
1	Order is placed
2	Payment is received
3	Payment clears
4	Order is shipped to customer
5	Order is received by customer

Table 3.5 Status values for an order transaction.

Sequence	Transaction Step	Order Status
1	Order is placed	Order Opened
2	Payment is received	Payment Received
3	Payment clears	Payment Cleared
4	Order is shipped to customer	Order Shipped
5	Order is received by customer	Order Received

Table 3.6 Status changes for an order transaction.

Sequence	Transaction Step	Order Status	Date
1	Order is placed	Order Opened	5 Jan
2	Payment is received	Payment Received	8 Jan
3	Payment clears	Payment Cleared	10 Jan
4	Order is shipped to customer	Order Shipped	11 Jan
5	Order is received by customer	Order Received	14 Jan

However, there is something special about status: it is updated when a transaction changes its state, and this is done at a particular point in time. Consider again the example of an order being processed, this time with dates on which each step occurs, as illustrated in Table 3.6.

On 9 Jan the transaction is in the status "Payment Received." If there is a requirement for the transaction to record its current status then it is only necessary that the status be captured with the transaction; for example, there could be an *Order Status* column in the `Order` table. However, if on 15 Jan someone asks, "What was the status of the transaction on 9 Jan?" no answer can be given because only the *current* status is recorded on the transaction record, and that was set to "Order Received" on 14 Jan. The database design that gives rise to this problem is illustrated in Figure 3.2. This is a common problem in transaction-based systems: it is

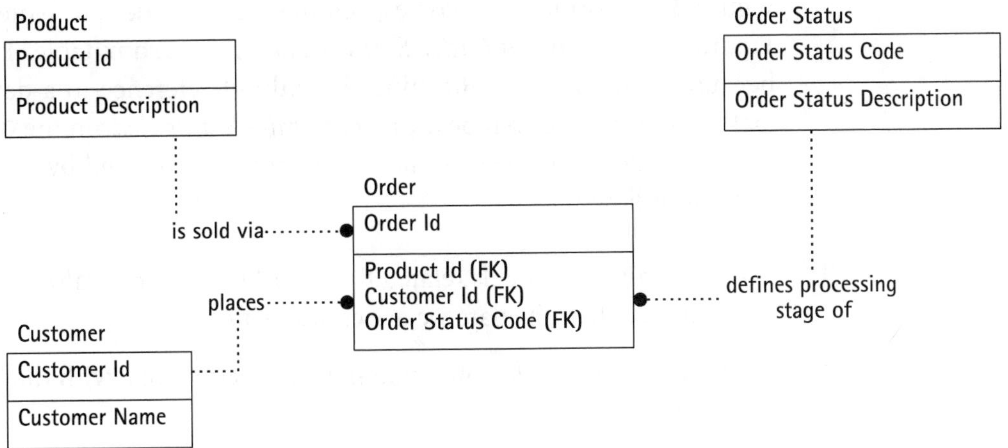

Figure 3.2 Database design using "current" Status Code.

impossible to report on transaction status from a historical viewpoint because only current status is recorded.

In reality each change in status is associated with a different date (or datetime) attribute. Thus when the status changes, the corresponding date attribute is given a value. Table 3.7 illustrates the date attributes that may be associated with the different order statuses in our example.

Table 3.7 Status changes for an order transaction.

Sequence	Transaction Step	Order Status	Date	Date Attribute
1	Order is placed	Order Opened	5 Jan	Order Opened Date
2	Payment is received	Payment Received	8 Jan	Payment Received Date
3	Payment clears	Payment Cleared	10 Jan	Payment Cleared Date
4	Order is shipped to customer	Order Shipped	11 Jan	Order Shipped Date
5	Order is received by customer	Order Received	14 Jan	Order Received Date

Figure 3.3 illustrates the corresponding database design. Note that Figure 3.3 has *Current Order Status Code* in the `Order` table. This is because *Order Status* is meaningless without reference to a date. In fact there need not even be a *Current Order Status Code* in the `Order` table. Instead the value of *Order Status* could be derived by an algorithm as follows:

(a) Determine date fields related to Order Status whose value is equal to or less than the date we are considering.

(b) From the date fields obtained in (a), select the one with the highest value.

(c) Select the *Order Status Description* associated with the date field selected in (b).

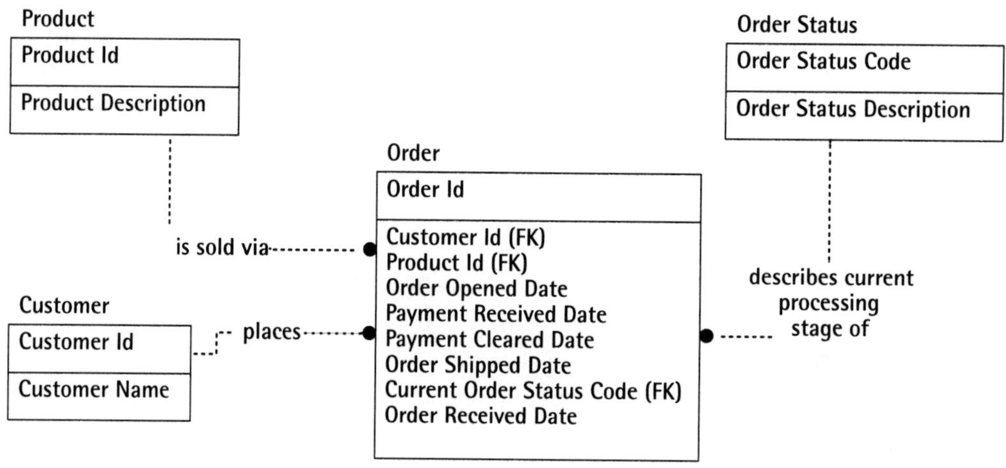

Figure 3.3 Database design incorporating dates to record change of status.

Completely removing the relationship between `Order Status` and `Order` in Figure 3.3 might seem anathema to many data modelers, but the fact is that the value of *Order Status Code* always depends on the reference date supplied by a user when performing a query. Most data modeling tools do not support the linking of two tables via this kind of business rule instead of an identifying or non-identifying relationship.

However, even the design shown in Figure 3.3 may not be flexible enough in all circumstances. Suppose some `Orders` do not flow in a nice linear manner through the statuses shown in Table 3.7. For instance, a damaged order could be returned by a customer and a new one might have to be shipped out. This implies that the `Order Status` is reset to "Order is shipped to customer." The design lacks flexibility because it requires a database change if new statuses are introduced. Suppose the business wanted to introduce a new status of "Order rejected by customer." A new date field would have to be added to the `Order` table in Figure 3.3, as well as a new record to the `Order Status` table. Figure 3.4 shows a more flexible way of handling complex status life cycles and the introduction of new statuses.

The design in Figure 3.4 has been improved by the addition of a new entity called `Order State`. This entity can record all the changes of `Order Status` that can happen to an `Order`—the entire history can be captured by the entity. Note that it has the attribute *Order Status Datetime* as part of its primary key. This allows for the inclusion of multiple records with the same status for a given item (so an item can cycle through the same statuses more than once). These records can also be for the same day (which would not be possible if the attribute were only for date and not datetime). The denormalized attribute *Current Order Status Code* has been retained in `Order`. It is still calculated by the same algorithm as described earlier. However, there is considerably less need for it now since current status can be derived by finding the record with the latest date in `Order State`.

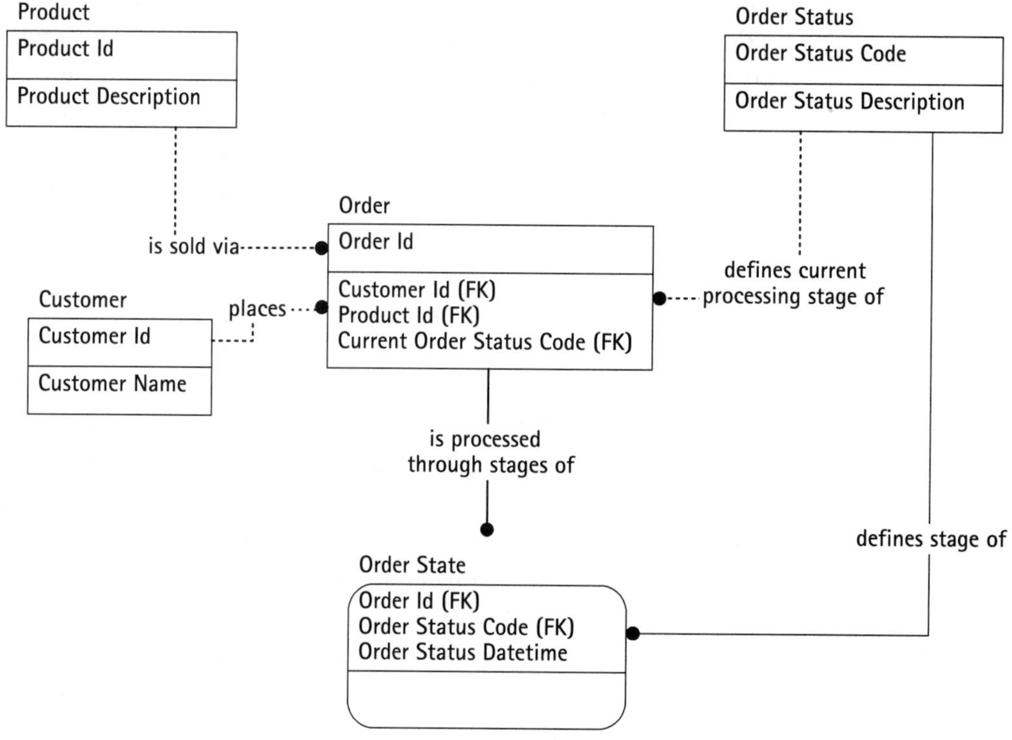

Figure 3.4 The introduction of the Order State entity.

The design shown in Figure 3.4 is also flexible enough to permit the addition of future anticipated states. This would require that extra columns be added to `Order State`, so an actual datetime can be distinguished from a predicted, or expected one. Forecasting future states can be an important consideration when dealing with entities that change their state over time (i.e., entity life cycles), and designers should bear this in mind.

There is usually important business logic controlling how an entity proceeds through different statuses in its life cycle. For instance, there may be a business rule that prohibits an `Order` from being shipped until it has been fully paid for. Thus the actual values of status codes become used in business rule logic. This in turn means that changing or deleting the values of these status codes can have major consequences, and their meaning also has to be communicated effectively to those responsible for the analysis and implementation of the business rules.

Status codes share something in common with type codes: they apply (or should apply) to only one entity. Just as type codes defined the subtyping of a single entity, status codes should define the life cycle of a single entity. It is reasonable to say that if a status code reference data table is used to constrain the life cycles of two or more entities in a database design, there may well be a design problem.

Constant Values

So far we have been discussing character data where descriptions are represented by codes. However, reference data can exist as datatypes such as numbers or dates. These can be called by a variety of names, but here they are referred to as *constant values* because they typically change very slowly.

Tax rates are a good example of numeric reference data. For example, the 2000 New Jersey state sales tax is 6%, except in some localities where it is 3%, and it has been at this level for several years. End of fiscal year is an example of a date constant. For U.S. government agencies this would typically be 30 September of any year. Unlike character codes and descriptions, constant values are not multivalued things, and so can exist only as non-key attributes of other tables.

Table 3.8 Incorporating sales tax in a State table.

State Code	State Name	General Sales Tax	Enterprise Zone Sales Tax
NJ	New Jersey	6.0000	3.0000
NY	New York	8.2500	Null

Going back to the sales tax example, imagine a table of U.S. States, where the sales tax rate could be included (Table 3.8). Over time, constant values such as these are subject to change, although it typically happens infrequently. Therefore a wise database designer will want to assign an effective date to the constant values, which means they have to be broken out into distinct tables.

Figure 3.5 shows how a `State Sales Tax` table has been created to hold the information on sales tax, and how it is qualified by an effective date. This is a dependent table, which is a child of the independent `State` table.

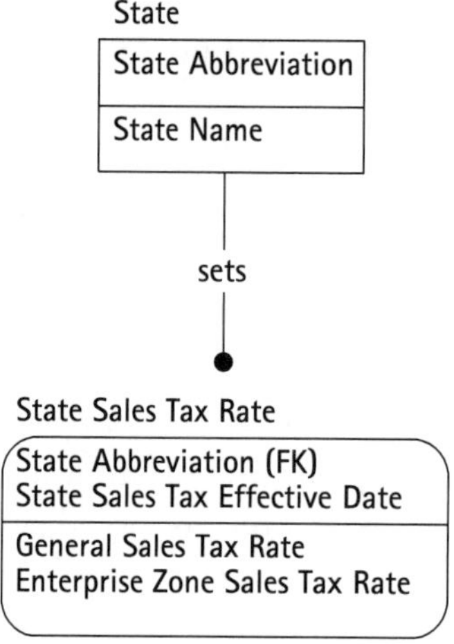

Figure 3.5 Constant values in a separate table.

Figure 3.5 is not the best design for describing how a sales tax may be set because it implies that *General Sales Tax Rate* and *Enterprise Zone Sales Tax Rate* change synchronously. Furthermore it is not general enough to store information about sales taxes that may be set by legal authorities other than states. Figure 3.6 describes a more general way of modeling the situation. In this model constant values sit within a reasonably complex related subset of entities in a database design, rather than within the context of a simple relationship to a reference data table.

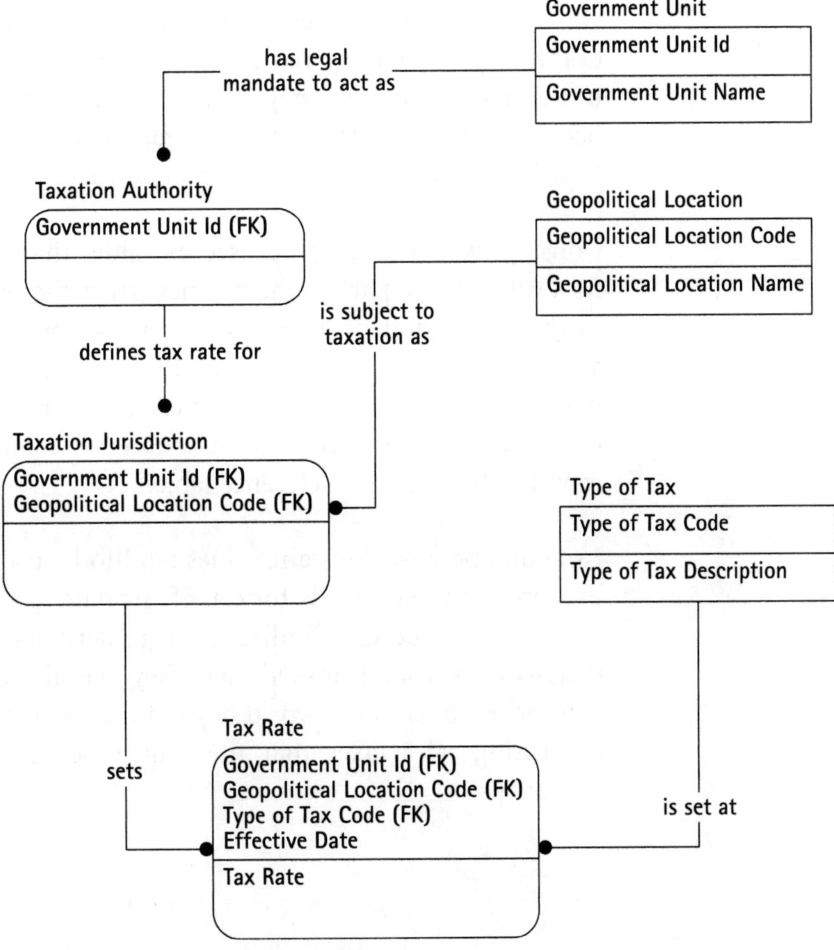

Figure 3.6 A more general model for tax rates.

This illustrates some important facts about constant values:

- Constant values do not have independent tables created for them in databases, nor are they found as keys in database tables. This is because they are not independent things and do not describe anything else.
- Constant values are nearly always qualified by an effective date (or datetime).

Constant values may sometimes be subject to a greater rate of change than other reference data. Foreign exchange rates are a good example. They may be recorded in a table on a daily basis, or even more frequently. Yet they can be considered as reference data because they are never created by transactions in a business application, but are taken from a market somewhere.

Constant values tend to be used as values that are input into business rules, or are part of the business rules themselves. For instance, in the calculation of sales tax it is important to know what each applicable current tax rate is. Another business rule may determine if a transaction belongs to the current or prior fiscal year by comparing a reference date on the transaction to an end of fiscal year day/month value held in a reference table.

Note that because constant values tend to be used in business rules, they are not used directly for classifying data in a database. However, they may well be used indirectly (e.g., deriving a fiscal year that is then used to group transactions). They may also be used to relate the enterprise's data to the world beyond the enterprise itself, such as in calculating sales taxes that then must be paid to a government authority.

Global Data

Some data exists as global data for an enterprise. It belongs in a single table, with one record, as it should change rarely during the lifetime of the enterprise. For example, a corporation may decide its fiscal year ends on 31 May of any year. A `Global Corporate Information` table may look like the example shown in Table 3.9. There could actually be many other data attributes in this table. It is surprising how often the need to hold global information arises in database design. This may be global at the level of the database being designed, or global for the enterprise as a whole.

Default data may also be held in a table like this. A default is one value from a set of values for a column that is used when a new record is being added to a table. For instance, the country in an address could always be defaulted to "USA" when a new record is added to any database table that contains an address. Of course, there are other design alternatives available for defaults, including building them into the database server.

Table 3.9 A single record in a table of global corporate information.

Attribute Name	Attribute Value
Company Name	The Great XYZ Company Incorporated
Company Acronym	XYZ Inc.
End of Fiscal Year - Month	05
End of Fiscal Year - Day	31

Global data is different from defaults, even though both may be held in the same table, and has a special design to ensure it is universally applied.

- Global reference data is typically held in a single table in a database that contains a single record.
- If global reference data can change, then the single table in which it is held should have a primary key of *Effective Date.*

While global data can often be considered reference data, it may also contain data that is there purely to be shared among the information systems of the enterprise and is not used to classify other data, or to relate any other data to information held beyond the boundaries of the enterprise. Such internal, shared data is called *common data* in this book (see Chapter 1 for a definition). However, in the context of global data it looks and behaves almost exactly like reference data.

Classification Schemes

Classification schemes are an important part of reference data. They are used to classify the transactions of a system into special categories that are meaningful to users in terms of information analysis. At first sight classification schemes may appear as just another set of codes and descriptions, but they are *profoundly* different from the other kinds of data found in a database and demand special attention.

Suppose a zoo has a database that lists all the individual animals in its collection. For each animal there are many facts that need to be recorded: identification number, gender, date of entry into the collection, purchase price, and so on. All these are objectively verifiable facts about each animal. In addition each animal must be classified scientifically: as a mammal, bird, reptile, amphibian, fish, and so on. In fact each animal will be classified down to the species level. Our zoo may wish to go beyond this and categorize the species in its collection as "Highly Endangered," "Endangered," and "Not Endangered." After all, one of the functions of modern zoos is to ensure the continuity of species that are in danger of becoming extinct. The zoo may classify its animals in other ways also, such as how popular they are with the general public. Figure 3.7 illustrates this situation, with `Popularity With Public`, `Species`, and `Endangered Status` as classification schemes.

Thus the zoo's database contains a set of objective facts about its collection and a set of "facts" that are ways in which the animals have been classified: scientific names, level of endangerment, and popularity rating. These classification schemes are human inventions although they may be based on observable facts. A lion has certain characteristics that can be used to classify it as a mammal, but the term *mammal* is a human construct based on an arbitrary (from a database viewpoint) set of values for certain attributes. For example,

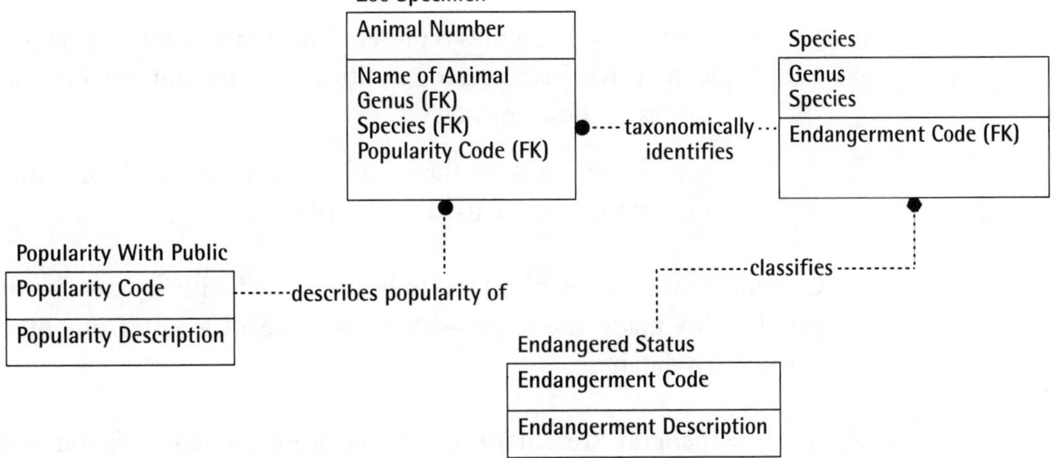

Figure 3.7 The use of Classification schemes.

If animal suckles its young
Or animal has hair
Or animal has teeth with many roots
Then animal is a mammal.

Scientific classification is well understood, but classification schemes can be infinite in number. Every person on the planet could potentially come up with different lists of animals they really like, animals they like a little, animals they dislike a little, and animals they dislike a lot. Beyond this, it is possible to invent completely different classification schemes ad infinitum. Animals can be categorized by how poisonous they are to humans, whether their consumption is restricted by religious dietary laws, whether trade in them is restricted by international convention, and so on.

Classification schemes are particularly sensitive to fads and fashions. For instance, in the 1970s during the oil crises, it was common to categorize economic activities based upon the amount of energy they consumed. When oil became cheaper there was considerably less demand for this kind of information.

We can summarize this discussion as follows:

- Classification schemes represent information about how people perceive instances of entities and are not intrinsic attributes of these entities.
- There is no limit to the number of different classification schemes that can be used to describe an entity.

Classification schemes also tend to be associated with "owners"—the people who made them up—which is quite different from other entities in a database.

A more general treatment of classification schemes is possible where it is acknowledged that they are being used for measurement. In the theory of measurement, the nominal or classificatory scale is regarded as the weakest level of measurement—that is, when symbols are used to classify an object, person, or characteristic. This scale of measurement has certain formal properties, particularly the following:

- All subclasses are mutually exclusive; that is, a transaction can only be assigned one value in a given classification scheme.
- The classification scheme must be complete—that is, there must be no transactions that cannot be assigned a value in the classification scheme.

Unfortunately these are not recognized as formal elements in the methodologies on which data modeling tools are based. However, the designer must recognize and understand the unique properties of classification schemes if they are to be used successfully.

Buckets

Buckets is an unfortunate and clumsy term but, alas, one that is gaining ground at a grassroots user level, particularly in the financial industry. It represents a parallel (though not a complete one) to classification schemes. Just as classification schemes are used to categorize instances of entities, buckets are used to categorize numeric data

Bucketing involves accumulating numeric data (often financial information) into derived fields called buckets. This may be done by simple summation or by using complex logic defined by a user.

An important feature of bucketing is that it is user driven. Users often find it difficult to appreciate the abstract nature of data modeling, and some of the concepts are quite unfamiliar to them. Professionals involved in database design may occasionally forget this and may become frustrated as they try to understand users' data needs. Part of this frustration may arise from the fact that some data needs are very short term. For instance, a user may have a need to calculate a certain number today, but the number will only be used for reporting at the end of the current month, and then never again. This kind of requirement is not something that a database designer likes because it is so transitory. On the other hand, users often view fields in databases as pigeonholes where they should be able to place anything they want. The database designer has to explain that this is not the case, and that every attribute has a distinct meaning and cannot contain data that means something different. Such an explanation is not helpful to the user, who may actually know of attributes in the database that are not really used, and who may be inclined to ask why these cannot be used to hold their new calculated number.

The problem does not stop at this point. It may also involve the business rules behind any calculations. For instance, a credit card company will process payments received every month. A user may wish to total up all the principal and interest received each month in order to show how profitable the business is to potential investors. Let us suppose that the database involved has no attribute in its design to hold this information, and that the investors have different ideas of what constitutes principal and what constitutes interest.

Investor 1

Principal = Principal payments for purchases

+ Cash advance principal payments

+ Cash advance fee payments

+ Credit card annual fee payments

+ Late payment charges

Interest = Interest payments on purchases

+ Interest payments on cash advances

Investor 2

Principal = Principal payments for purchases

+ Cash advance principal payments

+ Credit card annual fee payments

Interest = Interest payments on purchases

+ Interest payments on cash advances

+ Late payment charges

+ Charges for bounced checks

+ Charges for exceeding the credit limit

In this example Principal and Interest are buckets—monthly totals of financial information that can be calculated in a variety of different ways. Both the buckets and the rules to derive them are user defined, and there is no limit to the number of buckets that can be defined for a set of financial data. Each investor who looks at this data may have a different way of calculating principal and interest. Indeed, different investors may want to calculate some numbers that are totally unique to them and not used by any other investor.

Naturally if the designer wishes to record more than one way of calculating principal (or interest), these must be separate attributes. However, as has been noted above, users may not be able to know these data requirements at design time. This problem is thus frustrating for all concerned and can lead to poorly considered implementations that are little more than workarounds or fixes. It is particularly acute in finance, where accumulating transaction data into buckets based on a variety of business rules is a common practice. Indeed, a number of financial software packages come with the option of "user-defined fields" to meet this need.

Can buckets be considered reference data? Classification schemes are certainly reference data (and "look" like reference data with tables of codes and descriptions). Buckets, by contrast, are non-key numeric attributes. Nevertheless, they are like classification schemes in that they are user-defined interpretations of the underlying data, and there is no upper limit to the number that can be invented. Buckets do not classify individual instances of entities as is the case with classification schemes, but they do categorize sets of columns across one or more tables. Whereas classification schemes have values that contain descriptions, buckets have their descriptions only at the level of metadata—as attribute definitions. Or, to put it another way, classification schemes have metadata physically implemented in tables in a database, instead of in a data dictionary or repository.

Buckets may also be calculated at a different frequency than that for which transaction data is populated, such as when daily activity is closed, or at the end of a month. This argues that buckets should be considered closer to reference data than to transaction data, even though database designers and system developers may be unfamiliar with thinking of them in this way. However, this is not to say that any numeric field can be considered a bucket. As noted earlier, buckets are calculated numbers, not knowable at database design time, which are based on other attributes that are known at design time and do exist as distinct columns in the database.

There is a common link between classification schemes and buckets in many databases, although it is not usually formalized. Figure 3.8 illustrates the relationship.

Figure 3.8 has several buckets in the `Classification Scheme` entity. These may be simply assignments of fields in the related `Transaction` table, or the buckets may be populated by complex calculations involving the fields in the `Transaction` table. The point is that the values in the `Classification Scheme` are used to create a distribution of instances derived from data in the `Transaction` table (analogous to the *x*-axis of a histogram), and the buckets are used to hold such items as financial balances (analogous to the *y*-axis of a histogram), which are properties of the `Classification Scheme` and not of the transaction.

The situation represented in Figure 3.9 is more complex, with all the buckets placed in the intersection entity `Transaction Classification`. Here the buckets are calculated periodically using transaction data for a particular time period. For example, at the end of every month, buckets are calculated based on the transaction activity for that month. Note that the buckets in Figure 3.9 are at a much

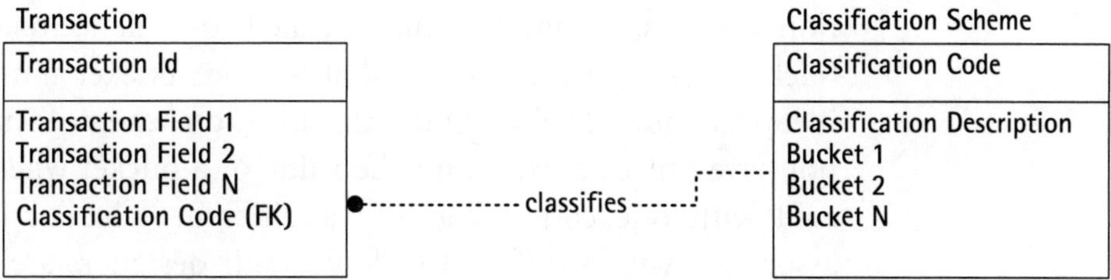

Figure 3.8 The relationship between Classification Scheme and buckets.

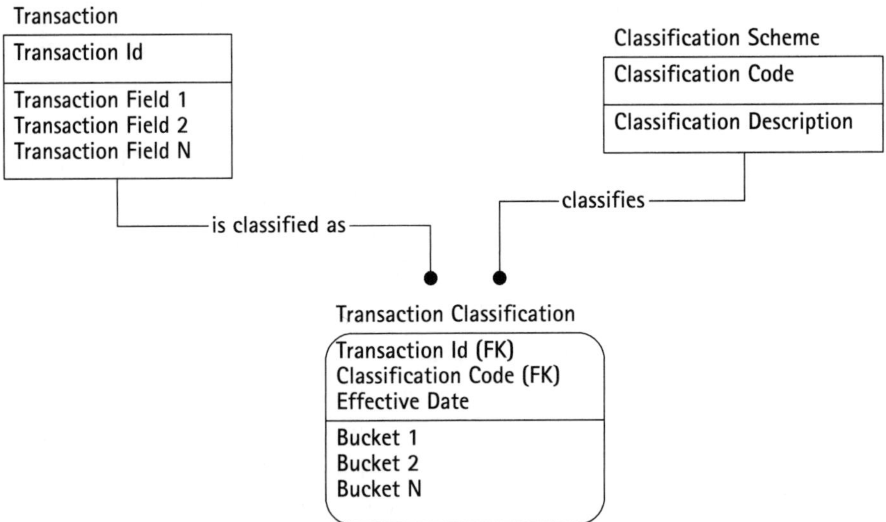

Figure 3.9 A more complex relationship between Classification Scheme and buckets.

lower level of aggregation than those in Figure 3.8. They are at the level of the individual transaction (although they are still dependent on `Classification Scheme`), whereas those in Figure 3.8 are aggregated across all transactions. It is possible to find buckets at intermediate levels of aggregation between these two extremes.

If we return to the theory of measurement, which covers classification schemes, we find that the so-called equivalence relation governs buckets. This basically states that a given bucket must be derived identically for all values in the classification scheme. That is, we cannot have one calculation for the value of a bucket when it is associated with one code value and a different calculation when it is associated with a different code value. If designers are to tackle the problem of buckets, they must beware of giving loose verbal definitions to buckets and then finding that programmers assign values to these buckets using different algorithms based on the associated classification code value.

This discussion can be summarized as follows:

- Reference data can be associated with non-key attributes used to store numeric data derived from the underlying transactions. These attributes are often known as buckets. They may be simple aggregations or based on more complex logic. However, their calculation should not vary with different values of the primary key in the individual reference tables with which they are associated.

What Is Not Reference Data

We began the discussion of what constitutes reference data by discussing codes and descriptions in general. Type codes, status codes, and classification schemes have been discussed as special categories of tables that contain codes and descriptions. However, there are many tables in which codes are used to represent descriptive texts. Are all of these considered reference data?

Databases often contain tables with descriptions represented by *identifiers*. For instance, a sales database may have a `Product Type` table with a key attribute *Product Type Id*. It is true that this is a code that represents the description of a `Product Type`. However, `Product Type` information is added, changed, and deleted all the time in such a database, which is quite unlike reference data. Also the `Product Type` table will have many non-foreign key attributes, which is also not typical of reference data.

Sometimes such identifiers are what is commonly called *intelligent keys*—that is, a primary key attributes composed of subgroups of reference and transaction structuring data. The use of intelligent keys is a very poor database design practice. For example, a company may have an *Account Code* like this:

USA-111-222222-33-444

where

- "USA" represents country
- "111" represents a division of the company
- "222222" represents an account code
- "33" represents a subaccount
- "444" represents a type of expenditure (e.g., office supplies)

This violates the basic rule of data modeling that requires each piece of data to be identified separately. In practice it leads to program logic having to parse the key values to determine what the individual pieces of data are—something that makes it very difficult to change the key structure.

Fortunately reference data is very rarely implemented using intelligent keys to represent descriptions, even by designers with the poorest skills. Unfortunately intelligent keys are not uncommon in tables that store transaction data.

One main difference between reference data tables and other tables that use codes to describe things is that reference data represents things that are not changed by the business processes of an organization. No organization has business processes that will cause countries, states, currencies, or languages to come into being, change their characteristics, or disappear. However, an organization can manage customers, products, and employees.

Indicators and Flags

An *indicator,* or *flag,* is a common systems term for a boolean datatype that has two states: true and false. Such logical datatypes are found in many database server platforms. They should be used only to describe the presence or absence of a characteristic of the entity to which they belong, but unfortunately they are often misapplied with respect to reference data.

One example in which an indicator can be used is in recording whether or not an employee is a high school graduate. The employee is either a high school graduate, or is not a high school graduate, and there are no other possibilities.

The characteristic in question may be derived from a business rule. For example, customers of a corporation may be eligible for deferred billing based upon their payment history. In this case an attribute called *Eligible for Deferred Billing Indicator* would be set on the `Customer Account` table.

Problems arise with the temptation to think that an indicator can be used in the case in which there are two alternative states, rather than the presence or absence of a particular characteristic. For instance, marital status could be represented by an indicator with *true* meaning *married* and *false* meaning *single.* However, when reference data like this is represented by indicators, two problems arise:

- The indicator is being used like a coded value, but there is no place in the database to store the corresponding descriptions. This means that the descriptions must be hard-coded into programs and reports.

- The set of values is not easily changed. For instance, if it is necessary to add *widowed* and *divorced* as additional options for marital status, the indicator will have to be converted to a datatype capable of holding more values.

This is a trap that a designer should not fall into. Instead, the designer should be careful to distinguish between

- the presence and absence of a particular characteristic
- two different values with different meanings

In summary, therefore, indicators and flags are usually not reference data, but they can be used in such a way that they hide the presence of reference data.

Conclusion

The preceding discussion shows that there are several kinds of reference data. They can be summarized as follows:

- **Data about things external to the enterprise.** Things that are not managed by an enterprise's business processes, but that the enterprise needs to refer to. This data usually comprises simple tables of codes and descriptions.
- **Type codes.** Tables of codes and values used to categorize subtypes. Their values are known at the time database tables are designed.
- **Status codes.** Tables of codes and descriptions that describe a life cycle of a transaction or ways in which a transaction can change over time. They are fundamentally associated with time and a set of business rules that governs how their values are assigned.

- **Classification schemes.** Tables of codes and descriptions that can be used to categorize other information in a database. These reflect the enterprise's perceptions or judgments about the objective data in a database, and there is no limit on the number that can be created.
- **Constant values.** These are numeric and date attributes that are not managed by an enterprise's business processes. They exist as non-key attributes in tables where there is usually an effective date as part of the primary key. However, they represent just another set of information about things that are external to the enterprise.
- **Global data.** Data that pertains to the entire enterprise that a database serves. It can also pertain to individual systems or databases. It is often implemented as a table that contains one record and does not have a meaningful key, because the key is the enterprise, or system, or database.
- **Buckets.** Non-key attributes of reference data tables that store numeric data derived from transactions related to these reference data tables. Buckets may be simple aggregations or derived via complex business rules.

Reference data is therefore quite heterogeneous. It consists of a number of different categories, each with somewhat different properties.

Additionally, it is important to remember that codes and descriptions play a very important role in reference data but are not used in all reference data. Furthermore, codes can be used for tables that are not reference data.

Figure 3.10 summarizes the preceding discussion to illustrate the broad categories of reference data that exist.

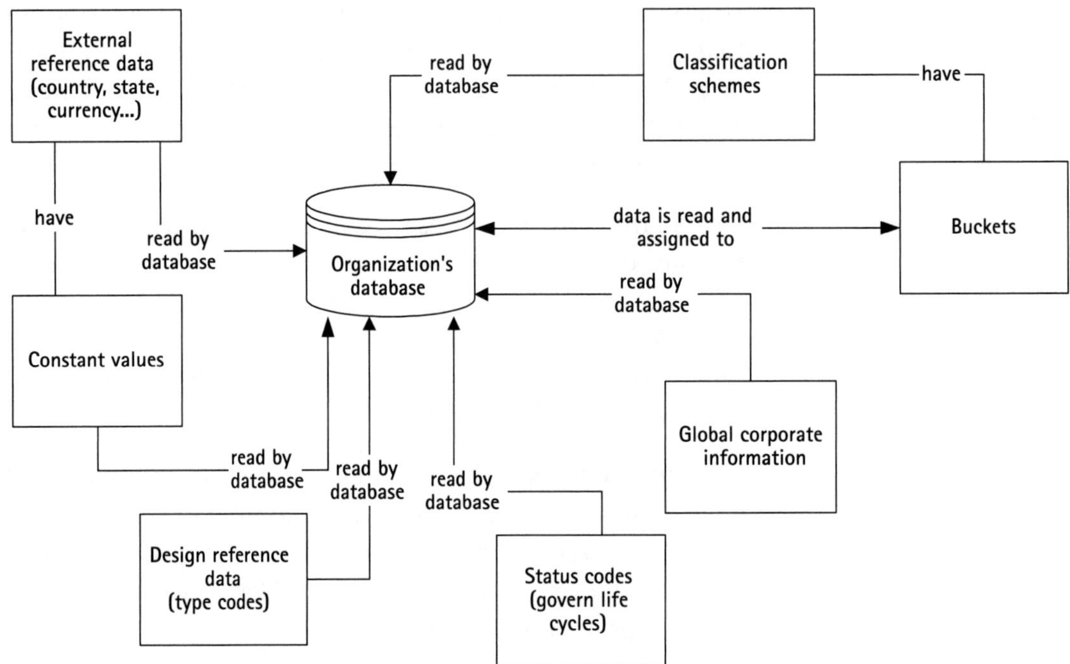

Figure 3.10 A summary of categories of reference data and their typical usage.

CHAPTER 4

Characteristics of Reference Data

THE PREVIOUS CHAPTER explored the key features of different kinds of reference data. However, there are a number of characteristics that these different categories often have in common, and they are discussed in this chapter. These characteristics are more general than the ones we have examined before and are more relevant to how reference data behaves rather than to how it should be defined.

Rate of Change

An important characteristic of reference data is the rate at which it changes. Reference data nearly always changes much more slowly than the other data in a database. Some reference data may never be subject to addition, change, or deletion in the entire lifetime of a database. Type codes are an example of this.

Constant values are recognized as somewhat more prone to change, as discussed in the previous chapter. That is why they often have an effective date (or datetime) as part of their primary key.

This slow rate of change leads some designers to dispense with thinking through how to handle change when it does happen. Two common problems can arise because of this:

- Information systems are created with reference data tables that are populated when the system first goes into production but lack any mechanism for updating them in the future (except via direct intervention by programmers or database administrators).
- Information systems are built on the assumption that values in reference data tables will never change or be deleted. When this does happen, referential integrity problems arise that can severely affect information quality and may even cause system failures.

These issues are explored more fully in Chapters 12 and 14. To avoid these and other problems, the designer must plan for change in reference data. This means considering both how the reference data tables will be updated and how to manage the effects of these changes on the rest of the data in an enterprise's databases. Chapter 13 describes how change can be managed.

Not all reference data is slow to change. Foreign exchange rates can be considered reference data, and they can change at any moment in time.

Scope

Reference data is usually, but not always, broad in scope, although what is meant by scope varies somewhat among the different types of reference data.

For a code representing a description, scope is primarily the number of columns in database tables outside the original reference data table (i.e., the one with both code and description) where the code is found. For instance, the attribute *State Abbreviation* may be found in many tables containing address and location information in a single database. It may even be found more than once in a single table (e.g., a customer may have a billing address and a mailing address, each requiring a state attribute).

Scope for codes is also important in terms of the outputs of a system, whether these are printed or displayed on screens. Very often these outputs contain information sorted and grouped by coded values, although descriptions are increasingly being used for sorting and grouping.

While codes in general may have a wide scope, this is not always true. Type codes, as noted in the previous chapter, have a very restricted scope. They are nearly always found only in the reference data table where they are defined, the table whose subtyping they control, and nowhere else.

Status codes are similarly restricted in scope as they typically describe the life cycle of a particular entity. Again, they exist in the reference data table where they are defined, the entity whose life cycle they describe, and nowhere else.

For constant values, scope is a different matter. They are not used for organizing information but rather for participating in process logic.

The calculations, and the other logic in which constant values participate, are usually termed *business rules.* Business rules are another big topic in information technology and also exist in relation to plenty of things that have nothing to do with constant values. The number of business rules in which constant values participate, and the number of times these business rules are executed, represent the scope of constant values in a system. Unfortunately business rules are often buried in program code, so it can be very difficult to assess the actual scope of constant values.

Volume

The volume of reference data, in terms of the numbers of records in reference data tables, is typically not high. For instance, there are only about 200 countries in the world and a similar number of currencies. Low volume, together with slow rate of change, seems to lead some professionals to underestimating the importance of reference data, or not thinking hard about it in database and process designs.

On the other hand, low volume does allow designers to do some interesting things, such as physically clustering reference data on disk storage such that reference data tables are very close together. Thus when information is read from one table, the others are buffered and available without further physical disk access. Such designs can improve system performance.

However, if numbers of database tables are considered, volume may not be so low. It is often the case that quite a high percentage of the tables in a database house reference data. This fact may be overlooked because these tables are slow to change. Furthermore, the reference data tables may have large numbers of relationships with other data tables. This can annoy data modelers who want to concentrate on the tables that house transaction structuring and activity information.

Numbers of reference data tables and their relationships may be even higher as a percentage of the total number of tables and relationships in data warehouses and marts. Here there tend to be a few fact tables and many dimension tables, and reference data is always found in the dimension tables.

Low volumes in terms of record counts makes issues like database table space allocation relatively easy. However, high numbers of reference data tables relative to other database tables make database administrative tasks more complex for both database designers and database administrators. For instance, it may make it less easy to distinguish a reference data table from a transaction table. Naming conventions can help with this problem of lots of "little" reference data tables crowding out the "main" tables of a database.

Risk

Unfortunately the scope of reference data means that if something bad happens to it, the consequences are usually widespread. There are three main types of risk:

- Operational risk, which is the risk that transactions, including outputs of a system, are incorrect or nonfunctional due to errors in reference data.
- Distribution risk, which is the risk that changes in reference data are not propagated throughout the databases of an enterprise. This may give rise to irreconcilable differences in reporting from different systems or databases.
- Design risk, which is the set of problems that may be encountered when some design change involving reference

data is needed in a system (perhaps due to an incorrect initial design).

There is a widespread appreciation of the risks associated with reference data among more experienced information systems professionals. Careful management of reference data is needed to reduce these risks, and Chapter 19 explores ways in which this can be achieved.

Metadata and Meaning

Metadata is a term that is becoming more and more important in information systems. Larry English [En1999] notes that the term has not yet been included in the *Oxford English Dictionary* or *Webster's Unabridged Dictionary*, and defines it as follows:

> *A term used to mean data that describes or specifies other data. The term metadata is used to define all the characteristics that need to be known about data in order to build databases and applications and to support knowledge workers and information producers.*

The business definitions of tables and columns in a database are among the most important types of metadata. In the case of reference data, values themselves sometimes have business definitions, which is a very unusual property to have. For instance, individual values of type codes have definitions since they serve to subtype a table. Consider the `Employee Position Type` table shown in Table 4.1.

Table 4.1 Employee Position Type table.

Employee Position Type Code	Employee Position Type Description
A	Administrative
P	Professional

This table contains two records, one to classify an employee position as administrative and another to classify an employee position as professional. But the company may have a complex definition of what constitutes each of these job categories. Perhaps temporary hires are always considered administrative, or perhaps computer consultants are considered professional, and so on. The point is that each record contains data values that represent different business definitions.

This is not confined to type codes; values in classification schemes have definitions also. For instance, a company may wish to classify transactions according to market sector and will create a `Sector` table for this purpose, like that shown in Table 4.2. The descriptions seem easy enough to understand, but when a number of users have to apply them in a consistent fashion to the company's transactions, they really need to know how they have been defined.

Table 4.2 Sector Classification table.

Sector Code	Sector Description
01	Banking
02	Insurance
03	Brokerage
04	Real Estate
05	Government

The need to understand definitions at the instance (i.e., row) level applies only to codes, and not to constant values. This is because codes represent instances of "things," including ideas, whereas numeric constants do not. Codes are by definition keys of a reference data table, unlike constant values.

When Reference Data Values Are Known

Another characteristic of reference data is that actual values are often known during the design phases of databases and systems. This arises because

- Much reference data is maintained by organizations external to the enterprise. Therefore it is available at any time.
- In many organizations reference data has been used since the introduction of computing, and so it is widely known. The same reference data will probably be used for any new database or system, and so it is known at design time.
- Reference data associated with database design decisions, such as type codes and status codes, has to be elaborated before the design can be finalized.
- Reference data that controls processes has to be elaborated before program specifications can be completed.

When a new system is built, the designers, if not the business analysts, often record the reference data values so that they can be entered into the database as soon as possible. This is to enable testing of other components of the system to begin quickly. However, the reference data may only be recorded on paper or in electronic documents, and so it may have to be entered into database tables directly by programmers. This can spell trouble, particularly during the testing and production implementation phases. Production implementation is a particularly critical phase. It is nearly always the case that reference data must be fully available at the point a system or database goes live.

One of the more difficult things to manage is the dissemination of the actual reference data values (and associated metadata, as mentioned in the prior section) among the parties that need to know it in a systems development project team. If reference data is not actively managed, then it will be addressed in some other way—for example, programmers may simply make up values if none are provided to them.

The main point to consider here is that real reference data values must be managed during the design phases of systems projects. In this regard it is quite unlike other data that is stored in databases. These issues are discussed more fully in Chapter 14.

Discrete Sets

Codes and descriptions tend to exist as discrete sets of values, unlike transaction data which simply keeps growing and has a continuous set of values. Thus transaction data has to be aggregated to summarize it, but coded reference data is rarely aggregated, and individual values tend to appear in system outputs.

Constant values are a little different. Because they are usually associated with an effective date, they can be viewed as consisting of one current record and the remainder as historical records.

The fact that reference data occurs as discrete sets is something that is necessary for its primary function of providing a means for distributing transaction data in analyses.

Independence

Codes and descriptions typically exist as independent entities in a database. This is hardly surprising as so much reference data represents things found outside the boundaries of the enterprise. Typically there are few relationships among different types of reference data, although they do exist (see Chapter 6). Where such relationships exist, they are of a non-identifying kind, so it is comparatively rare to find hierarchies of reference data entities linked together by identifying relationships.

This characteristic of reference data makes it more possible to deal with reference data tables one at a time, which would not be possible if they were all tightly coupled together by identifying relationships.

Constant values typically have to depend on a parent entity (usually another reference data table) for their existence, and they are non-key attributes of these dependent tables. Thus the parent entities of the entities that contain constant values must be addressed before constant values themselves can be fully addressed for either design or implementation.

Source of Update

A significant characteristic of reference data is that it is often updated with data that is not created by the business transactions processed by the enterprise. Instead it comes from some external source and is entered by a user or interfaced into the system somehow.

This is another feature that sets reference data apart from the other data in a database. It has several implications for the management of reference data:

- The external source of the reference data must be known.
- There must be a connection to this external source so that the enterprise can receive information about updates to the reference data.
- Whenever new information is received from the external source, it must be checked for changes. For example, the meaning of a particular coded value may have changed, and the format of the reference data may also need to change. It is also necessary to verify the data quality.
- Information about the source of the reference data may be important within the enterprise to users of the reference data, and it may also have to be stored (thus becoming another kind of metadata).

Conclusion

In the previous chapter we looked at the different kinds of reference data, and in this chapter we reviewed the general characteristics of reference data. These characteristics determine how reference data behaves. They are quite different from the characteristics of most of the other data found in a database, which supports the idea that reference data should be managed independently from the other data. The management needs brought about by the way in which reference data behaves have been briefly mentioned and are discussed in much greater detail in subsequent chapters.

CHAPTER 5

Assigning Values to Codes

MUCH REFERENCE DATA, perhaps even most, consists of codes that represent real-world names of things. When databases are built with tables designed to hold these codes, decisions need to be made about what values to use for the codes. The descriptions can be regarded as objective facts, but the values used for the codes that represent them are another matter. In theory a code can be any value, but it makes sense to have some kind of scheme that bears a relationship to the descriptions. In many cases the code values must be invented from scratch, but sometimes acronyms are used for descriptions within a user community, or even within an entire industry. For example, "USA" is commonly used for "United States of America." Such acronyms, therefore, exist in their own right and are natural candidates to use as codes.

The alternative to acronyms is to use a scheme of sequence numbers or randomly created alphanumeric codes. Whatever scheme is chosen, it is important to remember that deciding what values to assign to codes can affect the design of the reference data tables and related program logic. In addition, designers often have to populate certain reference data tables with real production data prior to implementing a system, and so they are forced to choose actual values. If they do not, programmers are likely to choose these very important values for them.

There is no equivalent problem for constant values, which never occur as foreign keys, nor represent something else in the same way that codes do.

This chapter reviews the issues surrounding how values are assigned to codes and explores particularly the benefits and drawbacks of using acronyms as codes.

Descriptions without Acronyms

Often a database will contain descriptions that are not represented by acronyms in use by the business community. The values for their codes must therefore be invented by someone, as candidate values (that is, preexisting values from which you can choose) cannot possibly exist. Type codes are often like this. The nature of type codes is such that they usually all have to be entered into tables prior to the implementation of a system. This forces the database designers, programmers, or other technical staff to choose the values that are implemented.

Let's look at using `Employee Position Type` to subtype the `Employee Position` table (Figure 5.1). Table 5.1 shows the records that may be entered for `Employee Position Type`. In this example the codes "A" and "P" have been used. Since the organization in which this table is implemented does not use acronyms for Administrative or Professional, only the descriptions "Administrative " and

"Professional" have meaning to users, and the codes "A" and "P" would typically not appear on any outputs.

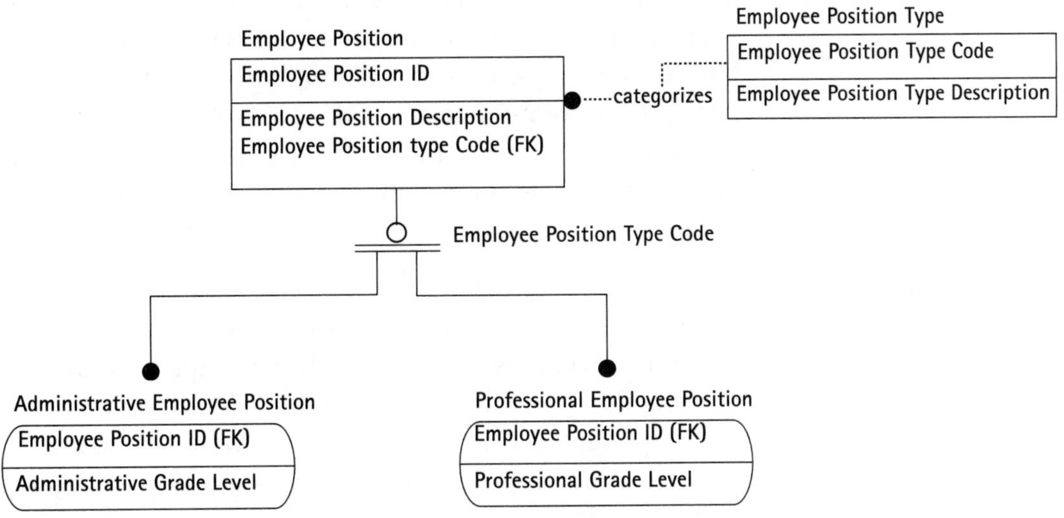

Figure 5.1 Employee Position Type Code.

Table 5.1 Employee Position Type table.

Employee Position Type Code	Employee Position Type Description
A	Administrative
P	Professional

Even in this simple scenario, there are a number of design points that need to be considered:

- Will the codes play any role in the sort order in which the data in the table is presented? If so, it is better if the codes sort in the same sequence as the descriptions. This tends to make designers use abbreviations of the descriptions, which in turn means the datatype of the code must be character. This issue tends to be less important in more modern systems that present users only with sorted lists of descriptions and never show the underlying codes.
- If the codes are to be used in program logic, it also helps to have abbreviations of the descriptions. Suppose that in the `Employee Type` table "0" represented "Administrative" and "1" represented "Professional." There would be more of a chance that a programmer would do something wrong when writing code like

```
IF EmpPosType.EmpPosTypeCode = "0" Then
     <Program logic for Administrative positions>
Else
     <Program logic for Professional positions>
End if
```

It is easier for the programmer to associate "A" with "Administrative" and "P" with "Professional." Again, this is a reason why the code should have a character datatype.

- The datatype used for the code must be long enough to permit codes for all possible descriptions. In the `Employee Position Type` table there are only two descriptions, so a Character(1) field would suffice. It is worth being liberal in this regard, because if the set of codes grows so large that it exceeds what the code attribute can hold, there could be a need for major reprogramming. A Character(2) field can hold 676 different codes using alphabetic characters (more if both upper- and lowercases are allowed).

- The use of spaces in the codes should be avoided. If a Character(2) field was chosen, then even if there were only two values, they should each be represented by 2-character codes—for example, "AD" and "PR." The potential for errors is increased if different codes have different lengths. Tables 5.2 and 5.3 illustrate this point.

Table 5.2 Pay Grade table with character codes of different lengths.

Code	Description
1	Pay Grade 1
2	Pay Grade 2
3	Pay Grade 3
4	Pay Grade 4
5	Pay Grade 5
6	Pay Grade 6
7	Pay Grade 7
8	Pay Grade 8
9	Pay Grade 9
10	Pay Grade 10
11	Pay Grade 11
12	Pay Grade 12

Table 5.3 Pay Grade table with character codes of the same length.

Code	Description
01	Pay Grade 1
02	Pay Grade 2
03	Pay Grade 3
04	Pay Grade 4
05	Pay Grade 5
06	Pay Grade 6
07	Pay Grade 7
08	Pay Grade 8
09	Pay Grade 9
10	Pay Grade 10
11	Pay Grade 11
12	Pay Grade 12

Tables 5.2 and 5.3 show records in a reference data table for pay grades, where the code is a Character(2) field. In Table 5.2 if the codes are sorted, “10”, “11,” and “12” will sort between “1” and “2,” because they all begin with “1.” By contrast, the codes in Table 5.3 will sort correctly. Also, depending on the programming language, the following program logic fragment may treat the codes “1,” “10,” “11,”and “12” identically, which may be an error.

```
If PayGradeCode = “1” Then
    <Some logic>
Else
    <Some other logic>
End if
```

Again, this problem will not happen to the code values used in Table 5.3 because there are no spaces in the values and the values less than 10 have a leading zero.

Descriptions with Acronyms

An acronym is an abbreviation formed from the first (or first few) letters of a series of words (or their syllables), such as

LIBOR—**L**ondon **I**nter**b**ank **O**ffered **R**ate

When confronted with a long description, and an acronym, it seems only human to use the acronym. Everyone knows what DNA is, but people rarely refer to it as deoxyribose nucleic acid. Even in business an acronym may become so widely used that many people are unsure of exactly what it represents, as is the case with LIBOR.

In these situations, the database designer will need to decide if the acronym should be used as the code value. There are two basic design alternatives:

- Use the acronym as the code value.
- Use another scheme to create the code value, but record the acronym as well as the description.

There are advantages and disadvantages to both alternatives. The advantages of using the acronym as the code value (i.e., the primary key of the reference data table) are these:

- Wherever it is used in the database, it is recognizable to users. There may be less of a need to program joins back to the parent table to pick up the description. Users may in fact prefer to see the acronym rather than the full description on screens and reports.

- Programmers and analysts can instantly recognize the acronym when browsing raw data in tables. This can be a big help in testing and debugging.
- If programmers have to embed a code value in program logic, it is better to use the acronym than some other code. It is less likely the programmer will make a mistake, and it is easier for anyone else who has to understand the program.
- If data from one database has to be merged with data from another, acronyms are likely to make the process easier (although there is no guarantee of this).
- If users have to enter codes directly on screens, rather than select from lists of descriptions, acronyms are easier for them to remember.

The disadvantages of using the acronym as the code are as follows:

- If an acronym has been used on screens and reports and then it changes, problems can result. Very often acronyms do not change, but this is far from universally true. A good example is the European Union. This seems to change every few years and has been variously

  EEC European Economic Community

  EC European Community

  EU European Union

  If the screens and reports must reflect the latest acronym, then the entire database has to be updated when an acronym changes—not just the reference data table where the description is located. Such a change can be achieved by the database management system having a referential integrity constraint to cascade the update from the reference data table to every other table where the acronym has been used. More often special programs must be written to implement the change.

There is also a problem if an acronym has been hard-coded in program logic. If the acronym changes, the program logic must be updated to reflect the new acronym. This in turn means that the affected program logic has to be retested and moved to a production setting.

An even bigger headache occurs when information from one system or database is interfaced with another. The acronym may be changed in one database at one time but not changed in all databases of the enterprise at the same time. This can then lead to all kinds of problems when the new acronym is imported into or interfaces with an information system in which the old acronym is still in use. The kinds of problems that arise in this situation can be very difficult to diagnose and correct.

- There is a risk that the code will be designed for an acronym of a maximum length but that this will be exceeded after the database is put into production. For example, say Character(3) is chosen, but later an acronym that is four characters long has to be added; then either the new acronym will have to be shortened or the database restructured to increase the length of the columns affected.

After making a commitment to use an acronym, it is unfortunate if longer acronyms have to be abbreviated. However, changing column sizes and possibly program logic, screens, and reports is not attractive either, especially because this inevitably requires a lot of testing to ensure that changes have not introduced any bugs.

This problem can be avoided if a suitably large column size is chosen at the outset, irrespective of the longest acronym known at the time. Acronyms never seem to exceed Character(10), so this is a good choice as a standard datatype length.

Using Sequence Numbers to Represent Descriptions

The alternative to using acronyms as codes is to use another coding scheme (usually numeric) and to record the acronym with the description. Table 5.4 shows an example of this design. In such cases the code is usually a sequence number. A sequence number of 1 is assigned to the first record inserted into a table. After that, each successive record is given a key value of 1 greater than the previous record inserted. This sequence number becomes the foreign key value that is used in other database tables, and if the acronym is required, it can only be obtained from the reference table.

Part of the attraction of using sequence numbers is that it is an excellent design approach for other kinds of data in a database. For instance, in an order entry system, each new record in the `Order` table could automatically be assigned a value for the attribute *Order Number.* To do this the system finds the last sequence number assigned and increments it by one. Some software tools even have special datatypes for just this purpose—for example, Microsoft Access has an Autonumber datatype.

Table 5.4 Country table with a sequence number as the code.

Country Code	Country Acronym	Country Description
001	USA	United States of America
002	FRA	France
003	IRE	Ireland
004	SWE	Sweden
005	UKM	United Kingdom

An alternative to a sequence number is a randomly generated alphanumeric string. These are not integer datatypes (which sequence numbers are) and specify no order, which a sequence number does. However, they serve the same purpose as sequence numbers.

It is not unusual for designers who reflexively use sequence numbers to blur the distinction between reference data and data for structuring business transactions and recording transaction activity—even though each type uses slightly different terminology. For instance, a designer may refer to a *Transaction Id* or a *Transaction Number*, but not to a *Transaction Code*. Similarly, a designer will refer to a *Reference Data Code*, but not a *Reference Data Id* or *Reference Data Number*. Despite this perhaps subconscious distinction, many designers are inclined to use sequence numbers for codes in reference data. This may or may not be justifiable, but it should be a conscious design decision because it has widespread and long-term consequences.

There are differences between reference data and the kind of data used to structure an enterprise's transactions (e.g., product, customer, employee, account). For instance, reference data values stand a much higher chance of being referred to in program logic, and a much higher chance of being used in other systems to which data has to be interfaced. Therefore, some thought ought to be applied before deciding to use sequence numbers simply because they are used in important tables that do not contain reference data.

Information Float

We discussed earlier how acronyms and descriptions can change over time. There is an additional problem connected with such change called *information float*. Information float is the time it takes for a new fact that arises in the real world to be fully represented in the databases of an enterprise, and it has implications for the ways in which values are assigned to codes.

Since reference data often represents data completely external to an enterprise, there can be a time lag before a change in this data becomes known to an enterprise. Sometimes this problem can be handled very well. For instance, when the Euro (the new unified currency used in several European countries) was introduced in 1999, there was an advance publicity campaign which made a great number of interested parties aware of the new currency.

On the other hand, there can be instances when new reference data arises that is not communicated to the enterprise. If the enterprise does not really need to know this reference data, there is not much of a problem. For instance, when the country Zaire changed its name to Democratic Republic of the Congo, enterprises with no data that could be related to this country were not really affected.

However, the opposite can also occur. A fact about reference data can become known to an enterprise, but the external body responsible for standardizing that data may be slow to incorporate the new fact into the standard. Going back to the Euro, it took some time before the official new ISO Currency Code of "EUR" was issued. Yet a number of financial institutions wanted to test their information systems to see if the new code would work before it was officially issued. As it happened, it was a fairly safe guess that "EUR" would be the code, although "EUR" was actually at odds with ISO's own conventions for creating currency acronyms. The general problem is that official bodies responsible for maintaining standards used as reference data do not necessarily move at the same speed as the enterprises that use this data. Nor do they always move at the speed at which this data changes. This means that if enterprises use official acronyms as their way of representing reference data, they may be caught in a difficult position in which they have to use reference data for which no official acronym yet exists.

The use of sequence numbers as the code—the primary key of the reference data table—overcomes this problem. The acronym and description are stored as non-key attributes in the reference data tables, so if they have to be changed, this needs to be done in only one place.

Providing Data to External Parties

An enterprise often has to provide data to external parties—other organizations or people that are not part of the enterprise. Such data may be provided in electronic or printed form. In all such cases it is better for the enterprise to use official acronyms to represent reference data than to use internally assigned sequence numbers. Where recognized standards occur, such as ISO Currency and Country codes, the enterprise can direct the party to whom it is sending data to the official standard for the interpretation of the coded values. If the enterprise provides internally assigned sequence numbers to represent reference data, then it has to be responsible for answering queries about translating these code values to the real things they represent.

As discussed earlier, a great deal of reference data is used to relate the enterprise's data to the world beyond the enterprise. Wherever possible recognized standards should be used for this data. It may make sense for the enterprise to assign its own values to codes to represent these standards for internal use. However, these codes lose their meaning when data passes back from the enterprise to the world beyond it, and so the official standard should be the only one used to represent reference data in any data provided to external parties.

Multilingual Issues

Multilingual issues are described more fully in Chapter 16. However, they have an important impact on the use of acronyms as primary key values for reference data tables. Acronyms may differ from language to language. This is especially true for organizations; for example, the United Nations is known by the acronym "UN" in English, but "ONU" (Organización de las Naciones Unidos) in Spanish. These two acronyms are obviously different, including a difference in length.

If reference data is to be used in information systems where multilingual usage is required, acronyms become much more difficult to manage and are considerably less attractive as primary key values for reference data tables. Sequence numbers are a much better alternative.

Conclusion

Reference data often represents things and resides in tables where codes are used to represent official descriptions of these things. There may be well-known acronyms that represent these descriptions, or official standards that have created codes (often acronyms) to represent the descriptions.

While acronyms (or official codes) can be used as coded values for the primary keys of reference data tables, there is a design alternative of using a sequence number (or similar code) within an enterprise to represent reference data descriptions.

The advantages of using sequence numbers are

- If an acronym changes, it is simply changed in the parent reference table, and there is no need to cascade it to other parts of the database.
- Problems related to information float are greatly reduced.
- An additional way of sorting the table is available. The code can be used to sort the descriptions in a way that users find easier to deal with. However, sorting issues can be dealt with in other ways that do not involve code values.

The disadvantages are

- Acronyms are nearly always needed and have to be stored as an additional column in the reference data table.
- A join needs to be made back to the parent reference table when either the acronym or description is required.
- Analysts, programmers, and perhaps users have to relate sequence numbers back to descriptions. The sequence numbers exist as foreign keys outside the parent reference data table and in program logic. They represent something else that has to be understood and managed.
- Merging the same reference data from different systems that use different sequence numbering schemes is difficult. The enterprise must use the same sequence numbering schemes across all databases containing the same reference data (which may be a challenge in some organizations).

Basically sequence numbers are the safer alternative but need more management, while acronyms are generally easier to use but create significant problems whenever they change. Acronyms may be used for ultraslow-changing reference data like type codes and status codes, but beyond these kinds of situations, they can be risky (as primary keys, that is—they must at least be non-key attributes of reference data tables).

CHAPTER 6

Relationships within Reference Data

SINCE REFERENCE DATA EXISTS to be "referred to," the reference data tables in a database always have relationships with other tables. In any given database design, there may be many of these relationships, perhaps creating an entity-relationship diagram with so many relationship lines that it can no longer be easily read. These relationships can be classified into three main groups:

- Relationships between reference data tables and transaction data tables.

  Example: A `Country` table may be related to many transaction tables that store address information, in order to permit recording of the country of the address.

- Relationships between reference data tables and other reference data tables.

  Example: A `Country` table and `Region` table may exist, and each country may be assigned to one region.

- Business rules that bind reference data to transaction data (or even other reference data). These relationships do not show up in an entity relationship diagram.

  Example: (State Sales Tax Due) = (Total Amount of Sale) x ((Current Sales Tax Rate) for (State Where Sale Made))

The first and third of these classes of relationship are discussed elsewhere in this book. The relationships between reference data tables are important because they gives rise to some unique issues which this chapter explores.

Extending Tables Containing Codes and Descriptions

At a simple level a table designed to hold codes and descriptions will hold just that—a column for a code, a column for a description, and perhaps a column for an acronym. Indeed it is often the case that reference data tables do not hold a great deal of non-key data (unlike tables designed to hold transaction data). However, this is not always the case, and reference data tables can sometimes contain non-key data.

Consider the example of the `Country` table in Figure 6.1. Here we see a simple reference data table with two attributes: *Country Code* and *Country Description.* Suppose we are implementing a pharmaceutical sales tracking database for an international drug company, and our users have the following requirements that involve `Country` and need to be put into the design:

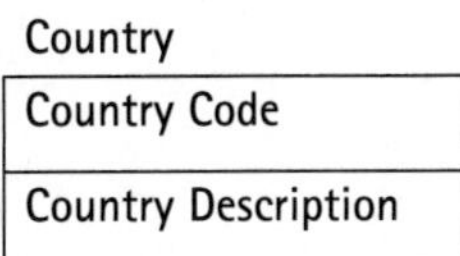

Figure 6.1 A simple design for a Country table.

- Sales must be tracked by country and region. Each country will be assigned to one region.
- We sell a lot of our products in Third World countries. Because they have fewer regulatory issues, fewer liability claims, and a market that cannot afford high prices, we sell to them using a different pricing regime than that used with developed countries. So we need to be able to distinguish between industrialized and developing countries.
- In some countries we have no presence; in others we market directly; and in others we have one or more distributors. We refer to this as "National Marketing Strategy" and need to record it.
- We do not have offices in all countries. Sometimes an office in one country is responsible for sales efforts in one or more neighboring countries.

The list of requirements could go on, but the design is already starting to get fairly complex.

Figure 6.2 shows the design to incorporate the requirements. We now have a `Country` table with relationships to several other reference data tables (including itself)—even before we have made any relationships from the `Country` table to any transaction data tables.

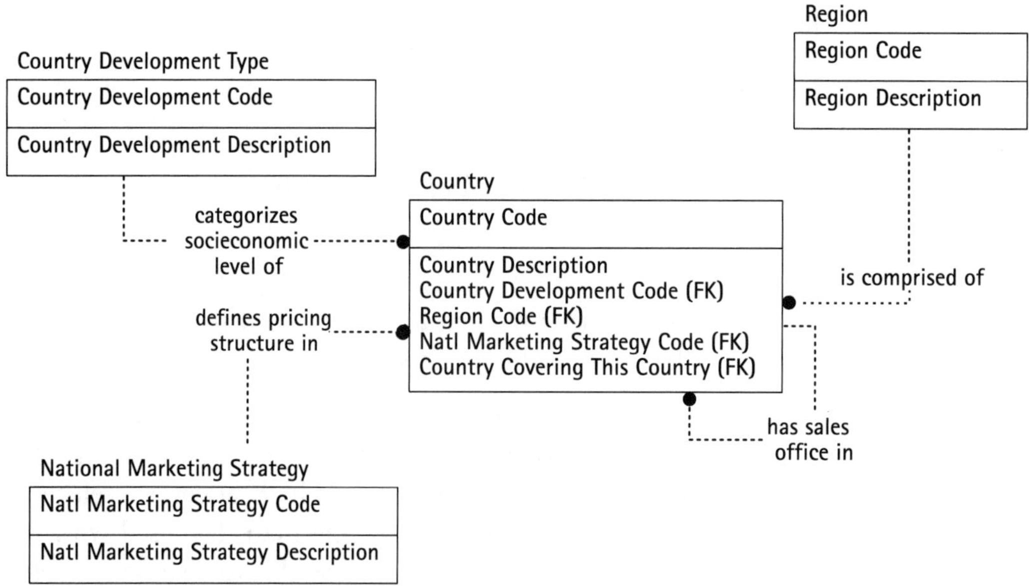

Figure 6.2 A Country table with relationships to other reference data tables.

What is interesting about this design is that all the non-key attributes of `Country` are foreign keys, except for *Country Description*. This example is not unusual; reference data tables often contain attributes that are foreign keys to other reference data tables.

As we discussed in Chapter 1, reference data is used to categorize other data that represents an enterprise's structure and activities. Therefore if reference data tables contain foreign keys, the latter cannot, by definition, come from tables that hold information about the enterprise's transaction structure and activity. These foreign keys can come only from other reference data tables.

Implications of Relationships between Reference Data Tables

One of the biggest implications of having additional non-key columns in reference data tables is that data entry screens used to update these tables will be more complex. In the example shown in Figure 6.2, the data entry screen(s) for the `Country` table must include not just *Country Code* and *Country Description*, but must also record *Country Development Code*, *National Marketing Strategy Code*, *Region Code*, and *Country Covering This Country*.

There is a tendency to think that reference data tables are simple and that the components of applications required to update them are simple also. However, this is not always the case, and reference data tables can sometimes be surprisingly complex. It is a mistake to think that all tables containing codes and descriptions are design clones of one another and can be accommodated within a common architecture for managing them, such as an identical update screen for each table.

Hierarchies of Reference Data

So far we have considered examples of non-identifying relationships between reference data tables, but identifying relationships can also be present. Identifying relationships exist when a table relies on another table for both its existence and identification. Consider an example of an industry classification system that exists at two levels.

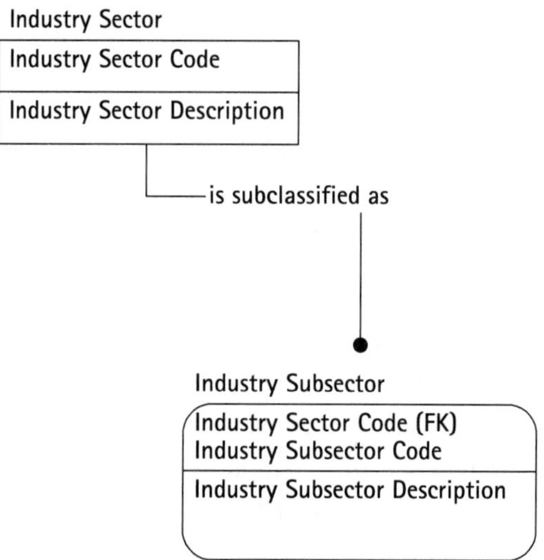

Figure 6.3 Industry Sector classification.

Figure 6.3 shows the design for this scheme with a higher-level `Industry Sector` table and a lower-level `Industry Subsector` table. Tables 6.1 and 6.2 show some examples of the records contained in these two tables. It is important to notice in this design that the primary key of the higher-level `Industry Sector` table becomes part of the primary key of the lower-level `Industry Subsector` table.

Table 6.1 Industry Sector table.

Industry Sector Code	Industry Code Description
01	Health
02	Energy
03	Transport
04	Agriculture
05	Food Services

Table 6.2 Industry Subsector table.

Industry Sector Code	Industry Subsector Code	Industry Subsector Description
01	01	Hospitals and Clinics
01	02	Physicians
01	03	Public Health
02	01	Electrical Power Generation
02	02	Hydrocarbon Fuels

When the Industry Subsector table is related to some other table, both fields of the primary key are migrated. An example is shown in Figure 6.4 where the `Company` table is related to `Industry Subsector`, presumably because the users of our database need to know what industry subsector each company belongs to. As can be seen, both *Industry Sector Code* and *Industry Subsector Code* are migrated into the `Company` table.

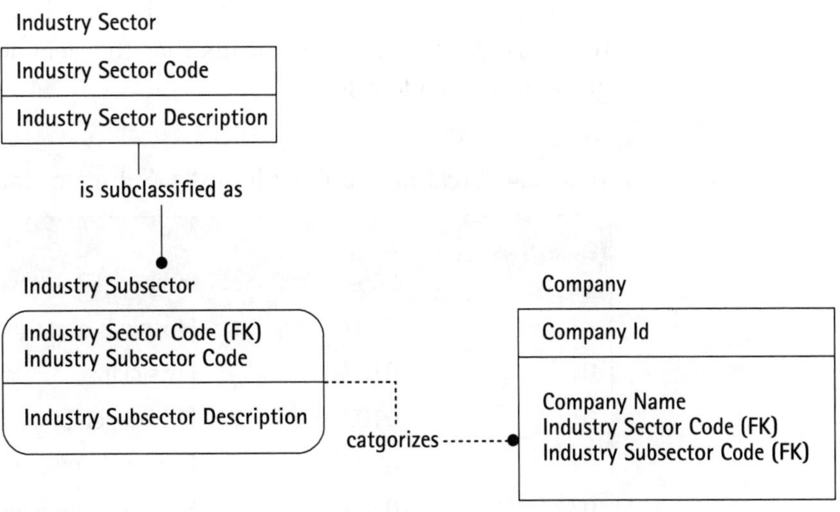

Figure 6.4 Usage of Industry Sector and Subsector.

Some designers do not like this approach because it complicates database design and application development in terms of writing program logic, queries, and reports when you have two key fields instead of one in a reference data table, and both fields migrate to other tables where they are used as a foreign key.

This is not necessarily a big problem, but some designers prefer to limit the key of a codes and descriptions table to one field—a single column that is also a coded value. Such a column is called a *surrogate key* because it has no business meaning and is used to represent the columns that do have business meaning and that are the real key of the table.

Having all code and description tables use only one code column as a key does make some issues easier. For instance, programming joins is a little easier this way, and it makes for a more understandable database design for users, perhaps lessening the difficulties of constructing queries.

If a designer really wants to achieve this result, the identifying relationship in the hierarchy must be changed into a non-identifying relationship. This in turn means that the dependent table must be given unique code values.

Table 6.4 Creating a unique Industry Subsector table.

Industry Sector Code	Industry Subsector Code	Industry Subsector Description
01	0101	Hospitals and Clinics
01	0102	Physicians
01	0103	Public Health
02	0201	Electrical Power Generation
02	0202	Hydrocarbon Fuels

Table 6.4 shows how the *Industry Subsector Code* can be made unique in the `Industry Subsector` Table by the very tempting method of prefixing each value with the corresponding value of *Industry Sector Code.* Figure 6.5 shows the revised database design with a non-identifying relationship that now links `Industry Sector` to `Industry Subsector`. The primary key of `Industry Subsector` is now only the *Industry Subsector Code.* Thus, when `Industry Subsector` is related to another table, like `Company`, only the single attribute *Industry Subsector Code* will be migrated into the related table as a foreign key.

While the structure of the tables is fine, prefixing *Industry Subsector Code* with *Industry Sector Code* is definitely not a good design. The reason is that we have now embedded two different pieces of information in one attribute: both *Industry Subsector Code* and *Industry Sector Code* exist within the new *Industry Subsector Code.* This can cause all kinds of problems, such as clever programmers parsing the value in their program logic to extract the *Industry Sector Code* instead of using SQL to join to the `Industry Sector` table to retrieve it. Ultimately data quality problems can arise from this kind of approach, and it makes the overall system very sensitive to changes, for example, in the length of the *Industry Sector Code.* Although it may appear unlikely at the outset, such changes are far from remote possibilities.

This so-called intelligent key problem is properly resolved by using a sequence number (or randomly valued code) as discussed in Chapter 5.

Returning to the new database design, let us assume that we have created a new key value for `Industry Subsector`, called *Industry Subsector Key,* which is a sequence number. Of course in terms of data modeling, this is cheating. `Industry Subsector` should be modeled as shown in Figure 6.3. Still, it is a comparatively small bending of the rules.

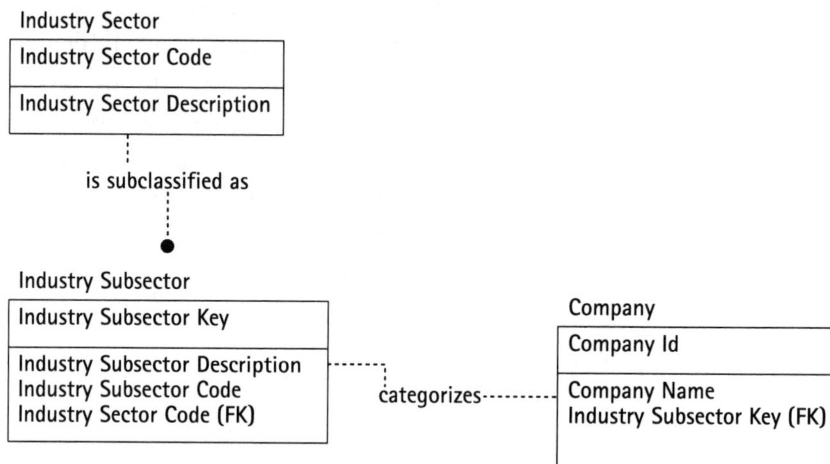

Figure 6.5 Conversion of an identifying relationship to a non-identifying relationship.

However, there is a new problem that affects joins. In the design using two columns for the primary key (see Figure 6.4), it is possible to join directly from `Company` to `Industry Sector`. Even though no relationship line exists between the two tables in Figure 6.4, there is in fact a relationship since both tables share *Industry Sector Code.* When `Industry Subsector` is changed to have a single column as its primary key, this is not possible. Figure 6.5 shows that `Company` must first be joined to `Industry Subsector`, and then an additional join operation is needed to `Industry Sector`. Alternatively this can be accomplished in a single SQL join of all three tables.

The design approach of using surrogate keys to avoid hierarchy and other issues in reference data was discussed more fully in Chapter 5. Traditional databases that handle transactions are more suited to the design shown in Figure 6.4. However, the designer must always be careful to select the design approach that best suits the goals he or she is trying to achieve.

Conclusion

There can be relationships among reference data tables. Data entry facilities for reference data must take account of these relationships and must not assume that reference data tables have very similar structures. These relationships are often non-identifying, but not always. Where identifying relationships exist, the child reference data tables contain multiattribute primary keys. It is more difficult to design update and retrieval functions for transaction data tables that are related to such reference data tables. Use of a surrogate key can help to overcome these problems.

CHAPTER 7

Redundancy of Reference Data

ONE OF THE CHARACTERISTICS of reference data discussed in Chapter 4 is its wide scope. Reference data is frequently related to many other tables in a database and is often used in program logic to create other information. The scope can also pass the boundaries of individual systems, so that the same reference data may be implemented repeatedly in different databases of an enterprise's information systems architecture. In situations like this, reference data is said to be *redundant* because multiple copies of it exist within the same general context. However, reference data can actually be redundant at a number of different levels, each with its own characteristics and different management needs. This chapter explores why this is so and how to address these management needs.

Redundancy of Codes and Descriptions

In a very basic way a code and its description represent the same piece of information. This redundancy is a deliberate design decision, for reasons discussed in Chapter 3. Even so, it does give rise to a couple of issues.

The first issue arises when a new record is added to a table containing codes and descriptions; both the code and description should be checked for uniqueness. Because the code is the primary key of the table, each record must have a different code (and this will probably be guaranteed if a sequence number is used instead of an acronym). After all, relational databases do not allow duplicate primary key instances in the same table. However, there is always a possibility that someone will forget that a particular description exists in a given table and try to add it again using a different code to represent it. The real piece of information being stored is the description, and duplicate descriptions cannot be allowed. Thus, whenever a description is being added or updated a check should be performed to make sure no other identical description exists in the table. Such a check may be time-consuming for the database engine because the description is not a primary key attribute of the table. Most database engines will automatically enforce uniqueness on codes (as they are the primary key of the table). However, they will not do this automatically for the non-key descriptions, so the check for their uniqueness must be done programmatically.

If acronyms are not used as primary keys, but are stored in reference data tables along with descriptions, then it is very important that they too are checked for uniqueness when records are updated. Again, since they are not primary keys, this will have to be done programmatically.

Another problem that can arise when dealing with both codes and descriptions is the divergent sorting of results sets for reporting purposes. This is especially true when acronyms are used as codes. Table 7.1 illustrates the problem. In this table, if *Country Code* is sorted alphabetically, then "JOR" comes before "JPN," but if *Country Name* is sorted alphabetically, then "Japan" comes before "Jordan." Because the code is the primary key, it may seem more natural to some programmers to sort by it. If the sort sequence of the codes is almost identical to that of the descriptions, programmers may assume that they both sort identically. Of course, this is an erroneous assumption.

This problem can become even more difficult if the codes involved are acronyms that are well known to users of the system. Table 7.2 shows some of the official acronyms and names of United Nations agencies. The acronyms do not always match the names because over time the official names have changed, but the acronyms were so well known that it was decided they would not be changed. For example, "UNFPA" used to stand for "**U**nited **N**ations **F**und for **P**opulation **A**ctivities," but several years ago the name of the agency was changed to United Nations Population Fund. The acronym was retained and is still "UNFPA."

Table 7.1 Fragment of a Country table.

Country Code	Country Name
JAM	Jamaica
JOR	Jordan
JPN	Japan

Table 7.2 Fragment of a United Nations Agency table.

UN Agency Acronym	UN Agency Name
UNCTAD	United Nations Conference on Trade and Development
UNDP	United Nations Development Programme
UNFPA	United Nations Population Fund
UNICEF	United Nations Children's Fund

Obviously the acronyms in this table will sort in a different sequence than the agency names. Which sequence is correct? There is no easy rule to apply in this situation except to ask the users of a system at design time if they want the information sorted by acronym or by official name. Some organizations do have standards for sorting outputs, such as always sorting by official name. Such standards make it easy to achieve consistency among outputs, but they are comparatively rare. The worst thing to do is to ignore the problem and have different reports sort by acronym or description for no reason other than programmer choice.

Redundancy across Databases

As noted above, the scope of reference data virtually guarantees that it will be implemented redundantly across an enterprise's information systems architecture. Very few organizations, except perhaps the smallest, have a single central database. Most have a set of operational systems (each with its own database), and perhaps data warehouses or data marts into which information is gathered for analysis and reporting. The situation may be even more complex if a given system is implemented in a number of different places, with a local copy of the database at each location.

Redundancy of reference data tables in different databases gives rise to a number of management issues, which are discussed below.

Synchronization of Data

If the same reference data is implemented in different systems, it may get updated more promptly in one system than in another. It may even get updated with different values in different systems. Many organizations experience these timing and data quality problems. They may be ignored until a problem occurs, such as reported information from one system does not match reported information from another system.

A better approach is to have a strategy to ensure that reference data is the same across all of an organization's systems. Unfortunately strategies of this kind are not easy to implement because of cost, organizational barriers, and technical difficulties. The best approach is for an organization to commit to central administration of reference data and to have one copy of reference data maintained by a centralized group. This approach is discussed further in Chapter 19.

Even if an organization has a central repository for reference data, the data still needs to be available to the organization's systems. There are three general ways of approaching this problem:

- A single reference database can be used by all systems. These systems would no longer contain reference data tables. The advent of Web-enabled databases makes this more of a possibility.
- Reference data can be exported from a central repository and imported into the databases of individual systems. This implies the design of the reference data tables in these systems is a very close match to the design of the central repository.

Some technical advances, like replication in certain database management software tools, may make this task a little easier.

- Personnel responsible for maintaining reference data in individual systems can be informed of changes in reference data by the group responsible for central reference data administration. They can then update their systems via user interfaces.

Perhaps the most important step that an organization can take in this area is to actually implement a strategy to manage reference data across multiple systems, even if the strategy is suboptimal in terms of achieving complete synchronization.

It should also be recognized that this is a very complex problem to solve. To some extent the best approach to take will depend on the information architecture of a given organization; factors such as the geographical distribution of systems and the reliance on legacy systems may be particularly important. These issues are explored in more depth in Chapter 19.

Replication of Maintenance Functionality

When the same reference data is implemented in different systems, there is a temptation to build the functionality to maintain the reference data into each system. Maintenance functionality consists of the processes needed to add, change, delete, and report on reference data. Creating such redundant functionality results in a duplication of effort and reinforcement of an architecture that views information systems as islands of automation and data.

Several reasons may lie behind this approach:

- There is no enterprise-level strategy for reference data, so no alternative is even considered.

- There is an enterprise-level strategy for reference data, but the team building a particular system decides to build the required functionality because
  - it wants to avoid dependencies on any other part of the organization;
  - the effort required to implement the functionality is viewed as minimal;
  - reference data is needed as soon as possible for other functionality to be built and tested;
  - the reference data is thought to pertain only to the system being built and to no other.

It is important to understand what the consequences of this design are.

Cost

The cost of building and supporting the same functionality over and over again represents wasted resources. Consider that the components that are typically built include

- screens and menus
- database tables and columns
- programs
- reports
- systems documentation
- user documentation

The functionality that is typically implemented is

- Add / Change / Delete reference data

- View reference data
- Query and report on reference data

The processes required to develop this functionality are

- design
- program
- test (unit test / systems test / user acceptance test)
- implement
- initial data load
- ongoing support

It may be argued that the functionality to maintain reference data represents perhaps only 5 to 10% of the total effort to develop an average system. However, this is still a real cost to an enterprise, and it means that on average for every 10 to 20 systems built, there is an unnecessary expenditure of the resources needed to construct one of these systems.

The recurrent annual cost of ongoing support—fixing bugs and implementing enhancements—is another issue. If functionality exists, the potential for bugs exists too. If a change occurs in the structure of reference data, the supporting functionality will have to be changed also. These costs will quickly add up across an enterprise with many systems.

The actual work done by the users of the systems in updating data via these separate components represents yet another cost. This may add up to a significant number, as well as increasing the chances of user error in data entry, leading to data quality issues.

Design Risk

If many different systems development project teams implement functionality to maintain the same reference data, the risk of someone getting his or her design wrong increases.

For instance, a table of `Industry Sector` may exist with *Industry Sector Code* incorrectly implemented as Character(3) in one system and correctly as Character(4) in another. The first system will work until a code with more than three characters is encountered. This could be days or years after implementation.

Adding to this risk is the fact that in many organizations there is no central repository of knowledge about reference data. Knowledge of individual tables may be dispersed among different business users. Many systems professionals may think that they know the reference data based on experience with prior systems, whereas in fact they do not.

Different Implementation

Charles Darwin found that animals with the same common ancestor evolved differently on different islands. The same can be true of reference data in "islands" of different systems within the same enterprise.

Tables 7.3 to 7.5 show three different ways of representing currency data in three different systems. Unfortunately these examples are drawn from real life.

Table 7.3 A simple approach in a system that deals with only two currencies.

Currency Code	Currency Name
C	Canadian Dollar
D	US Dollar

Table 7.4 Using Country Code to represent currency.

Currency Code	Currency Name
CAN	Canadian Dollar
MEX	Mexican Peso
USA	US Dollar

Table 7.5 Using ISO Currency codes to represent currency.

Currency Code	Currency Name
CAD	Canadian Dollar
MXP	Mexican Peso
USD	US Dollar

Table 7.3 is taken from a system in which all amounts were in U.S. dollars, and which was later enhanced to accept transactions in Canadian dollars. Table 7.4 is taken from a system in which it was decided that the country acronym could represent currency. This is not actually a good design because some countries have more than one currency and some currencies do not belong to a single country (e.g., the Euro). Table 7.5 shows an example that uses currency codes defined by the International Organization for Standardization (ISO).

The consequences of this kind of redundancy between systems are increased costs of maintaining different data representing the same thing, and serious problems if data from one system ever has to be merged with data from another.

Many organizations are implementing data warehouses and data marts, which take data from operational systems and make it available for analysis and reporting. One of the implementation problems they can encounter is the use of different codes to represent the same reference data in the source systems. This is discussed more fully in Chapter 10.

The "evolution" of codes into different forms does not end with different coding schemes. Even worse is the introduction of semantic incompatibilities. *Semantics* in this case refers to the meaning of codes and descriptions. Ideally a table of, say, countries will contain only real countries, but with redundant implementation of reference data, the chances increase that things that are not countries will be introduced.

If a reference table can be updated in a given system with no restrictions beyond simple edit checks, then the data quality can easily get out of control. Remember that users like to classify data, but it takes time to add new tables to a database to contain the classification schemes. There is a strong temptation to use existing tables to contain these classification schemes.

Table 7.6 shows an example in which regions (Europe and North America) have been added to a reference table for `Country`. This may be easier than implementing a separate `Region` table, but it violates the basic rule of database design that each entity and attribute has only one definition. The precise definition of *Country Code* can no longer be "a unique code which represents a country," since it can now represent a country or a region. Similarly, the definition of the `Country` table can no longer be "countries and dependent territories in which our company does business."

Table 7.6 Adding regions to a Country table.

Country Code	Country Name
CAN	Canada
EUR	Europe
FRA	France
IRE	Ireland
MEX	Mexico
NAM	North America
SWE	Sweden
UKM	United Kingdom
USA	United States of America

Suppose the data in Table 7.6 is used in a company's sales system to record where sales occur, and sales in European countries other than France, Ireland, Sweden, and the United Kingdom are recorded for "country" "EUR." The results for one month are shown in Table 7.7.

Now suppose that all payments for the company are received only in France, Ireland, Sweden, and the United Kingdom, irrespective of where sales occurred, and recorded in an accounts receivable system that has a `Country` table without the record for "EUR." The payments received for the same sales shown in Table 7.7 are summarized in Table 7.8.

Table 7.7 Summary report of Monthly Sales Results.

Country Code	Monthly Sales
EUR	20,000
FRA	50,000
IRE	30,000
SWE	10,000
UKM	60,000

Table 7.8 Summary report of Payments Received.

Country Code	Payments Received
FRA	60,000
IRE	32,000
SWE	13,000
UKM	65,000

The reports from these two systems will total to the same amount, but they cannot be reconciled at the country level. If the accounts receivable system had included "EUR" in the `Country` table, it would have been possible to record payments to match the sales system, but this would have been semantically wrong because "EUR" represents a region, not a country. The correct design would involve having a reference data table with all the countries in Europe (and no regions) and transaction tables that indicate both the country where a sale was made and the country where payment was received.

This example may seem a little artificial, but it is not that far from what happens in real life. The basic issue is that if the same reference data is implemented in different systems, there is nothing to stop it from drifting apart if it can be updated independently in these systems. The problems that arise from this situation may be glaring but are more often subtle and difficult to foresee.

These kinds of problems can be prevented if the enterprise as a whole has a strategy for dealing with reference data. Chapter 19 discusses how such a strategy can be developed.

Global Redundancy

So far we have been considering the redundancy of reference data within the context of a single enterprise, but some reference data is used by many different organizations.

It is not uncommon for enterprises to exchange data. This involves many of the same issues as exchanging data among different systems within a single enterprise, but when an external party is concerned, the process is usually treated more seriously. A major problem that is often encountered is reconciling differences in the reference data used by the two enterprises. For example, one enterprise may wish to send a mailing list to another enterprise. The first enterprise may use numeric codes to represent countries, and the second enterprise may use alphabetic codes.

Fortunately, there is something that can be done to facilitate the exchange of reference data, and that is to adopt the use of officially recognized standards wherever possible. A number of international coding standards exist, and any serious database design effort should determine if these standards will cover any coded reference data included in the database. If an organization adopts these standards, it is in a very strong position when it must send data to an external party and can probably avoid having to map reference data to a different format used by the external party.

Using international standards is good practice even if there are no plans to exchange data with other organizations. The standards are the product of a great deal of thought and effort, and there should be no reason why an organization would need to reinvent them. However, once adopted they must not be "polluted" by the addition of nonstandard codes. This requires an organizational approach to the maintenance of reference data, which is discussed in Chapter 19.

In Chapter 15 we review representative examples of these standards and the bodies responsible for them. The ISO, located in Geneva, Switzerland, is one of the more important bodies, and two of its standards, for Currency Codes and Country Codes, are reproduced in Appendices 1 and 2, respectively.

Conclusion

Reference data can exhibit redundancy at a number of levels. If the redundancy is not managed, it can lead to a waste of resources and to problems with data quality. Particularly serious problems can arise when different organizations exchange reference data. The use of recognized standard reference data can reduce these problems.

CHAPTER 8

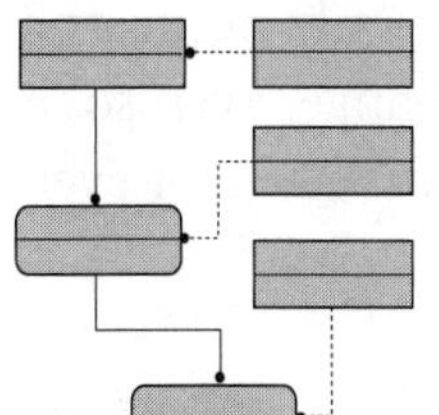

The Reference Data Life Cycle

INEVITABLY REFERENCE DATA VALUES have to be updated as time goes by. Additions, changes, and sometimes deletions have to be carried out. Few concerns are usually raised about additions, but changes and deletions are often approached with great trepidation. The reason is that the wide scope of reference data is well understood and gives rise to well-founded fears that changing it may cause systems errors. This chapter reviews the issues that arise from the need to maintain reference data over time.

Current and Historical Reference Data

Codes and descriptions are often recorded in tables that contain no additional information relating to time. This is probably because reference data is generally perceived as changing very infrequently.

Such a perception is not unreasonable. There is a particularly strong case for type codes not changing. Because they define entity subtypes, adding a new record or deleting an existing one would imply a change in database structure. Ordinarily this would only occur as a result of a design error or a fairly major business change. Even so, it can never be guaranteed that such a change is impossible. Not even type codes are immune to change.

However, more "mainstream" codes and descriptions are nearly always subject to pressures that cause change over time. The examples of country and currency used throughout this book are good examples. Throughout the 1980s there was relatively little change in any `Country` table—a couple of countries changed their names, and a very few new ones came into existence. Then with the breakup of the Soviet Union, a sizable number of new countries suddenly appeared. `Currency` tables have always been more subject to change each year, even excluding the new currencies for the countries formed from the old Soviet Union. This happens, for instance, as countries reform currencies that have lost value, and in most years up to half a dozen changes can occur.

There is more acceptance that constant values change over time, although many are slow to change, such as tax rates that change only by legislative action. On the other hand, exchange rates can change on a daily, or even an intraday, basis. That is why constant values nearly always have keys that include effective dates or datetimes.

The reality is that reference data does change, albeit slowly. Perhaps some of it may not change over the lifetime of a system, but this cannot be predicted during the design phase of the system. For a system that is designed to last, say, five years, the probability is that more reference data will change than the designers anticipated. Such change can be planned for or it can be ignored. Planning for it does not require much extra effort, but ignoring change can be costly.

Codes and descriptions are somewhat different from constant values in terms of their maintenance requirements, so they are dealt with first in the following section.

Changing Codes and Descriptions

There is a limited set of actions that can be taken to update codes and descriptions:

- Adding a new code and description (and possibly an acronym)
- Changing a code
- Changing a description (and possibly an acronym)
- Deleting a code and description (and possibly an acronym)

The functionality to perform these actions must be present in some way (for instance, through data entry or batch interface). The most serious issues surround changing a code or deleting a record. With reference data these two actions always raise the fear—usually with good reason—that the change will cause system problems.

Referential Integrity

If a coded value is to be updated or deleted, referential integrity (RI) can be a useful tool for managing the change. Even if RI is not available, the concepts it uses to handle changes are very useful to know about and can be applied in a wide variety of situations.

Many database management systems have implemented RI, which is an automated way of ensuring that foreign keys are kept consistent. RI is set up within the database and is invoked whenever any kind of update actions occur.

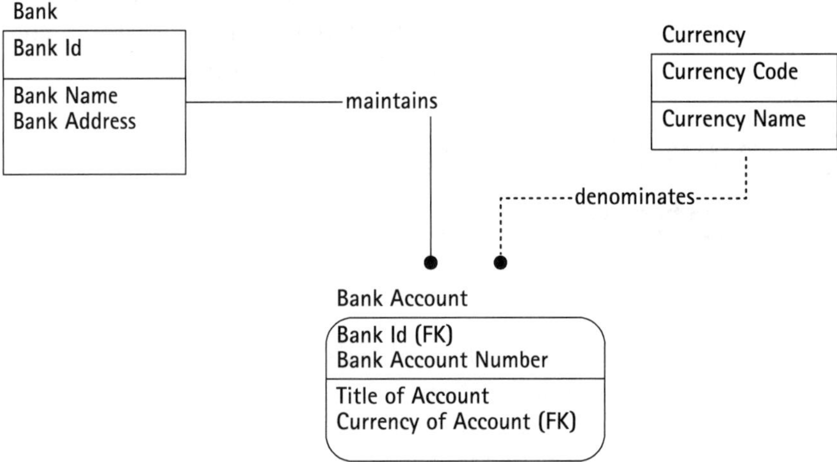

Figure 8.1 Physical database design fragment showing relationships.

In RI a series of possible choices are associated with adding, changing, or deleting either the parent or child record in a foreign-key relationship. This is illustrated in Figure 8.1, which shows the two kinds of relationships that can exist in a database:

- Identifying: where the primary key of the parent is migrated into the primary key of the child. For example, the key of `Bank` (parent)—that is, *Bank Id*—is migrated into `Bank Account` (child).
- Non-identifying: where the primary key of the parent is migrated as a non-primary key column of the child. For example, `Currency` (parent) is migrated to `Bank Account` (child) *where Currency Code* is renamed to *Bank Account Currency* in the child.

For each relationship there are six RI cases that need to be considered:

1. **Parent Insert.** What action is to be taken if a new record is inserted into the parent table?
2. **Parent Update.** What action is to be taken if the primary key of a parent record is changed?
3. **Parent Delete.** What action is to be taken if a parent record is deleted?
4. **Child Insert.** What action is to be taken if a new record is inserted into the child table?
5. **Child Update.** What action is to be taken if the primary key of a child record is changed?
6. **Child Delete.** What action is to be taken if a child record is deleted?

In the context of managing reference data, numbers 2 and 3 above matter most, because the reference data table is always the parent, and adding a new record should have no effect on other tables. For each of these cases there are five possible actions that can be taken. These are as follows:

Parent Update

- **Restrict.** Do not let the code be changed if it is used in the child table. For example, if the code "USA" is supposed to be changed to "USD" in the parent `Currency` table, this cannot happen if "USA" is being used in *Bank Account Currency.*
- **Cascade.** Carry the change down to all related records in the child table. For example, if the code "USA" is changed to "USD" in the `Currency` table, then the database will automatically change all "USA" values to "USD" in *the Bank Account Currency* column of the `Bank Account` table.
- **Set Null.** This should be used with caution, if at all. It will result in the child values being set to nulls. For example, if

"USA" is changed to "USD" in the `Currency` table, all the values "USD" in *Bank Account Currency* will be automatically set to null by the database. This option cannot be used for identifying relationships because no column of the primary key in the child table can be null.

- **Set Default.** This should be used with caution, if at all. It will result in the child values being set to a default value. For example, if the default is "USD," and "CAN" is changed to "CND" in the `Currency` table, then the database will automatically change "CAN" to "USD" in *Bank Account Currency.*
- **None.** This means that if the code is changed in the parent record, the database takes no action on the child. This should not be used.

Parent Delete

- **Restrict.** Disallow the deletion of the parent record if corresponding child records exist. For example, if the record to be deleted in the `Currency` table has a code value of "USD," the action will not be allowed if any record in the `Bank Account` table has a *Bank Account Currency* with a value of "USD." This option is widely recognized as being very safe.
- **Cascade.** Permit the deletion to occur, but also delete all corresponding records in the child table. For example, if the record to be deleted in the `Currency` table has a code value of "USD," then delete all records in `Bank Account` where *Bank Account Currency* is also "USD." This can be a very useful option to use for reference data, but its effects can be widespread and it should be used with extreme care.
- **Set Null.** Permit the deletion to occur, and change all corresponding values in the child table to null. For example, if the record to be deleted in the `Currency` table has a code value of "USD," then update all records in `Bank Account` where *Bank Account Currency* is also "USD" to set *Bank Account Currency*

to null. This option could be justified under some circumstances—mainly if *Bank Account Currency* was an optional attribute in `Bank Account`. However, it cannot be used for identifying relationships because no column of the primary key in the child table can be null.

- **Set Default.** Permit the deletion to occur, and change all corresponding values in the child table to a default value. For instance, if the record to be deleted in the `Currency` table has a code value of "CND," then update all records in `Bank Account` where *Bank Account Currency* is also "CND" to set *Bank Account Currency* to "USD." It is difficult to see any value is using this option.
- **None.** This means that the parent record is deleted, but the database takes no action on the child. This should not be used as it will create "orphan" records in the child table.

These, then, are the actions that could be taken for the case of a Parent Update or Parent Delete. One of the characteristics of reference data is that it is potentially a "service" to many other tables in a database. Thus one reference data table may be related to many other tables in a database, even to the extent that systems personnel may not be completely sure of all the places where it is used. This is an argument for a very conservative approach to modifying reference data, and the best RI constraints for this are

- Parent Delete—Restrict
- Parent Update—Restrict

These two choices will prevent a code from being changed or deleted in a reference data table if it is used at all in any child table.

Most modern database management systems support the implementation of RI constraints, usually as triggers. It is worth implementing *Parent Delete—Restrict* and *Parent Update—Restrict* if it is fairly easy to change reference data. There is little in the way of overhead to worry about, and the triggers will only be fired if someone tries to change or delete the reference data. One downside to doing this is that prior to production implementation, especially during testing, programmers and analysts may need to modify data in an unrestricted fashion. If the triggers are implemented at this point, they can fire and cause problems. To avoid problems, it may be advisable to enable triggers during the later stages of testing. However, triggers still need to be tested thoroughly.

Another downside to using *Restrict* referential integrity is that, as discussed above, there may sometimes be a genuine need to cascade a changed code. This could still be done by changing the triggers, or via the steps in the following example.

Let us say we need to change the code "USA" to "USD" in the `Currency` table. The description "US Dollar" will remain unchanged.

1. Add a new record to the `Currency` table with "USD" as the code and "US Dollar" as the description.
2. In every table that is a child of `Currency`, change the value "USA" to "USD" in the foreign key columns. This will be allowed because "USD" now exists in the `Currency` table.
3. Delete the record with "USA" from the `Currency` table. This will be allowed since "USA" is no longer used in any child table.

This set of steps could be performed by a specially written program or even by manually updating the system.

If RI is not implemented at the database level via triggers, it can be implemented in program logic, which may be the only alternative in some database systems. This option provides less security, which may be a concern.

Caution is advised if RI is implemented on the child side. For instance, it is possible to have a *Child Update—Cascade* which will add a record to the parent reference table if the code is not found there. As an example, if in the `Bank Account` table the user changes the *Bank Account Currency* from "USD" to "AUD," and "AUD" does not exist in the parent `Currency` table, then a new record will be inserted into the `Currency` table with a *Currency Code* of "AUD." Similarly a *Child Delete—Cascade* could be written so that when the last instance of a code is deleted from the child table, it is also deleted from the parent table. For example, if the last record with "CND" is deleted from `Bank Account`, then the record in the `Currency` table where the *Currency Code* is "CND" is also deleted from the parent reference data table. This is not a good idea since "CND" is no longer available as a choice for future transactions.

It is not a good idea to have RI, or indeed any program logic, update reference data tables without human intervention of some kind. There are simply too many issues involved in reference data and too great a potential for problems. Updates should always be made directly via data entry or through a specific batch interface based on operator-entered information.

Even when RI is implemented, there are limits to what it can achieve. One common problem is what to do with archived data. It is a common practice to "archive" transactions from a database once they have reached a certain age. The process of archiving involves removing older transactions from the database and housing them somewhere else. This could be in another database, a data warehouse, or some kind of mass storage, such as an optical disk. Without archiving, databases can become filled with transactions that are rarely accessed for any reason and grow in an unlimited fashion. However, once they are archived transactions are beyond the reach of RI in the originating database. There is less chance of RI being implemented in the archive database because in many cases they are not even relational database management systems. This leaves programming as the only realistic way to effect change.

The analyst must consider if the archived data actually should be changed. If the archived transactions have been reported under the old reference data, and this is then changed, any new reports may be irreconcilable with the old reports. This may even be illegal in the case of regulatory reporting or government regulations covering the archiving of data. On the other hand, if the archived transactions are to be used in trend analyses, they must be consistent over time, and so the old reference data will have to be changed to conform with the new. Once again the designer must choose the correct approach to solve the business problem at hand.

Succession of Codes and Descriptions

There is another dimension to changing codes and values besides the actual update actions that have to occur and the potential RI constraints. This dimension reflects the fact that the enterprise needs not only to add, update, and delete reference data, but also to have one particular value succeeded by another value as time goes by.

Figure 8.2 illustrates the life cycle of a code representing a currency. Let us suppose "XXX" represents a currency that has an exchange rate of 10,000 to the U.S. dollar. The government of the country where it is now in use decides to introduce a completely new currency, initially trading at 1.00 to the U.S. dollar. The new currency will have a new name and by convention a new currency code, "YYY." There will be a date on which the new currency is introduced, perhaps a phase-in period when both currencies are in circulation, and a date when the old currency is no longer valid, leaving only the new currency in effect.

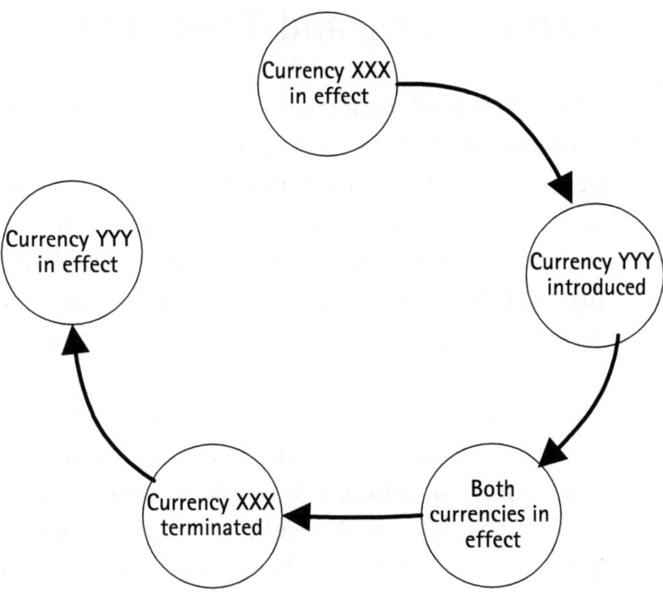

Figure 8.2 Currency code life cycle.

This example illustrates a number of characteristics that are involved in managing change in codes and descriptions. The two most important are:

- **Life span.** A code and its description become effective on a given date and terminate at a later specific date. The *effective date* and *termination date* apply to a set of transactions for the business. Optimally they apply to the business as a whole, but this is not necessarily true.
- **Succession.** A code is usually succeeded by another. This may not always happen, and it may happen in a complex way.

Dates, Times, and Time Zones

The life span of a code value is bounded by its *effective date* and *termination date*. A date—that is, a specific day—may not actually be precise enough in all situations. Fortunately most modern database management systems do have a datatype for datetime, which will permit a time as well as a date to be recorded, usually down to a millisecond. In databases that do not have a datetime datatype, it is necessary to hold the time in a separate data attribute.

However, even datetime may not be precise enough in a global environment, because it is measured with reference to geographical location, not in an absolute way. For instance, 6:00 PM on December 19 in New York City will be 6:00 AM on December 20 in Hong Kong. If a really precise datetime is required, then the concept of time zone must be introduced. Time zones can be named or can be represented as a time offset measured relative to Greenwich Mean Time (GMT, also known as Universal Time or UT), that is, the standard time on the prime meridian (which passes through Greenwich, England). GMT does not vary to accommodate seasons so there is no summer (daylight savings) and winter time. Each time zone has a GMT offset, which is the number of hours (and possibly minutes) it is ahead of or behind GMT. For instance, the U.S. Eastern Standard Time zone is designated as –0500 (two digits for hours and two digits for minutes) because it is five hours behind GMT. When a datetime is expressed with the related time zone, it can be converted to the corresponding datetime at any other place in the world. Thus if in addition to datetime, time zone is also captured, we can give totally precise effective and termination "dates" to a code value.

Time Zone is data that consists of codes and descriptions; for example, the code "EST" represents the description "U.S. Eastern Standard Time." *GMT Offset* is a different piece of data: the number of hours and minutes it differs from the time measured at its location relative to GMT. A database designer can put either (or both) in the database. *Time Zone* can be used to categorize data but requires some logic and calculations to derive the equivalent GMT. *GMT Offset* is easier to deal with mathematically but is not well suited to categorizing data (e.g., it has no description associated with it).

Some time zones differ in units other than a number of whole hours from GMT; for example, Newfoundland in North America is –04:30. A further complication is daylight savings time. U.S. Eastern Daylight Time is –04:00, whereas Eastern Standard Time is –0500. In the U.S. this is further complicated by the fact that some states do not have daylight saving time (e.g., Arizona and parts of Indiana). If an organization needs to record time zone information, it should use standard time zones rather than the daylight saving equivalents (e.g., always use U.S. Eastern Standard Time). It should also consider recording standard time rather than daylight savings time.

Figure 8.3 illustrates the gradual increase in complexity of database design as these concepts are implemented. Not all organizations need the greatest level of precision, but it is important to consider it for databases that deal in transactions from different time zones.

If a new system is developed and reference data implemented with effective and termination dates, the question arises as to what the effective date should be. In some instances an effective date may be known, but it is likely that for much of the data particular effective dates will not be available. The effective date should not be left null, as this would be confusing to program logic trying to determine if a particular code value was in effect at a particular time. The best solution is to adopt a default date or datetime. This could be the date the organization for whom the system is being built came into existence (if this is known), or a date so far back in the past that it could not have been recorded in any actual transaction in the system. This information could itself be global reference data (Table 8.1), recorded in a table that consists of a single record (see Chapter 3).

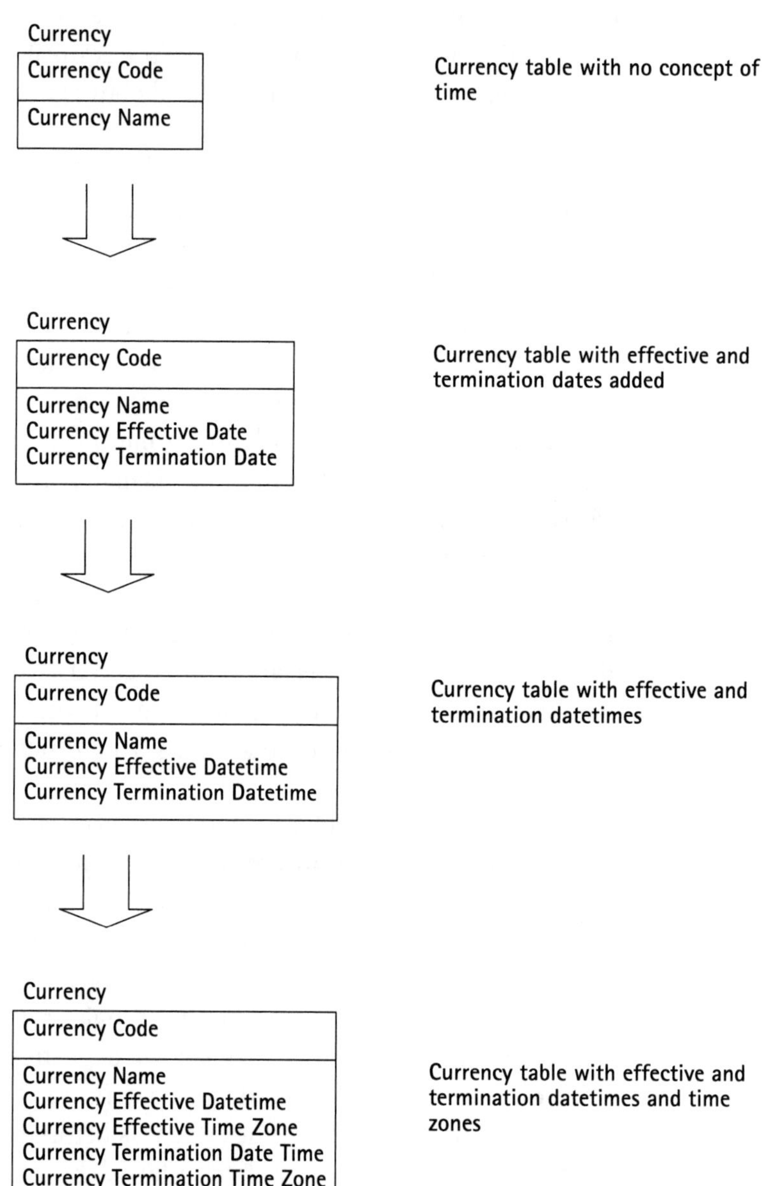

Figure 8.3 Database designs for increasing precision of code life span.

Table 8.1 Part of Global Default Table, showing default datetime and GMT offset.

Column	Value
Default Effective Datetime	01/01/1970 00:00:00
Default Effective GMT Offset	-0500

Correlating Transactions to Effective Reference Data

The dates, times, and time zones (or GMT offsets) of reference data, which set the boundaries of when it is in effect, represent only part of what is required. Transactions that make use of reference data must be able to access the correct reference data values. This means that each transaction recorded in the database must have a date (putting aside times and time zones for the moment in order to simplify the discussion) which can be compared with the *effective date* and *termination date* in the reference data. Such a date is called a *reference date,* and reference data is relevant to the transaction if the *reference date* of the transaction is greater than or equal to the *effective date* and less than the *termination date* of the reference data.

If the transactions do not have a *reference date,* then none of this is possible, unless it is assumed that the *reference date* is the current (today's) date.

Using reference dates also has implications when transaction data is updated in a database. The program logic must ensure that only reference data that may be applicable to a transaction based upon the *reference date* is available to update the transaction. Reference data that is not in effect for such a transaction must be filtered out from the update process.

Adding this kind of logic to a computerized system is an extra cost, but it can make the system more robust and give it a longer life span. Simply dismissing the issue, or failing to think about it during the design stage, is an error. It is also an error to introduce *effective dates* and *termination dates* into reference data tables if no use is to be made of them. A good designer must always consciously match the system design to the business goals that are to be met.

Succession

While dates, times, and time zones can define the life span of a reference data value, it is important to consider what happens when such values cease to be in effect. This raises the issue of succession—how new reference data values replace older ones over time.

It is possible that when a piece of reference data ceases to be in effect, it is not succeeded by any other data. In a reference table where this happens, the designer may wish to indicate that termination is final by including an additional data attribute such as an indicator.

It is also possible (and perhaps more frequent) that a reference data value is succeeded by one or more values after it terminates. There are a number of ways in which this can happen, some of which are fairly complex. Each of the ways in which succession can occur is examined in the remainder of this section.

- The reference data value is not succeeded by any other value after it ceases to be in effect.

Take, for example, a company that publishes magazines in a number of languages. The company might decide to discontinue publishing all magazines in a particular language. Figure 8.4 illustrates this situation. In the reference table implemented to contain the language codes and descriptions for the languages that the publisher publishes

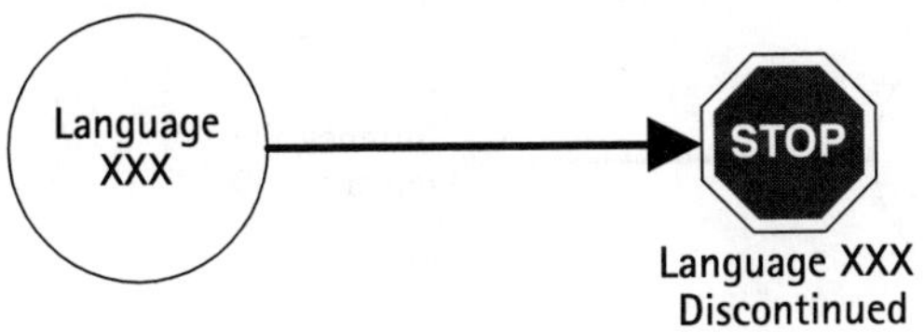

Publication Language
Language Code
Language Name Language Effective Datetime Language Effective Time Zone Language Termination Datetime Language Termination Time Zone Language Discontinued Indicator

Figure 8.4 Example of complete termination of a reference data value.

in, the designer has included an indicator to show that a code is no longer in effect and has no successor.

- The reference data value is succeeded by one other value after it ceases to be in effect.

Consider, for example, a currency that is replaced by another currency, as illustrated in Figure 8.5. The successor currency has been added as a column in the database.

- Several reference data values are merged into one.

An example of this is two or more countries that merge into one. Figure 8.6 illustrates such a situation. The database design is the same as that in which one value is replaced by one other, because each value is replaced by only one successor.

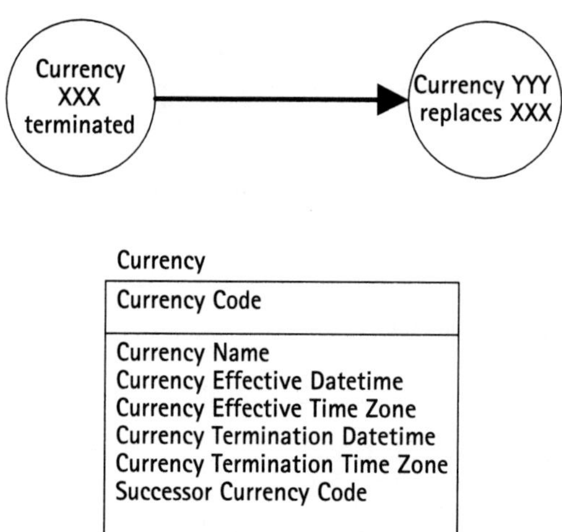

Figure 8.5 Replacement of one reference data value by one other value.

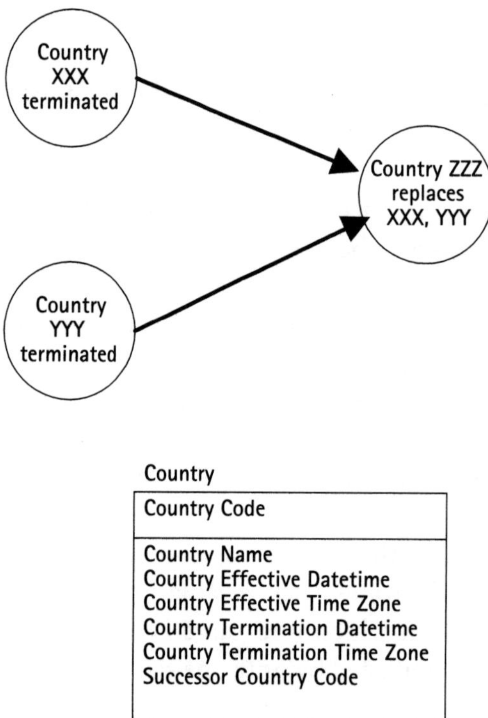

Figure 8.6 The merging of several reference data values into one other value.

However, there are some additional business issues involved here, the most important being how historical information recorded using the old country code will be handled. This is discussed more in the next section, *Business Issues Related to Succession.*

- One reference data value is split into two or more.

The splitting of a reference data value into two (or more) is more complex than the other scenarios described above. Figure 8.7 illustrates the situation. This situation cannot be supported simply by adding a data attribute *Successor Country Code* to the `Country` table because there is more than one successor. One solution is to create another table to hold succession information, as shown in Figure 8.7. This design is a general solution to handling all types of succession, because it handles the one-to-many of a value splitting and the many-to-one of a value merging.

An alternative, bad (but tempting) denormalized database design is shown in Figure 8.8. The `Country` table contains both a *Successor Country Code* and a *Predecessor Country Code.*

The idea is that when a *Country Code* value is succeeded by another value, then the *Successor Country Code* field can be filled in on the record for the old *Country Code*, and the *Predecessor Country Code* filled in on the record for the new *Country Code.* Unfortunately when several *Country Codes* merge into one, *the Predecessor Country Code* cannot be filled in on the record for the new *Country Code*, because there are several values, and not one. Similarly, when a *Country Code* splits into several new codes, the *Successor Country Code* cannot be filled in on the record for the old Country Code.

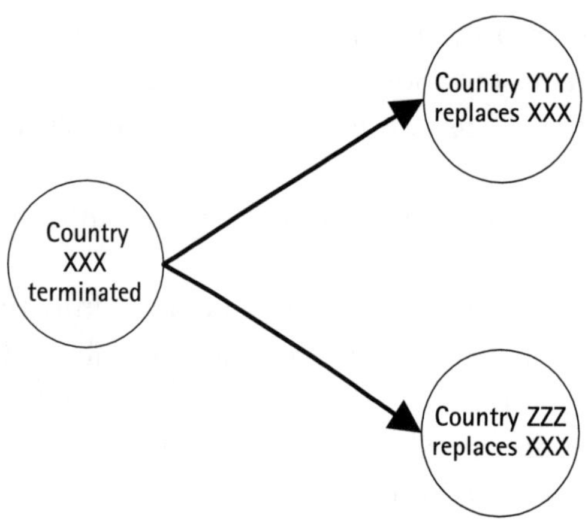

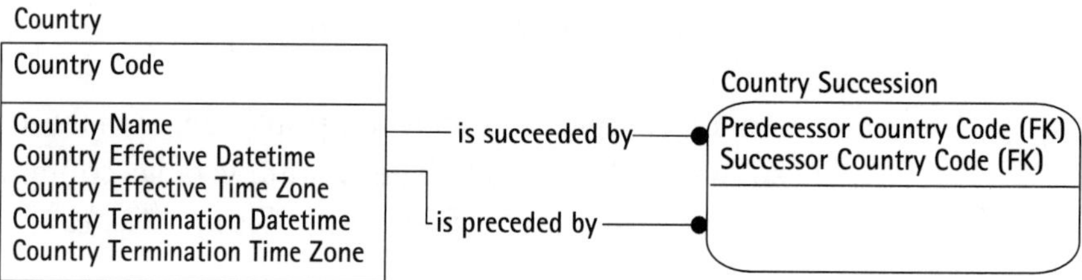

Figure 8.7 The splitting of reference data values into several other values.

Country

Country Code

Country Name
Country Effective Datetime
Country Effective Time Zone
Country Termination Datetime
Country Termination Time Zone
Successor Country Code
Predecessor Country Code

Figure 8.8 A flawed general way of dealing with succession.

Other deficiencies of this denormalized design are as follows:

- A *Predecessor Country Code* value may be null, even though the current code is a successor to another code (when several codes merge into one). This could be inferred by a *Country Effective Datetime* not being equal to some default value. Alternatively the database could be searched for records where the *Successor Country Code* is equal to the *Country Code* of the current record.
- A *Successor Country Code* value may be null, even though the current code has been succeeded by another (when one code splits into several others). This could be inferred by the presence of a non-null *Country Termination Datetime.*

The design is tempting because only one table is involved. However, it should not be used.

Physical implementations of database designs to deal with succession depend on a variety of factors that differ from project to project. Suffice it to say that the best logical design is that shown in Figure 8.7. Other alternatives, like that shown in Figure 8.8, may be considered but usually do not work in the long run.

Business Issues Related to Succession

There are some additional concerns that need to be addressed when reference data value succession happens.

One important issue relates to the reporting of historical data—*historical* meaning transactions that occurred before the succession. How will this data be reported? Either the data will continue to be reported under the old code, or it will be reported under the new code. If the first option is chosen, nothing more need be done. After all, the old code value is still in the reference data table where it always was. If the second option is chosen, there is a problem if an old code splits into several others. The question arises as to which new code the data for the old code should be reported under.

Suppose we had a company that did business in the old Soviet Union. After the Soviet Union broke up into many new countries, how would we report the data recorded under "Soviet Union"? One way would to be to assign a default value, say "Russian Federation." Another approach would be to go through each old transaction, try to figure out what new country (e.g., Russian Federation, Ukraine, Uzbekistan, etc.) it corresponds to, and update the transaction to indicate the new country.

These kinds of changes can be complex. For instance, there could be a business requirement to retain the old code value on the transaction and add the new one, rather than simply replacing the old with the new. As noted earlier in this chapter, there may even be legal requirements that mandate the retention of the old code.

There can be many business issues related to the succession of reference data values that are not easy to resolve. If an organization is serious about managing reference data, it should try to adopt a strategy prior to being faced with the need to implement a change. It takes time to research and think about these problems, and a poorly informed decision taken simply to implement a change quickly can have profound effects on information systems for a very long time.

Succession and Sequence Numbers

The use of sequence numbers as values for codes in reference data tables was discussed in Chapter 5 and contrasted with the use of acronyms. Many designers think that using sequence numbers provides automatic protection against all changes in reference data. This is just not true. All the issues of code succession discussed in this chapter pertain equally to codes represented by sequence numbers as to codes represented by acronyms. Sequence numbers have an advantage over acronyms when there is simply a change from one acronym or description, rather than a succession of values. Acronyms, having business meaning, are more susceptible to such changes from the user community, whereas sequence numbers are not. The designer should not choose to use sequence numbers to represent coded values, with the expectation that they are immune to changes.

Conclusion

Reference data cannot be assumed to be static over time, and changes need to be planned for in information systems. In particular, referential integrity needs to be maintained in an enterprise's databases. The problem of the evolution of reference data values over time (especially splitting and merging of values) can present additional challenges that should be planned for in database designs. A complete change management strategy should also address the needs of historical or archived data.

CHAPTER 9

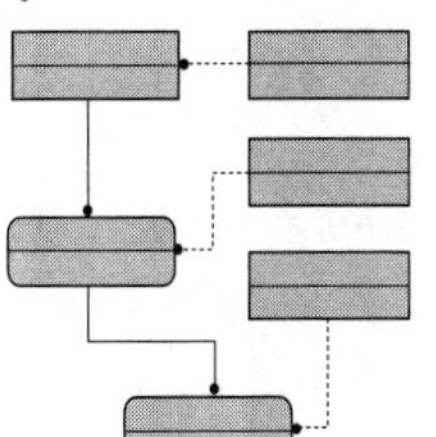

Monitoring the Usage of Reference Data

THE ISSUES INVOLVED IN THE MANAGEMENT of reference data are often different from those of managing other kinds of data in a database. One of these issues is a need to know what reference data is being used in a database, and how it is being used. However, there are differences in what usage means for the two main classes of reference data:

- Codes are defined with descriptions in one parent table and exist as foreign keys in other tables in the database. They usually exist as sets of values, and usage refers to the occurrence of these values outside the parent table.
- Constant values are not usually propagated into other database tables. Their usage is in process logic, often in distinct business rules.

The ways in which reference data is used, and how usage can be monitored, are discussed in this chapter.

Which Columns Are Codes Used In?

We will first consider the usage of reference data values represented by codes. To determine where codes are used in a database, it is helpful to have an entity-relationship diagram (ERD) of the database under consideration. With an ERD, the relationships from each reference table can be traced to the tables in which the codes exist as foreign keys.

Figure 9.1 is an example of an ERD that shows *Country Code* used as `Customer Account`.*Domicile Country of Account*, `Order`.*Order Shipping Address - Country*, and `Order`.*Order Origination Country*. *Currency Code* is used as `Order`.*Order Total Value Currency* and `General Ledger`.*Ledger Account Currency*. `Currency` should also have a relationship with `Customer Account`, and there should be an entity to represent Customer, but these have been omitted for readability.

Unfortunately many real-life databases are not documented well enough to show what columns are actually foreign keys from reference data tables. In these circumstances it can actually be quite difficult to find this information. The only real option—reverse engineering—involves looking at physical database tables, existing documentation, program code, and perhaps outputs of the system. There are some automated tools that can help, but they cannot make correct inferences for an analyst. For instance, it is possible to find column names in tables that are the same as the primary key column names of the reference data tables. However, it is not always true that a foreign key column in a table has the same name as the corresponding column in the reference table.

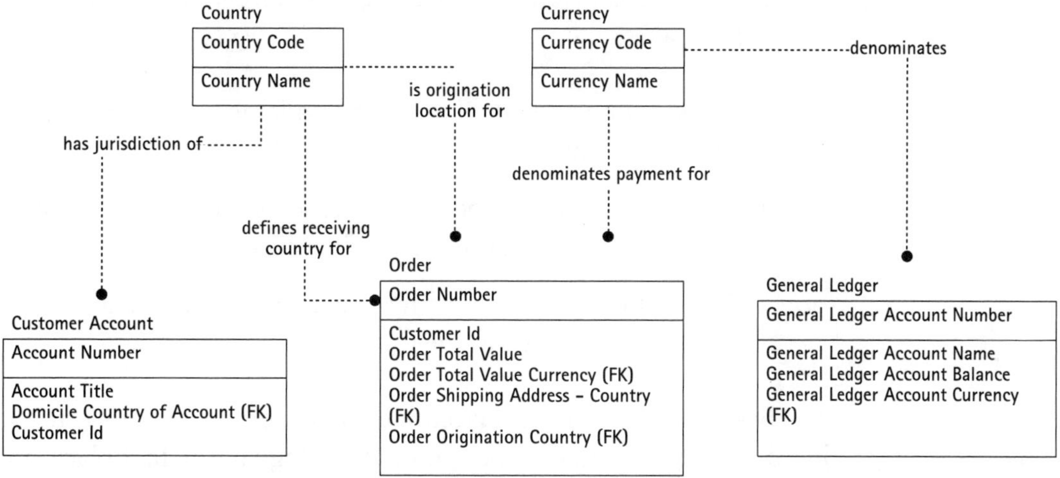

Figure 9.1 A simplified physical database design fragment showing the use of Country and Currency tables.

For instance, in the `Country` table the *Country Code* column may have a physical name of *CTY_C*, but in the `Order` table the *Order Shipping Address - Country* may have a physical name of *SHIP_CTY_C*. If it were called *CTY_C* instead of *SHIP_CTY_C*, we could be reasonably sure that it represents `Country Code`. Even so, in this particular example the way in which columns are named can still allow the inference that *SHIP_CTY_C* represents *Country Code*. Ultimately, it may be necessary to look at the values in the columns to try to determine which if any reference data table they come from.

It is even worse to find columns with identical physical names but completely different meanings. This can be a particularly serious problem for reference data. Some programmers may consider one code just the same as any other and always name the column containing the code value "Code," or "Id," or something similar in every reference table. Unfortunately this is not uncommon in legacy systems.

In these situations reverse engineering is required, but it has a number of drawbacks:

- It takes time and effort and can be a large, albeit hidden, cost in systems support.
- If inferences have to be used, a certain degree of guesswork is involved, and the results can be inaccurate.
- If the findings of the analysis are not documented, it may have to be repeated in the future.

The best way to avoid this inaccurate and expensive process is to follow a recognized database design methodology in the first place, and use enterprise-wide standards. If reverse engineering has to be done, try to involve personnel with experience in the area being reviewed. The results of reverse engineering should be captured in some kind of systems information repository, or at least in some consistent, centralized documentation.

Which Codes Are Being Used?

There are a number of reasons for wishing to know how codes representing individual reference data values are being used in a database.

- If a code is not used at all, it may not need to be included in reference data. Users may complain about having to select values from long lists, most of which are irrelevant to them.

  Example: A `Country` table may contain 200 entries, but in 10 years the organization has only had to use 18.

- If a code has to be changed, systems personnel may need to know what the potential effect will be. This involves knowing how often the code is used in transaction data.

  Example: Country X has just reformed its currency so it has an exchange rate of 1:1 with the U.S. dollar instead of 1:10,000. Has our organization ever used the old currency code?

- If there is a business question regarding a code, part of the analysis may involve finding out where it is used.

  Example: Our organization used to do business in East Germany (Country Code = "GDR"). After German reunification the code "GDR" should not have been used in any transactions. Are we sure this is the case?

- There may be data analysis questions pertaining to a specific code.

  Example: We are building a data mart that will include all customer information. The Country Code "EUR" exists in a reference data table in the order entry system, but not in the accounts receivable system. We will need to combine data from both systems. Has "EUR" actually been used in customer data in the order entry system?

Some of these questions will need special queries to be constructed to answer them. For others, it is worth considering if standard reporting should be implemented. Standard reporting means implementing reports that are produced at regular intervals (or on demand), rather than using a tool to create a query and report format each time the report is needed. The latter are termed ad-hoc reports, and staff may lose interest in having to recreate them repeatedly over a long period of time.

Standard reports can be used to quickly spot usage (or nonusage) patterns and possible anomalies in reference data. However, before creating any reports, the columns in which reference data is used must be known, as discussed in the previous section.

What would such standard reports look like? Figure 9.2 shows a minimum set of features.

- The reference data table whose codes are being analyzed must be identified—that is, `Country` in Figure 9.2.
- The target table and column being analyzed must be identified—that is, `Order` and *Order Origination Country,* respectively, in Figure 9.2.
- Each code value in the `Country` table should be shown, even those that are not used in the column being analyzed, such as “IRE” in Figure 9.2.
- If code values are found in the column being analyzed that do not exist in the reference data table, these should be included and flagged, such as “NET” in Figure 9.2. A situation like this would indicate that either invalid values have been entered into the target table, presumably bypassing edit controls, or that the reference data table has somehow lost records that were used to validate entry of codes into the target table.
- The number of occurrences of null values in the column being analyzed should be included. Null values represent the nonoccurrence of data and are catered for in most modern database products. It would certainly be surprising to see null values in a column that was thought to require the presence of a code.
- The grand total of all occurrences, including nulls, should be shown. This is the same as the number of rows in the table being analyzed.

Usage of Country Code, by Table and Column

Reference Data Table: Country

Target Table: Order

Target Column: Order Origination Country

Code	Description	Number of occurrences	
FRA	France	3	
IRE	Ireland	0	
NET		1	Error - No Code!
SWE	Sweden	3	
UKM	United Kingdom	5	
USA	United States of America	20	
	Subtotal:	32	
	Nulls	2	
	Grand Total:	34	

Figure 9.2 Reference Data Usage Report.

The report in Figure 9.2 could be enhanced to show a number of other things, if these were deemed useful, such as

- A count of the rows in the reference table
- Physical names of tables and columns
- The *Number of Occurrences* divided by the *Grand Total* and expressed as a percentage for each code value

Several modern database products do have built-in database consistency checking which can go some way to creating the kind of report illustrated in Figure 9.2. However, they may not report all the information needed to properly manage codes and descriptions.

Usage of Constant Values

Unlike codes, constant values are not used as foreign keys across a database. However, they are used in process logic in programs and can be particularly important in business rules, especially the rules that create derived data.

Consider the simple report from an order system shown in Figure 9.3. Table 9.1 shows the database records it is based on.

Order Number: 927546

Item	Cost
Item 1	35.00
Item 2	125.00
Item 3	40.00
Item 4	75.00
Subtotal	275.00
State Sales tax @ 6.000%	16.50
Order Total	291.50

Figure 9.3 Order Summary Report.

Table 9.1 Fragment of a Sales Order table.

Order Id	Order Item Number	Item Price	Item State Sales Tax
927546	1	38.00	2.10
927546	2	128.00	7.50
927546	3	40.00	2.40
927546	4	78.00	8.50

Table 9.2 Fragment of a State Sales Tax Rate table.

State Code	Effective Date	Sales Tax Rate %
NJ	1/1/1998	6.000
NY	1/1/1998	8.250

The data attribute *Item State Sales Tax* is calculated by the system, not entered by an operator. The business rule for its calculation is as follows:

Item State Sales Tax = (Item Price) x
((Applicable State Sales Tax Rate Percentage) / 100)

`Applicable State Sales Tax Rate Percentage` is the *Sales Tax Rate%* for the state in which the order was placed. *Sales Tax Rate%* is stored in a reference data table that contains tax rates by state and effective date, as shown in Table 9.2. The tax rate prevailing at the time of the sale is taken from this table.

Thus the `State Sales Tax Rate` table and the `Sales Order` table shown in Tables 9.1 and 9.2 are related by a business rule. Unfortunately business rules are often either not captured, or they are documented in a purely textual fashion. They do not show up as relationship lines on entity-relationship diagrams. The result is that there is no easy way to find out which business rules a given data attribute in the database participates in. Some more modern analytical tools are beginning to address this need, but for the vast majority of systems, determining the usage of constant values requires looking through system documentation or program code.

If reverse engineering must be performed on program specifications or program logic, then at a minimum the results should be retained so the process does not have to be repeated. The results should also be stored in a place where it is known they can be found and where it is easily accessible by any interested party.

Unlike codes and descriptions, constant values tend to be single instances of numbers, not a set that has to be implemented as a distinct table. Issues that might prompt questions about their usage could be concerned with the following:

- Format changes. Example: We need to add an extra decimal place to a particular rate. What will be the impact?
- Retiring a constant value. Example: The tax law has been amended so we no longer do a calculation involving a particular constant value. Can we safely eliminate it from the database?
- Database restructuring. Example: If we move *Sales Tax Rate %* from Table A to Table B, how much reprogramming will we have to do?
- Complex analytical questions that require a significant amount of research in addition to determining the usage of a constant value. Example: We can recapture sales tax on some items under certain conditions. What will the net savings be?

Coded values may also be used in business rules and other program logic. The same comments that are valid for constant values apply to them too.

Conclusion

There are many useful reasons for knowing how reference data is being used in the information systems of an enterprise. It may even be necessary to gather this information if "bugs" such as referential integrity problems arise in a system. Codes that represent reference data values are found as foreign keys in tables outside their parent reference data tables. Queries can be written to provide information about the values in these foreign key columns. Constant values, however, are used in business rules, which are usually turned into program logic. It can be much harder to find out how they are being used, and reverse engineering may be the only way. It should be remembered that code values can also be present in business rules.

CHAPTER 10

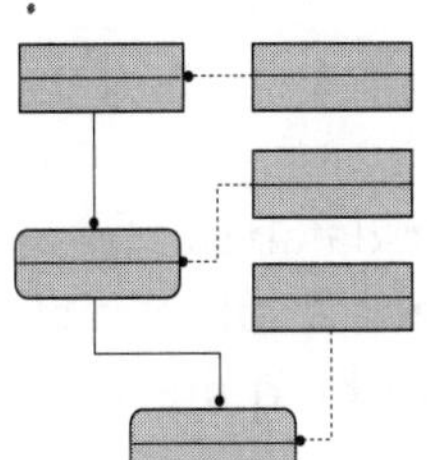

Mapping Reference Data

WHEN DATA IS EXCHANGED BETWEEN different systems, significant issues can arise with reference data. These issues center on how similar sets of reference data have to be merged in order to achieve consistency in the database into which the data is being placed. Unfortunately these issues are very common because systems and databases frequently exchange data. In transaction systems, feeds of data from or to other systems are not unusual, and when data warehouses and data marts are created, data has to be imported from operational transaction-based systems.

When the same reference data is implemented independently in two different systems, there is nothing to stop the two sets of data from diverging. This divergence can occur on a number of levels. Thus when these systems exchange data, the equivalent data from each system has to be identified, and any differences between them have to be reconciled —a process usually referred to as *mapping*.

The Need for Mapping

When data is exchanged there is a *source* system or database, from which data is extracted, and a *target* system or database into which the data is moved. The scope of data exchange can be quite variable. At its most simple, data from one or a few tables in a source system can be imported into a target system, perhaps merely to eliminate the need to manually reenter information, as illustrated in Figure 10.1.

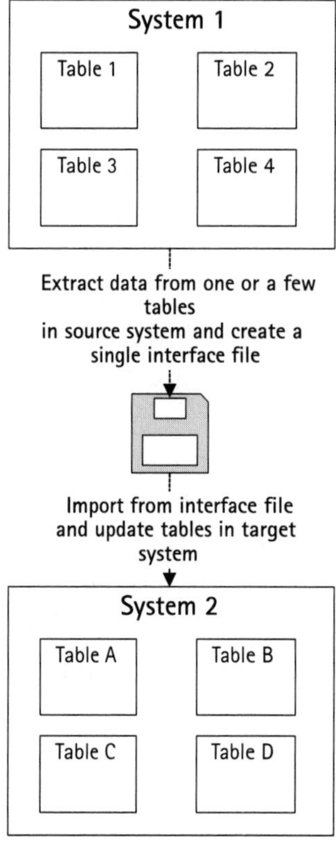

Figure 10.1 A simple interface file.

As system architectures become more open, there is more of a possibility for a system to directly read the data in the database of another system. This can eliminate the need for an interface file of the kind shown in Figure 10.1. However, the data mapping issues remain. Furthermore, this kind of interface can be more difficult to deal with since there is no intermediate file that can be examined to help in debugging problems of data quality.

At the most complex end of the spectrum, different systems can exchange *messages* containing transaction data back and forth in real time at very high rates. Also very complex is the extraction of all, or nearly all, data stored in a number of operational systems, which is then merged together to create an enterprise-wide data warehouse, as illustrated in Figure 10.2.

From the very simplest interface to the most complex, it is nearly certain that reference data will be included in the data being transferred. The whole topic of exchanging data between systems is too broad to be covered completely here, but there are a number of issues specific to reference data that need to be discussed.

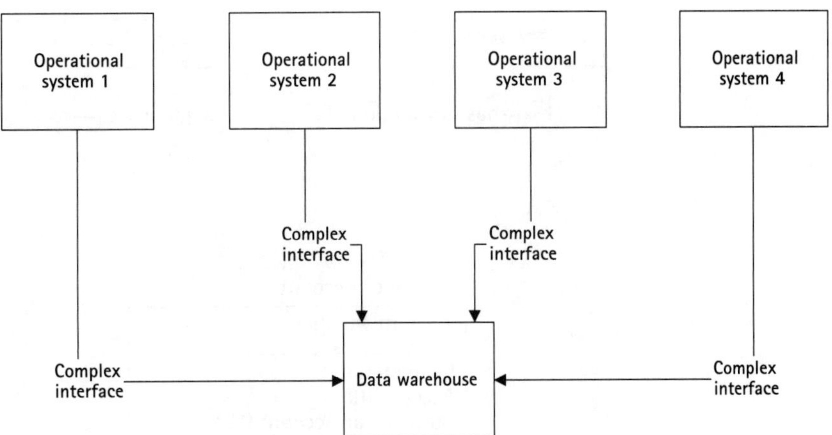

Figure 10.2 Interfaces to maintain a data warehouse.

It is very important to distinguish between reference data tables and reference data used in an *operational* setting (i.e., within transaction data) when considering moving data from one system to another. Figure 10.3 illustrates this, with `Country` and `Currency` tables that are used in the `Customer Account` table. There is a design issue that comes up very frequently here, namely, that there is a temptation when transferring reference data used in an operational setting from a source system to a target system to not transfer the parent reference data tables. The problem is that if the reference tables exist in both the source and the target systems, it is often thought that the data in both is completely identical. Suppose that `Customer Account` information, as illustrated in Figure 10.3, were to be taken from a source system to a target system. If the `Country` and `Currency` tables existed in both systems, it might be reasonable to think there would be no need to move them from one system to the other. Of course there is no guarantee that this assumption is correct. Unfortunately these kinds of assumptions are not always questioned when moving data from one database to another.

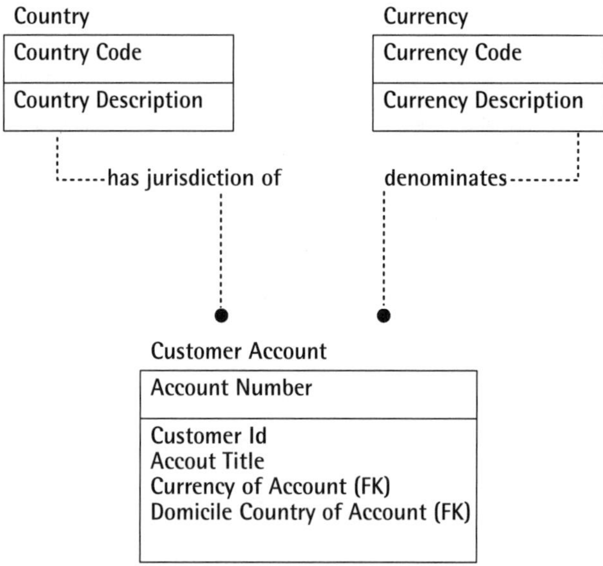

Figure 10.3 Reference data tables and their use in an operational setting.

There is a similar issue with constant values that are used to create calculated data. Figure 10.4 illustrates this issue. In the `Invoice` table there is a column called *Invoice Amount in US Dollars*, which is calculated as follows:

Invoice Amount in US Dollars =
(Invoice Amount in Invoice Currency) /
((Exchange Rate to US Dollar) for Invoice Currency on Invoice Date)

This business rule ties the `Exchange Rate` table to the `Invoice` table, even though in the database design there is no direct relationship between the two tables. Thus if data is transferred from the `Invoice` table to another system, if the data in the `Exchange Rate` table is not also moved, the *Invoice Amount in US Dollars* field cannot be recalculated.

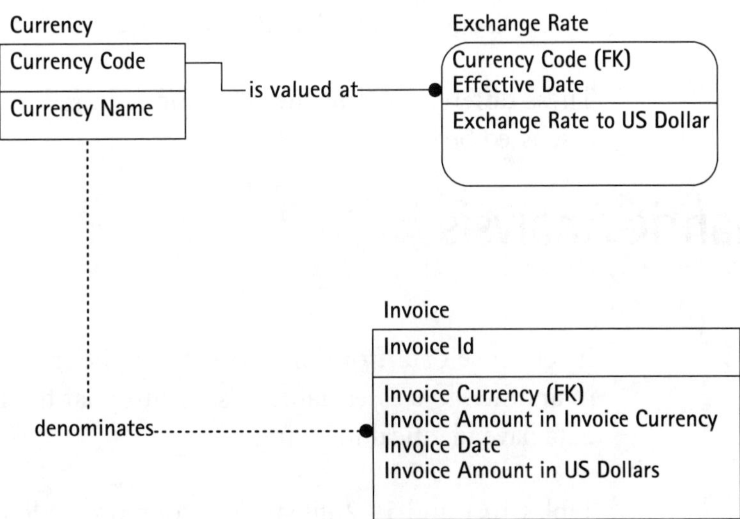

Figure 10.4 Usage of constant values.

Problems arise when there are differences in the reference data in the source and target systems. Then, the source reference data must be moved with the source operational data if it is to make sense in the target system.

Perhaps the best way to approach this issue is to think about the various ways in which reference data can differ between source and target systems and then see where mapping has to be performed. Differences can arise in the following areas:

- **Semantic differences,** where the meaning of reference data differs between the source and target systems
- **Coding scheme differences,** where the same reference data is implemented using different codes
- **Format differences,** where the same reference data is implemented using different datatypes
- **Value differences,** where one system may have data that is more up to date than another

These differences, and the mapping required to overcome them, are discussed below.

Semantic Analysis

If reference data from one system is to be mapped to reference data in another, it is essential to first ensure that the two sets of reference data have identical meanings.

Tables 10.1 and 10.2 illustrate a `Country` table implemented in two systems. Although the two tables are called `Country`, the table in System B contains regions as well as countries, so the two tables are really different in scope. These difficulties should be detected as early as possible in a project, certainly before programming or physical implementation begins. The best approach is to insist on conducting semantic analysis of the reference data. This means obtaining precise and complete definitions for the tables and the columns they contain. To do this, existing documentation should be reviewed and users interviewed. Data values present in the tables should be examined, along with the structures of these tables. Without semantic analysis, there is a risk that problems will only be detected when an interface is tested.

Table 10.1 Country table in System A

Country Code	Country Name
IRE	Ireland
FRA	France
SWE	Sweden
USA	United States of America

Table 10.2 Country table in System B.

Country Code	Country Name
IRE	Ireland
EUR	Europe
FRA	France
NAM	North America
SWE	Sweden
USA	United States of America

Relying simply on names of tables and columns, in place of proper definitions, is to take a risk. The risk is that the names of the tables and columns will not accurately convey their definitions. Sometimes there will not be a problem, but with the evolution of systems, the chances are that where many reference data tables exist there will be a greater chance of finding problems.

Reference data requires a further level of semantic analysis: determining what actual values in the tables mean. For instance, does "China" include Hong Kong, or is the latter considered as a separate country in our table? When semantic analysis must go beyond table and column definitions to value definitions, a great deal more work is involved.

If semantic differences are detected, what can be done? Where possible, the reference data used in the source system should be preserved in the target system (since it is usually the data of record), and the contents of the source reference data tables should be included if it is not already present.

Semantic analysis will allow reference data values to be matched up between the source and target systems. If differences are found, some form of data transformation will be needed if the transaction data from the source system is to make sense in the target system (even if the data of record is preserved). What is required depends on the problems that are found. Here are some of the more common ones:

- **Issue 1:** A reference data table in the source system has a different meaning from anything in the target system. This means that no mapping can occur. A new reference data table will have to be created in the target system for this information, if it is to be imported from the source system.
- **Issue 2:** A reference data table in the source system has values, some of which have identical meanings to those in the target system, but some of which do not. For example, the

`Country` table in one system has a record for China that includes Hong Kong, but in the target system China and Hong Kong are represented by two different records.

If the source system contains records for both China and Hong Kong, and the target system has only China, the values for Hong Kong can be changed to China in operational data extracted from the source system. This may be done by creating entirely new columns, so the original values are preserved.

If the source system contains only records for China, and the target system contains both China and Hong Kong, then there is a bigger problem. The target system `Country` reference table will need to have a record for Hong Kong added to it. The designer must find out if there is a business requirement that the imported transaction data is to be identified as either China or Hong Kong. Perhaps it can be left as China; otherwise the transaction data will have to be scanned to determine if fields where China is recorded really mean China, or really mean Hong Kong. This is usually hard to do programmatically but is even harder to do by human intervention if there is a great deal of data. Even if no action is taken, and the data is not modified, the problem should be carefully recorded so it is not forgotten.

- **Issue 3:** The reference data table in the source or target system has data quality problems that impact at the semantic level. For example, one of them contains regions in addition to countries, and this has been propagated into the operational data.

  There are no good alternatives in this case. If the real country cannot be determined in the transaction data, a default value may have to be substituted. If bad reference data values exist in the source system, they should not be added to the `Country` table in the target system, thereby corrupting it also.

Different Coding Schemes

When two reference data tables in two different databases are designed to hold the same information, entirely different schemes can be used for coded values, as shown in Tables 10.3 and 10.4.

Table 10.3 Country table in Database A.

Country Code	Country Name
IRE	Ireland
FRA	France
MEX	Mexico
SWE	Sweden
USA	United States of America

Table 10.4 Country table in Database B.

Country Code	Country Name
001	Ireland
002	France
003	Mexico
004	Sweden
005	United States of America

The same information is implemented in both tables. It can be matched up fairly easily. However, the analyst must be careful not to overlook any semantic differences and should try to understand precisely why a different coding scheme was used.

A variation of this issue can be found in unintended differences in coding schemes. For example, "M" could be used to denote Male in one system, and a lowercase "m" could be used in another system. Spelling mistakes and differences in case are not unusual in codes in legacy systems. More serious problems arise if data is to be interfaced from systems built in different countries where different human languages are used.

The best case, of course, is where there is an easy one-to-one correspondence between codes in one system and codes in another. The use of standard acronyms for primary key values in reference data tables can eliminate the need for mapping, but the practice carries other dangers (see Chapter 5). The use of sequence numbers may require mapping, unless an enterprise-wide scheme for managing these numbers can be implemented.

Format Differences

Even if a reference data table in a source and target system are identical in meaning and content, format differences can sometimes occur. For instance, the code in one table may be 8 characters long, and 10 characters long in the other table. Programmers in particular need to be aware of this issue.

When an analyst looks at a format difference of this kind, he or she can immediately appreciate that any code using more than 8 characters in the table where the code is 10 characters long must by definition not be found in the other table.

Value Differences

There can be differences at the value level in the same reference table implemented in source and target systems, quite apart from the semantic differences discussed above. Such differences can include the following:

- A description in one system is spelled differently from that in another, such as "China" versus "People's Republic of China." Quite often this causes no real difficulties, so long as it does not indicate an underlying semantic problem or a problem relating to one system being more up to date than another. However, it can sometimes be a major stumbling block, particularly in data warehouses and marts where quality and consistency of data are required.
- A record may be found in one table but not in another. It probably indicates that the system where is it found is more up to date than the other system. If it is found in the source system but not in the target system, it will have to be imported into the appropriate reference data table of the latter. Again, care must be taken to ensure there is no underlying semantic issue.

  If the record is missing from one table because it has been deliberately deleted from that table, then the analyst must find out why this has been done and may discover a more complex situation.
- There are differences in values because one code value has succeeded another. This topic was dealt with in detail in Chapter 8. It may not be easy to map values between the different systems in the operational data if this has occurred.

Undertaking a Mapping Exercise

Much of the key to performing mapping is to understand what is happening to the data in business terms. As noted above there are a number of problems that can arise to which there are no easy answers. They may require a decision that means that a data quality problem will continue to exist. These decisions should be reached in partnership with the knowledgeable business users. Furthermore, such mapping decisions, and the reasons they were arrived at, must be recorded and made available to users of the data so they can understand what they are looking at when they analyze the data. One place to put this information is in additional text fields in the reference data tables of the target system.

Data mapping is usually not an easy exercise; it can bring to the fore data quality issues, in both transaction and reference data, that may have gone unnoticed for years. The goal should always be to try to fix these problems in the source system, not the target system. Admittedly such a strategy may not always be feasible.

Conclusion

Data transferred from one information system to another typically involves transaction data. If the parent reference data in the source system is different from that in the target system, problems can occur. Beyond this, there can be issues at a number of levels when trying to match up reference data being taken from a source system with the equivalent data, and database structures, in the target system. Whenever data is copied or moved from a source system to a target system, or when any data mapping exercise between two systems is performed, it is important to pay attention to the special nature and characteristics of reference data.

CHAPTER 11

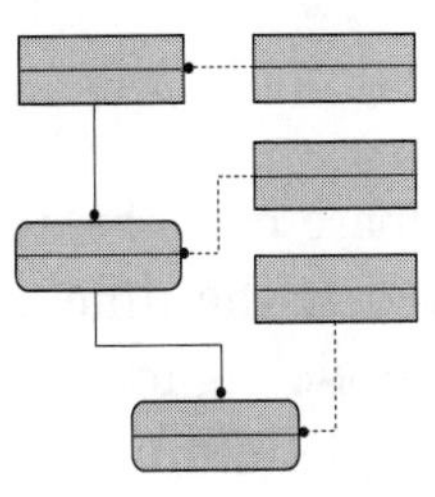

Understanding the Content of Reference Data

BECAUSE REFERENCE DATA WITHIN A SYSTEM can have a wide scope, it is important for users to understand what the data means, particularly what its business definitions are. Definitions and other data about data are known as *metadata.* Reference data is generally associated with more metadata than other types of data stored in a database.

One of the characteristics of reference data is that individual values may have complex meanings, although this tends to apply to codes and descriptions more than to constant values. The need for complex definitions at the instance level does not usually apply to other data (e.g., transaction data) stored in a database.

This chapter examines the metadata that applies to reference data, and why it is important to capture it, store it, and make it available to anyone who may use the reference data in any way.

Entity and Attribute Definitions

Each table (entity) and column (attribute) in a database has a business definition. These definitions should be captured at the time a database is being designed; analysts may use a data modeling tool to record them. Developers need to understand these definitions to build an application, but business users also need to understand them to utilize the database structure and the data it contains. For instance, a business user should never misinterpret data reported in the outputs of the system. It is therefore a very good idea to have the entity and attribute definitions in some form that the users can easily access. Most data modeling tools have interfaces that allow data to be extracted from them. By taking advantage of these interfaces, the entity and attribute definitions can be extracted and placed in a help file, or its equivalent, where they are available to users.

An alternative to a help file that is worth considering is to extract the information from the data modeling tool and place it in tables in the database itself. Figure 11.1 gives an example of a database design for this purpose.

A table called `Entity` has one row for every entity (table) in the database. It stores the business name and definition of the entity and the physical name of the table implemented in the database. The second table, called `Attribute`, has one row for every attribute (column) in the database. It contains the attribute's business name and definition and its physical column name and datatype. These tables can easily be modified to contain additional metadata, and they can also be used for other purposes besides storing definitions.

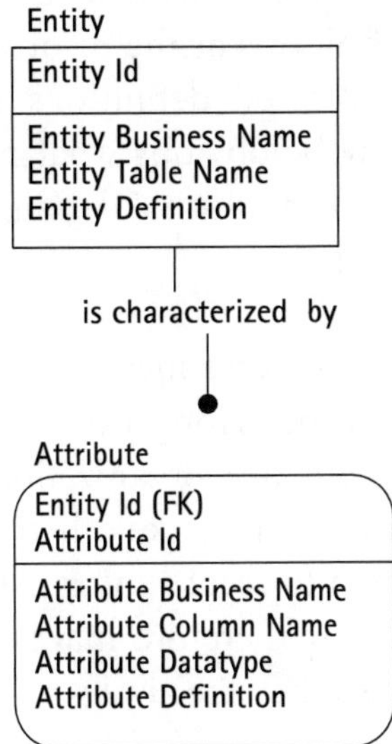

Figure 11.1 A simple design to hold entity and attribute definitions.

An advantage of storing the definitions in this way is that, if the definitions change in the data model, it is easier to move them into database tables than into a help file that must be rebuilt and distributed. Another alternative is to create an Internet web site where these definitions are always available and up to date.

Definitions of Values

While useful, the approach described in the previous section still does not help with the definitions required for individual reference data values. Furthermore, data modeling tools cannot record definitions for individual records (instances) within a table, because they deal only with designs, not with actual data.

It may be thought that most reference data tables are straightforward and there is no need for definitions at the record level. However, in many reference tables at least a few definitions are required. Consider a `Country` table. It may be obvious what most countries are, but this may not always be true, and some definitions may be necessary, as illustrated in Table 11.1.

The definitions in Table 11.1 provide a means of ensuring that a user will understand, for instance, that Hong Kong may be part of The People's Republic of China, but our organization considers it as a separate territory. The `Country` table, like other reference data, will be used widely within a system to record information on customers, sales, payments, and the like. It therefore makes sense to store the definitions in the table itself so they are always available with the reference data.

Table 11.1 Fragment of a Country table that includes definitions.

Country Code	Country Name	Definition
FRA	France	Includes French Overseas Territories (e.g., Guadeloupe, New Caledonia)
SWE	Sweden	
ESP	Spain	
POR	Portugal	
PRC	Peoples Republic of China	Excludes Hong Kong and Taiwan
HKG	Hong Kong	The former British crown colony. Although part of the People's Republic of China, it is considered a separate territory for our enterprise.
USA	United States of America	

Some reference data tables contain information that is especially prone to interpretation problems. A common example is the kind of table that seeks to classify the transaction data recorded in a database in order to serve some higher purpose. These classification schemes are often the result of careful analysis and tend to have long and complex definitions.

An example of this is shown in Figure 11.2, where an enterprise that manufactures laboratory equipment has decided to classify all of its product types in terms of some rather specialized industrial sectors. Table 11.2 shows some examples of the data values actually recorded in the `Industry Sector` table.

Without some guidance on the meaning of the various sectors defined in `Industry Sector`, it could be very difficult for business users to correctly classify product types. They would be left to infer their own definitions from the value of *Sector Description.* By placing definitions in the `Industry Sector` table, this problem can be avoided.

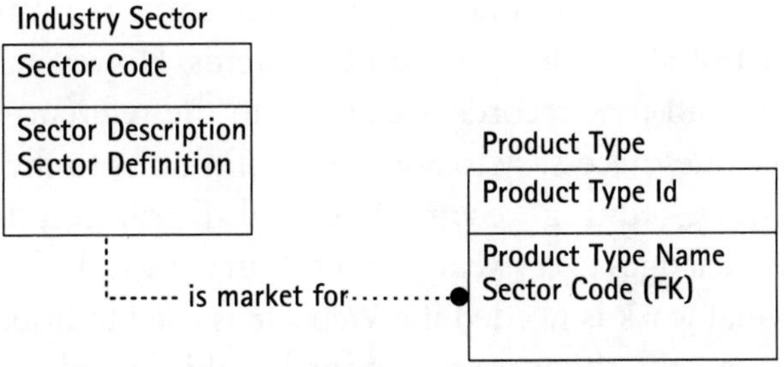

Figure 11.2 A database design to classify Product Type by Industry Sector.

Table 11.2 An example of an Industry Sector table.

Sector Code	Sector Description	Definition
01	Pharmaceuticals	The production of human and veterinary medicines
02	Biotechnology	The development of transgenic organisms to produce substances of industrial importance, but not the actual production of these substances
03	Brewing	The production of fermented human foodstuffs
04	Medical Equipment	The manufacture of equipment used in health care; excludes pharmaceutical products and chemical reagents

Distributing Reference Data Metadata

The entity and attribute definitions of reference data and the definitions of individual values can be placed in a help file or on a Web site. After all, online help in some form is regarded as a necessary part of all modern computer systems. However, if a help file is chosen, and new records are added to the reference data tables, it then becomes necessary to add their definitions to the help file. To do this requires editing, recompiling, and distributing the help file. Even a few changes every year can result in a great deal of effort. Some additional work is needed if a Web site is used to house the metadata, but at least the changes are confined to this one place.

An alternative design approach is to have definitions available from within the database itself, as illustrated in Figure 11.1 and Table 11.2. The database is by definition the central point accessed by users to obtain data, which solves the distribution problem. There should be little difficulty in programming the update functionality required: it is relatively simple to extend the user interface to permit data entry of definitions together with codes, descriptions, and constant values. Retrieval of the information (including sorting and searching) should also not be much of a programming challenge. For instance, the user interface can be designed to retrieve the definitions when the user accesses reference data.

It is quite possible that the metadata associated with particular reference data values can change, but the reference data values themselves do not change. For instance, in Table 11.2 the value "Medical Equipment" could have its definition expanded in the future to cover the area of gene therapy. Alternatively it may be "Biotechnology" whose definition is changed to include gene therapy. Having the metadata in a database makes managing such changes a lot easier than if it is present in more static media such as help files, written documentation, or static HTML.

Understanding the content of reference data is likely to be an increasingly important topic as use of the Internet permits the general public to interface directly with the databases of enterprises. Unless these new users can understand the content of these databases, they will not be able to use the data they are accessing.

Conclusion

There are costs and risks associated with not making the reference data metadata available to the users of the reference data, whether these are business user or information technology staff. Data quality can become degraded, and transactions may be corrupted if users do not know how to use the reference data correctly. The investment needed to capture and distribute the required metadata is usually relatively small, and it should be seriously considered.

CHAPTER 12

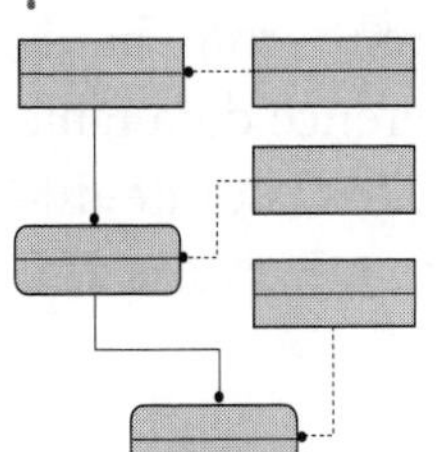

Programming and Reference Data

OTHER THAN DATABASE DESIGNERS, programmers are the only people who can have a profound impact on how reference data is managed by an information system. The way in which reference data is handled in program logic can have a long-term and far-reaching effect on the success of a system, especially its capacity for change, and may even determine its overall life span.

The issues that reference data presents to programmers are explored in this chapter.

Hard-Coded Reference Data

Unfortunately it is not uncommon to find reference data values defined in program code. Such *hard-coded* reference data can include code values, descriptions, or constant values. Being hard-coded means that the data is expressed as literals, although these may also be loaded into variables or arrays for later use.

A hard-coded *definition* of reference data is different from hard-coded *use*. A particular code value may exist in a reference data table and may be explicitly referenced in program logic. This is quite different from reference data values that do not exist in any tables and are only found in program logic.

Here is an example of hard-coded reference definitions in Microsoft Access 97 program code. The following lines of code set up various properties of a combo box called cmboCty on a form called Customer. The combo box is assigned values—country codes and names—that the user will choose from. These values do not come from a table but are defined in the program code itself.

```
Forms!Customer!cmboCty.RowSourceType = "Value List"
Forms!Customer!cmboCty.ColumnCount = 2
Forms!Customer!cmboCty.ColumnHeads = True
Forms!Customer!cmboCty.BoundColumn = 2
strList = "Country;Code;France;FRA;Italy;ITA;Spain;SPA"
Forms!Customer!cmboCty.RowSource = strList
```

The combo box could be used to update data in a transaction table.

Hard-coded use of reference data may also require values of reference data to be explicitly referenced in code, but this is not so much of a problem, so long as these values are not used to update tables. Suppose the combo box cmboCty was loaded from a reference data table, and there needs to be some special processing if Italy is chosen. The following is an example of how this might be done:

```
If Forms!Customer!cmboCty.Value = "ITA" Then
  ' special processing for Italy
```

```
Else
 ' processing for other countries
End if
```

In this example the reference to "ITA" is used to test a value and not to update a table.

Hard-coded use of reference data can be a problem if the data expressed as literals changes in some way in the reference tables. Consider the above example where "ITA" was used. What would happen if "ITA" were changed in a reference table—or even deleted? The problem of reference data values contained in program logic gradually becoming unsynchronized with the same data in reference data tables is difficult to control. The answer really lies in the way in which an enterprise approaches the implementation of business rules in computerized systems. If these design decisions are documented—that is, if the set of business rules is captured somewhere—then they can be searched for references to hard-coded reference data values.

Going back to defining (rather than using) reference data values in program logic, there is widespread acknowledgement of the problems associated with this practice. Here is a list of them, with particular emphasis on codes and descriptions.

- Very few people know what the set of reference data values is, unless they can find them in the program code. If a user tries to directly query the transaction data tables where such reference data is used, he or she will get some codes—probably not all—and no descriptions. The only way to see the full set of codes and descriptions is to invoke the system functionality—usually update processing—where the hard-coded values get presented onscreen.
- The descriptions are not kept in a table somewhere, so they have to be repeatedly hard coded, not only in update

program logic but also in reports and other outputs. This is a duplication of effort, and there is nothing to stop different descriptions from being used for the same code in different parts of a system.

- If an additional code value and description has to be added to a set that only exists in hard-coded form, the effort involves finding all the places where the code is implemented, and then adding the new code and description through reprogramming. Then the system must be retested and the updated components moved to the production environment. This is not only a waste of resources, but also increases the risk of introducing unintended errors.
- When hard-coded codes and values exist only in program code and not as database tables, a dimension of data is hidden from the users, and from many systems personnel as well. Users cannot use modern query tools to analyze transaction data by the hidden reference data because they cannot see it and its relationships to the rest of the database.

If there is widespread agreement on these problems, why do programmers sometimes define reference data in program logic? Reasons tend to involve saving time or improving system performance, as in the following:

- Some aspect of the database design is wrong or has been omitted, and a reference data table is required. However, implementing the new table in the database physical schema will take too long.
- There is a deliberate denormalization to get rid of a reference data table, perhaps to avoid an excessive number of joins.

Underlying these reasons is usually a lack of commitment to quality database design, a view of reference data as being relatively unimportant, and a judgment that long-term benefits of good design are outweighed by the need to reach some immediate goal.

Since the hard-coded definition of reference data is so widely acknowledged to be poor design, it is a feature to be looked for when a system is audited, its design reviewed, or it is reverse engineered to understand its functionality.

Preventing this problem is not necessarily easy. A good database design should be complete enough to identify all reference data structures and as many reference data values as possible before programming begins in a systems development project. The creation of additional reference data to solve programming difficulties should be discouraged by those responsible for the technical leadership of the project. The problems may be legitimate, and if they arise they should be carefully analyzed. If additional reference data really is needed, it should be placed in a database table.

Efficient Use of Reference Data

Programmers sometimes have problems using reference data. For instance, they may need to repeatedly read the same reference data, or they may encounter occasions when many reference tables have to be joined in SQL statements. These problems are connected with reading reference data, not updating it.

The need to repeatedly read the same reference data can be a problem in terms of performance. It can also be a problem if the programmer repeatedly has to create program logic to read the data. The programmer should try to modularize accesses to read the reference data, but it may not always be possible, for instance, if the data is needed for calculations as part of a SQL statement.

One design alternative to overcome this problem is to read reference data when a program is invoked and store it in memory variables. These variables should have the proper lifetime and scope to be available across a wide area of the system. For instance, when a user initiates a session in the system, the reference data could be read and stored in variables that can be accessed from any point in the program code for the remainder of the session. Alternatively some reference data might only be needed for certain sets of calculations and could be read when these calculations are invoked, rather than at the beginning of the session. The variables will be lost when the calculations are completed and control leaves the part of the system responsible for the calculations.

This design is good for constant values, which tend to exist as small sets of numbers. This is not always the case, however, and if the constant value is subject to change, or belongs to a very large set, it may not be a good idea. For instance, an exchange rate could vary from minute to minute, and finding the latest value would require a database read. Similarly a batch of transactions could be processed with a wide range of dates, requiring many records to be accessed in an exchange rate table.

The design can also be used for codes and descriptions. Both the code values and descriptions would have to be loaded, for which arrays are an attractive option. Again, the life and scope of the arrays need to be carefully considered. Codes and descriptions are usually needed for the user interface, whereas constant values are usually needed for calculations. Thus codes and descriptions might only be loaded into arrays when the part of the system providing the user interface is invoked. This could reduce memory usage and related overhead.

The limits to this approach are set by the amount of reference data that needs to be stored and the rate at which reference data changes.

Reducing the number of joins, or the need to repeatedly read reference data, can also be achieved by denormalized database design, which is covered in Chapter 14.

Using Reference Data as Inputs

Reference data is often input on screens as part of creating and updating transaction data. This has nothing to do with updating the reference data tables. It is usually confined to selecting a code value that is a foreign key in a table. Constant values are much less often input on screens.

Prior to the more modern software tools, it was common to input a code value by typing it into a field on a screen. With this technique, the program uses the input code to find (look up) a record in the parent reference data table, as illustrated in Figure 12.1. This verifies that the code is valid and perhaps also obtains the corresponding description which is then placed on the screen near to the code value. Sometimes a help feature is available to display the existing set of codes and descriptions. It may be activated by typing a question mark (?) into the screen field for the code value. The help screen may even permit the selection of a code value from the list displayed.

This method may still be employed in non-Windows and pre-Windows legacy systems and in systems that require the use of only alphanumeric keys. It has the disadvantage that it requires the user to know the code value. At a supermarket checkout, for example, when a bar code cannot be scanned properly, the checkout clerk will directly enter the stock-keeping unit (SKU) code. It is written on the bar code sticker, and it would be difficult for the clerk to select the right product if presented with a list of all products. In any case, the cash register is rarely set up with a screen on which such a list could appear.

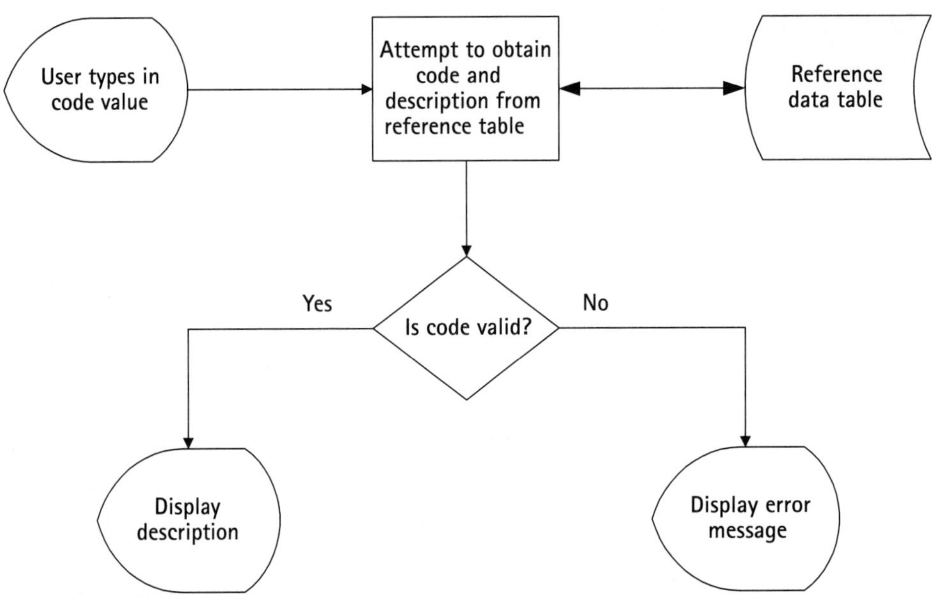

Figure 12.1 Validation of directly entered code values.

More modern software tools have special features to allow selection from lists, primarily combo boxes and list boxes, which are populated with descriptions (or both codes and descriptions) and then displayed to the user. The user can see the proper description right away and does not have to know the code. On selection, the code corresponding to the description selected is returned to the driving program. Figure 12.2 illustrates this concept.

There is no chance the user will obtain an invalid code value because he or she is selecting one of the valid values. Furthermore the user can look at all the possible values before making a selection. This design is thus less error prone and easier to implement than that shown in Figure 12.1. With some software tools the programmer simply needs to identify the reference data table to the combo box or list box control for the list to be created and presented to the user.

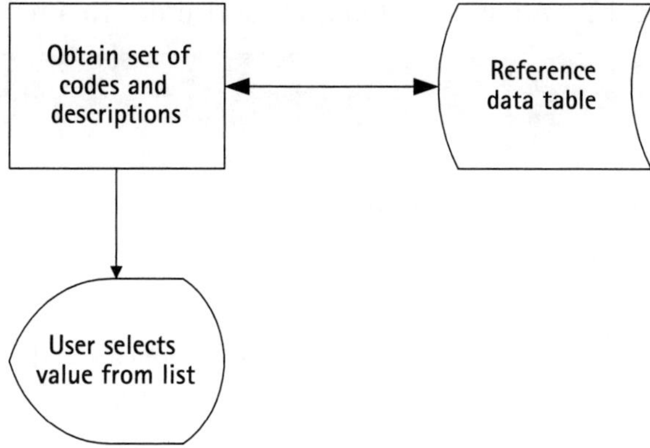

Figure 12.2 The user selects a code value from a list.

The list displayed to the user is usually based on the description, not the code value, and is sorted in the order of the description, not the code value. The code is usually not visible at all, although it is stored in the database. Sometimes, however, users are more familiar with acronyms than descriptions. In these cases acronyms as well as descriptions should be displayed. The acronym may or may not be used as the code value (a sequence number may be used instead).

Sometimes alphabetic sorting is not quite what users want. For instance, if the user has to select a country from a list, but will select "United States of America" most of the time, then it is irritating to have to scroll down to near the bottom of an alphabetically sorted list. One way to solve this is to add an additional column to the reference data table where the sort order can be defined. Table 12.1 illustrates this concept.

Another factor to remember about displaying lists of items for selection is that not all the reference data may be current. Codes and descriptions are sometimes no longer in effect, as described in Chapter 8. Once past its termination date, a code value should no longer be selectable. This can be achieved by selecting only those

Table 12.1 Adding a column for sort order to a reference data table.

Country Code	Country Name	Country Sort Order
AUS	Australia	2
FRA	France	3
IRE	Ireland	4
SWE	Sweden	5
USA	United States of America	1

records from the reference data that are in effect as of some reference date for the transaction being processed. The required logic can be executed when building the list to be displayed to the user.

Getting the transaction's reference date may require more analysis and programming than is usual in an approach to reference data where all codes are considered current. It may be worthwhile to adopt a programming approach where requests for reference data are handled by a centralized routine that accepts a reference date as a parameter and substitutes a default if the reference date is not passed to it. The default could be the current system date, and the central routine could perform other checks as well.

If it is accepted that reference data will have a life span defined by effective and termination dates, then it is important to ensure this is understood by the programmers as early as possible during design. In part this is because selecting subsets of the reference data in this way requires more complex programming than selecting all the records, and it may not be directly supported by the development environment of the software tool being used.

Other Issues with the Sequence of Reference Data

Programmers can experience other issues with sequence in which reference data is stored. These issues may not be immediately obvious to analysts and designers. For instance, consider the Standard and Poor's Long-Term Issue Rating codes shown in Table 12.2 (and more fully in Appendix 6).

These codes are arranged in order of quality. For instance, it is generally known that AAA (Triple-A) is the highest rating a bond can have. Suppose, however, that we have a business rule that states,

Table 12.2 Standard and Poor's Long-Term Issue Rating Codes.

Standard and Poor's Ratings
AAA
AA
A
BBB
BB
B
CCC
CC
R
SD
D
N.R.

"There should be no bond in our portfolio with a Standard and Poor's long-term rating less than A" (meaning that all bonds must rank as A or higher). A programmer might create logic such as

```
If Bond.SAPRating <= "A" Then
    ' Include in portfolio
Else
    ' Exclude from portfolio
End if
```

Unfortunately "A" will always sort ahead of every other value in Table 12.2. This collating sequence means that only bonds with a rating of A will be included in the portfolio; those with a rating of AA and AAA will be rejected, even though they are really of higher quality.

Thus the sequence of codes in a reference data table must match the uses to which they are put in program logic, as well as in screen presentation. Where problems occur, such as in Table 12.2, the reference data tables may need additional columns populated with values that behave in the way expected by the program logic. For instance, a new column could be added to Table 12.2 for a numeric rating factor with values that permit the correct comparison of bond quality in programs.

Using Reference Data as Outputs

When reference data is used in queries and reports, the major concern is that codes should be translated to descriptions. The most efficient approach is to translate the codes to their descriptions as the last step in gathering data from the database. In many cases, however, single SQL statements are the basis of queries and reports, and the descriptions will have to be obtained as part of this statement, thereby increasing the number of joined tables. If excessive joins become a real problem, then a denormalized database design may be an option, as described in Chapter 14.

An additional issue in dealing with descriptions is their length. Descriptions are usually too long to be used as column headings. If the code values that represent the descriptions are well-known acronyms, then they can be used as column headings. Overall it is more usual to sort and group alphabetically by description, which presents few problems.

It may sometimes be a good idea to include codes next to descriptions in outputs, particularly if the codes are acronyms that the users employ conversationally and may even be more commonly used than the descriptions. In these cases, it may even make more sense to sort and group by the acronyms.

Updating Reference Data from Transactions

Sometimes when transaction data is being entered, a new reference data value is found. For instance, when updating `Customer` information, a user may realize that the `Customer` is located in a country that is not included in the `Country` reference data table. What is the user to do in a situation like this?

One approach is to have the updating of reference data completely open, so that a user can go directly to this functionality and add the code and description for the new country. In some systems, there may even be some functionality on the transaction information screen that will take the user to the screen for updating reference data. The problem with this design is that having open access to reference data can result in the addition of duplicate or inconsistent reference data. This is a principal reason for having reference data administered centrally. However, in small systems with just a few users, it may be a practical approach. Even so, this can still be a headache for programmers, particularly if they have to implement complex security requirements for users to update some kinds of reference data but not others.

At the opposite end of the spectrum, the user may have to leave the transaction incomplete and contact the central function responsible for updating reference data. This will certainly reduce the programming effort required to maintain reference data in a particular system. Of course it may not be possible to leave some transactions in an incomplete state.

One possible solution to this problem is to have a special reference data value for "Unknown" that can be selected. The user can use this until the new reference data value has been implemented by the central group. Then the user can return to the transaction and change "Unknown" to the correct value. Unfortunately if the transaction has to be processed using a real value, or if its lifetime is shorter than the time the central group takes to do its work, this is not a viable alternative.

Before any programmer implements these kinds of solutions, the designer should find out how frequent the problems are and what the business consequences are of delaying the processing of transactions because of missing reference data.

Conclusion

Good programming practices are necessary if there is to be a successful enterprise-wide reference data management strategy because program logic can circumvent any such strategy. However, proper database design must take into account the ways in which reference data is used by program logic. There are a number of genuine issues concerning reference data that may be faced by programmers. Database designers should try to help find solutions that still maintain the integrity of any overall strategy.

CHAPTER 13

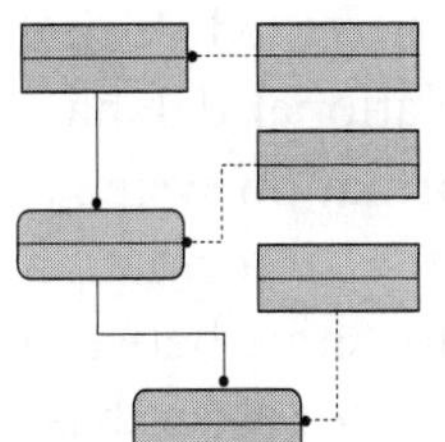

Implementing Reference Data in a Database

WHEN REFERENCE DATA IS IMPLEMENTED in a physical database, there may be performance and other requirements that the designer must take into account. These often impact the way in which a logical database design is translated into a physical database schema. Reference data tables do not usually hold many records, but this does not mean they play no role in database performance. This chapter reviews the ways in which reference data can affect performance and describes the design options available to the deal with these issues.

Fully Normalized Design

All other factors being equal, the best way to design any database is to create a fully normalized design. However, as we shall see later this is not always practical, although for systems that process transactions it is generally the best design choice.

Normalization is a term that describes the process by which database designers arrive at a database design where every entity contains attributes that depend completely on the primary key of the entity. It is a practice that has matured and become widely accepted during the past 25 years, following the introduction of relational database management systems as central components of information systems. Normalization eliminates redundancy among the information stored in a database, correctly represents the relationships between the data stored in the database, and ultimately provides a database whose design does not have to change except to keep pace with changes in the way the enterprise does business.

A good database designer aims to get database designs into what is known as *third normal form.* In third normal form, each table contains attributes that are fully and completely dependent on the primary key columns of that table. There are many excellent books on database design that cover this topic in depth (e.g., [Fl88], [Br92]). However, before we discuss the implications of normalization for reference data, let us very briefly review what first, second, and third normal form are.

In *first normal form,* any repeating groups are removed from a database table and placed in a separate table. In Figure 13.1, the `Order` table initially can hold information for up to three order items. These repeating data attributes are placed in a separate table—`Order Item`—and the design is in first normal form.

However, the design is not in second normal form. To be in second normal form, the information in each table must be dependent on the whole key, not just part of it. There is one customer per order, so *Customer Id* and *Customer Credit Rating* are dependent on *Order Id,* not *Order Id* plus *Order Item Number.* In Figure 13.2 these attributes are moved to the `Order` table, and the design is in second normal form.

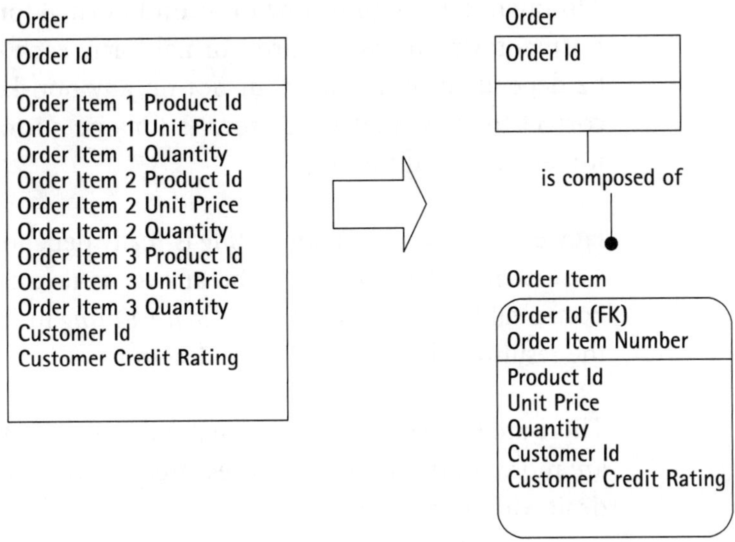

Figure 13.1 First normal form: removing repeating groups.

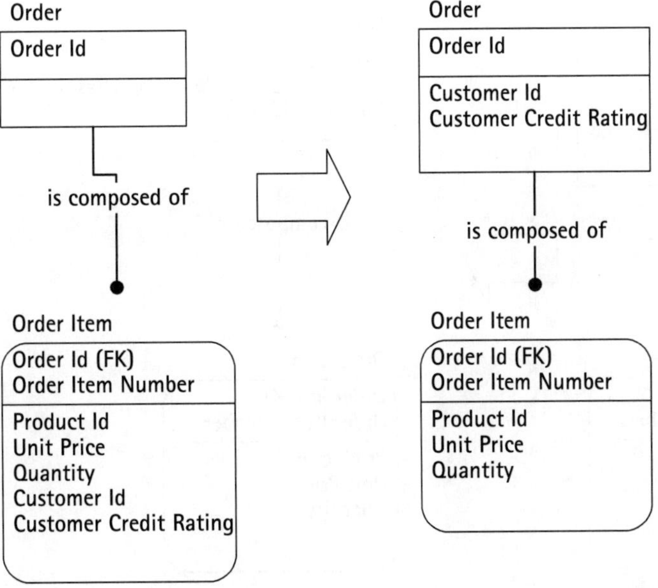

Figure 13.2 Second normal form: attributes depend on the whole key.

Although the design is now in second normal form it is not in third normal form. To be in third normal form, each data attribute must be dependent on the key, but not on any non-key value. It is more correct to show that each order is for one customer and each customer has a credit rating.

However, *Customer Credit Rating* is really dependent on the non-key *Customer Id*, not *Order Id*. The answer is to create a separate `Customer` table and put *Customer Credit Rating* in it. Figure 13.3 shows the resulting third normal form design.

There are higher orders of normal form (fourth, fifth, etc.), but these are more subtle and relatively less frequently encountered, so are not dealt with here.

There are several benefits that come from having a database design in third normal form. Let us briefly review them.

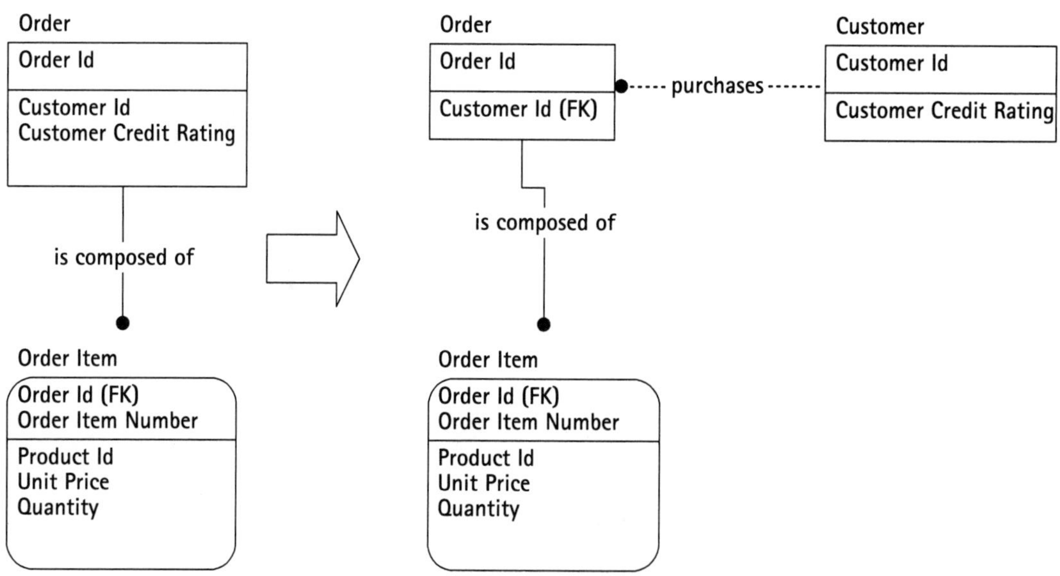

Figure 13.3 Third normal form: attributes depend only on the key.

Benefit 1: Effects of Change Minimized

With a fully normalized design, the database will change only to accommodate new business practices; it will not be forced to change for purely technical reasons. For example, if a new reference table has to be implemented, then the addition of that table and related foreign key columns in other tables are the only changes that need to be implemented. Other tables remain untouched. Thus if the designer decides there is a need to categorize customers by industry sector, all that must be done is to create a `Sector` reference table with *Sector Code* and *Sector Description* and add a column for *Sector Code* to the `Customer` table.

Each reference data table is also free to evolve on its own, independent from the others. For example, if a new non-key column has to be added to a reference data table, there is no change to any other reference data table. Thus if the designer needs to add a column for *Population Size* to the `Country` table, only this table is affected, and no other.

Restructuring a database is always a major event. It is not only the database that is affected. Programs, screens, and reports will most likely need to be changed in keeping with the database. There follows the usual cycle of design, programming, unit testing, systems testing, user acceptance testing, changes to existing documentation, and implementation in production. The changes are always implemented in a development environment first, where they can be tested, and moved to the production environment after testing is complete. There should be no doubt that changing a database design usually entails a lot of work.

Restructuring a database has less of an impact if it means the introduction of completely new tables and columns into a design for a valid business reason. With a normalized database design, these new components will have relatively little effect on the existing functionality of a system because there is no preexisting functionality that references the new columns and tables.

If restructuring means rearranging an existing database design, however, that is quite a different matter. The latter nearly always requires changes to existing system functionality (program logic, screens, queries, and reports), which is always difficult to justify if it is disproportionate to the new business functionality being introduced. In extreme cases there may be database changes but no new *business* functionality at all being introduced. In these cases the best result is that the system works exactly as it did before; still there may be significant downside exposure—that is, a real risk that system problems with perhaps unforeseeable consequences will occur. No systems manager wants to be in such a position, which is a good reason for insisting on a high-quality database design in the first place. Such a database will be immune to the need for restructuring because of poor initial design.

An example of poor design would be a `Country` table containing records for both countries and regions. It may eventually be necessary to separate the two because as new reports are added to the system, the amount of program logic needed to distinguish between countries and regions in this table becomes excessive. A normalized design would have had a `Country` table and a `Region` table from the start. To implement this change every piece of program logic that references the old `Country` table has to be reviewed and perhaps changed. So too do screens, reports, and queries that reference the `Country` table. There will also have to be a cleanup of the data to separate `Country` data from `Region` data. This is a lot of work, but from the users' perspective there are no changes—they still get exactly the same functionality provided by the system as they did before the changes. No designer wants to be in the position of implementing a change like this.

Benefit 2: Database Navigation Made Easier

In a fully normalized design, different sets of reference data exist in different tables, whereas in denormalized designs they are often merged into fewer tables.

Denormalized designs can mean that logic must be applied to navigating within a table to distinguish among the different types of record. This can be difficult enough for a programmer to deal with, but it can be much worse for a user. One of the goals of modern systems development is to provide users with the capacity to extract information by themselves from a database. Very often this is thought of simply in terms of buying and deploying end-user tools. It is just as important that the users understand where the data they want in a database is located and how to get at it. While end-user tools can help in this area when dealing with a normalized database design, it is usually impossible to provide them with the logic rules needed to extract different sets of reference data records from a single table. This is important because users typically need to analyze many different types of transaction data by the same reference data (e.g., sales by region, expenses by region, planned results by region, staffing costs by region).

Taking again the example of the `Country` table that includes region data (e.g., Europe, Asia, etc.), there may be a `Region Indicator` column which indicates that a particular record in fact pertains to a region, not to a country. Thus to obtain only countries, all records must be selected from the `Country` table where the indicator is not set. If there were distinct `Country` and `Region` tables, this need would not arise.

Not all denormalized designs cause problems for users. Indeed, denormalization can be used successfully in data warehouses and data marts to make it easier for users to construct their own queries. However, there are many different kinds of denormalization, and the one that is most dangerous when dealing with reference data comes from merging reference data tables so they lose their distinct identities.

Benefit 3: Dimensions of Data Made Explicit

Closely related to the ease of navigating around a database ensured by a normalized design is the explicit representation of dimensions of data. *Dimensions* are all the possible ways in which transaction data can be analyzed (extracted, sorted, grouped, aggregated, etc.) in a database. By definition reference data represents a large percentage of the available dimensions. If reference data is merged in a denormalized design, these dimensions become less apparent, particularly to users.

Consider Figures 13.4 and 13.5 which show a normalized and a denormalized design, respectively, for a database fragment of an offshore bank. In Figure 13.4 it is clear that there is a `Country` table, and every country belongs to one region (e.g., "France" belongs to "Europe"). It is also clear that each `Customer` resides in a single country (a rule of the bank is that each customer can declare only one country of residence). It can also be seen that each `Account` is denominated in a single `Currency`. From this design, it is immediately apparent that `Customer` can be analyzed in terms of `Country`, `Region`, and (indirectly in terms of the entities concerned) `Currency`.

In the denormalized design of Figure 13.5, the `Region` table has been merged into the `Country` table. Each country is still assigned to a single region, and the attribute *Region of Country* holds the code for the region. The table also contains one record for each region (which will have its *Region of Country* attribute set to null). In these "region" records the *Country Name* attribute holds the *Region Name*. A *Region Code Indicator* has been introduced to indicate when a record represents a region rather than a country. The

Country table has a recursive relationship to reflect the fact that a record for a country can have a parent record for a region in the same table. Additionally, Currency has been incorrectly merged with Country, by assuming that a country is the same as a currency (e.g., "France" is the same as "French Franc"). *Country Code* now represents currency. This is a design error because some currencies are not necessarily associated with a single country, but it is an error that exists in many real-life databases. The end result is that it is no longer apparent that Customer can be analyzed by Country, Region, and Currency.

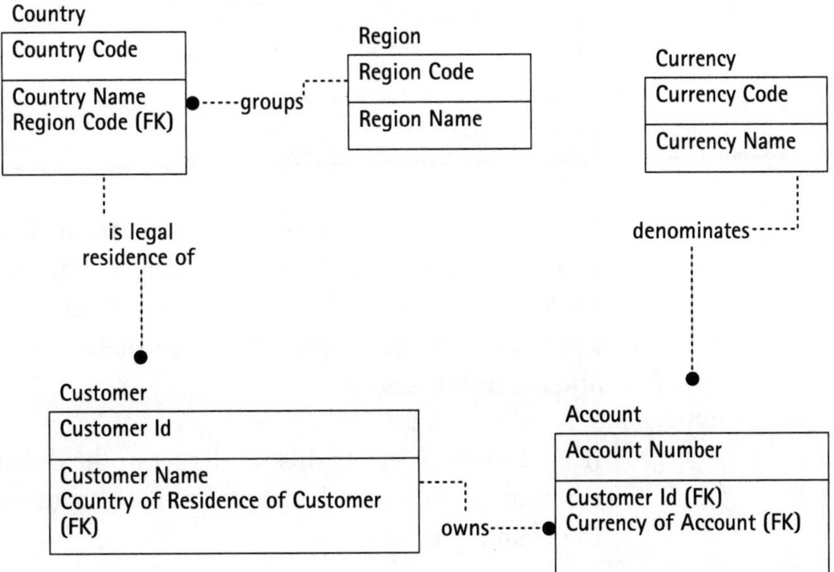

Figure 13.4 A normalized design.

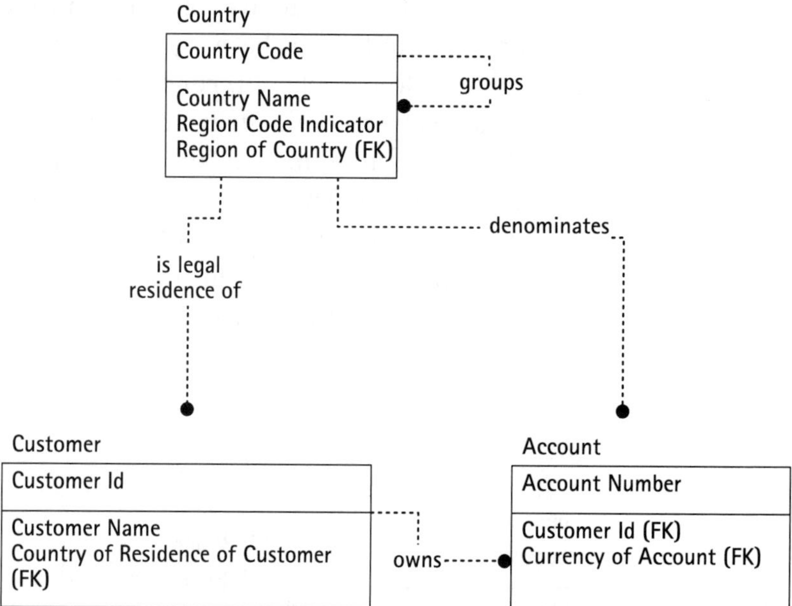

Figure 13.5 A denormalized design.

There are other problems that result from this. One is that SQL, which is based on normalized database design, becomes less easy. Table 13.1 shows the SQL needed to extract all European customers from the `Customer` table in the normalized design of Figure 13.4, and the results set.

If we want to replicate this results set in the denormalized design, we run into the problem that there are two sets of records we need from the `Country` table:

- the records that are joined to the `Customer` table
- the record for the region "Europe," which of course cannot be joined with any record in the `Customer` table

A simple approach is to disregard getting the official name for "Europe," as illustrated in Table 13.2.

Table 13.1 SQL and results for extracting all European customers from a normalized design.

```
SELECT CUSTOMER.*, REGION.*, COUNTRY.* FROM CUSTOMER,
REGION, COUNTRY
    WHERE REGION = "EUR"
    AND REGION.REGION_CODE = COUNTRY.REGION_CODE
    AND CUSTOMER.COUNTRY_CODE = COUNTRY.COUNTRY_CODE
```

Region Code	Region Name	Country Code	Country Name	Customer Id	Customer Name
EUR	Europe	FRA	France	00034	Customer 34
EUR	Europe	FRA	France	00017	Customer 17
EUR	Europe	IRE	Ireland	00122	Customer 122
EUR	Europe	SWE	Sweden	00004	Customer 4
EUR	Europe	UKM	United Kingdom	00067	Customer 67

Table 13.2 SQL and results for extracting all European customers from a denormalized design.

```
SELECT CUSTOMER.*, COUNTRY.* FROM CUSTOMER, COUNTRY
    WHERE COUNTRY.REGION_OF_COUNTRY = "EUR"
    AND CUSTOMER.COUNTRY_CODE = COUNTRY.COUNTRY_CODE
```

Region of Country	Country Code	Country Name	Customer Id	Customer Name
EUR	FRA	France	00034	Customer 34
EUR	FRA	France	00017	Customer 17
EUR	IRE	Ireland	00122	Customer 122
EUR	SWE	Sweden	00004	Customer 4
EUR	UKM	United Kingdom	00067	Customer 67

If we want to get the official name for "Europe, we will have to merge the results set from Table 13.2 with the following SQL:

```
SELECT * FROM COUNTRY
    WHERE COUNTRY.COUNTRY_CODE = "EUR"
    AND COUNTRY.REGION_CODE_INDICATOR = "Y"
```

There are a number of ways of doing this, such as by placing the results set from Table 13.2 in a temporary table and then joining back to the `Country` table to get the record for Europe. The point is that the complexity has increased as the dimensions of data required by SQL for easy access, and for the user's understanding, have disappeared.

Another consequence of the denormalized design shown in Figure 13.5 is the loss of objects to which metadata can be attached. As noted earlier, metadata is data about data, such as definitions of tables and attributes. In a database design, the minimum set of objects that can possess metadata is *tables*, *attributes*, and *relationships*. Table 13.3 shows the definitions for the normalized design in Figure 13.4.

Table 13.3 Data dictionary for the normalized design in Figure 13.4.

Table	Definition
Region	A group of countries and territories. The enterprise has one regional office per region, responsible for all activities in that region. The head office is responsible for defining regions and assigning their codes.
Country	An internationally recognized country or territory in which the enterprise does business.
Currency	The set of valid ISO currency codes and their descriptions. Only ISO codes are allowed as we send wire transfers by S.W.I.F.T. which requires their use.
Account	A type of product where a customer can deposit money for later withdrawal.
Customer	Any person or organization to whom the enterprise sells its products. Potential customers are not included; at least one sale must have occurred.

Table 13.3 (continued)

Attribute	Definition
Region Code	A unique alphabetic code that represents a region
Region Name	The official name the enterprise gives to a region
Country Code	A unique code that represents a country or territory
Country Name	The official name by which a country or territory is known, in English
Currency Code	The ISO currency code
Currency Name	The ISO currency name
Customer Id	A unique sequential number given to every customer
Customer Name	The full name of the individual or organization that is the customer
Customer Country of Residence	The country in which the customer officially resides
Account Number	A unique number for each account
Currency of Account	The currency in which the account is denominated

Relationship	Description
Region-Country	Each country belongs to one and only one region. Once defined, the region to which a country is assigned cannot be changed if that country has been used for a customer. A country must be assigned to a region as soon as it is entered into the database. A region cannot be deleted or have its code changed once it has been assigned to a country.
Country-Customer	A customer must reside in only one country. This is the country in which the customer pays taxes.
Customer-Account	A customer can have one or more accounts.
Currency-Account	An account can only be denominated in one currency. Once this is defined, the currency of the account cannot be changed. No currency record can be deleted if it is associated with an Account. No currency code can be changed if it is associated with an Account.

Table 13.4 has the corresponding information for the denormalized database design in Figure 13.5.

Table 13.4 Data dictionary for the denormalized design in Figure 13.5.

Table	Definition
Country	An internationally recognized country or territory in which the enterprise does business. The country also represents its national currency. This table also includes regions. A region is distinguished from a country by the Region Code Indicator being set to "Y."
Account	A type of product where a customer can deposit money for later withdrawal.
Customer	Any person or organization to whom the enterprise sells its products. Potential customers are not included; at least one sale must have occurred.

Attribute	Definition
Country Code	A unique code that represents a country or territory, or region.
Country Name	The official name by which a country or territory is known, in English. For regions, this is the name given to the region.
Region of Country	The region to which a country belongs.
Region Code Indicator	Indicates that the record is for a region, not a country, if set to "Y."
Customer Id	A unique sequential number given to every customer.
Customer Name	The full name of the individual or organization that is the customer.
Customer Country of Residence	The country in which the customer officially resides.
Account Number	A unique number for each account.
Account Currency	The currency in which the account is denominated.

Relationship	Description
Country-Country	Each country belongs to one and only one region. Once defined, the region to which a country is assigned cannot be changed if that country has been used for a customer. A country must be assigned to a region as soon as it is entered into the database. A region cannot be deleted or have its code changed once it has been assigned to a country.

Table 13.4 (continued)

Relationship	Description
Country-Customer	A customer must be associated with a country of residence as soon as the customer is entered into the database. A country cannot be deleted or have its Country Code changed if it has been associated with a customer.
Country-Account	A customer must be associated with a country, representing a currency, as soon as it is entered into the database. A country cannot be deleted or have its Country Code changed if it has been used to represent a currency for a customer.

If we compare Tables 13.4 and 13.5, it is immediately obvious that there are fewer tables in the dictionary for the denormalized design than there are in the dictionary for the normalized design. Thus if this metadata were available to users (or systems personnel) to help them understand the database design, they would not realize that region and currency information existed by reading the list of tables. They would have to read the definition of the `Country` table in detail to figure it out. The denormalized design is thus more difficult to understand and prone to misinterpretation.

Tables 13.3 and 13.4 show an unintended consequence of a denormalized database design—the hiding of table and relationship definitions and the increased complexity of all types of definition. The result is that the database is much more difficult to understand. Systems personnel are usually better able to cope with such problems than users. If it is intended that users actually write queries and reports by themselves to extract data from the database, the metadata does not support this goal in the denormalized design.

The importance of metadata, and the need to make it widely available, is gradually becoming better understood in systems development projects. Metadata is particularly important for reference data because of its wide scope and its usefulness in analyzing transaction data.

Controlled Redundancy of Descriptions

A fully normalized design can provide a lot of benefits, but it can also present operational problems with the performance of a system. One of the main problems is the need to resolve every code value to its corresponding description when outputting data. This is more of a problem in data warehouses and data marts, where the whole purpose of the database is to provide information for analysis, than in operational systems designed to process transactions.

When a query is run or a report is executed, there is typically a sequence of events that involves gathering data from database tables, performing calculations, sorting and grouping the results, and finally formatting the output. This last step is often the one in which descriptions are gathered for code values. In a fully normalized design, this may require selecting data from a number of reference tables. One denormalized design option is to include the descriptions in the data tables to which they are related.

Figure 13.6 shows an implementation of this design approach. Wherever a code appears, its description is also included in the table. The designer should be careful, however: this approach can sometimes be justified in a data mart or warehouse, but never in an operational system that processes transactions.

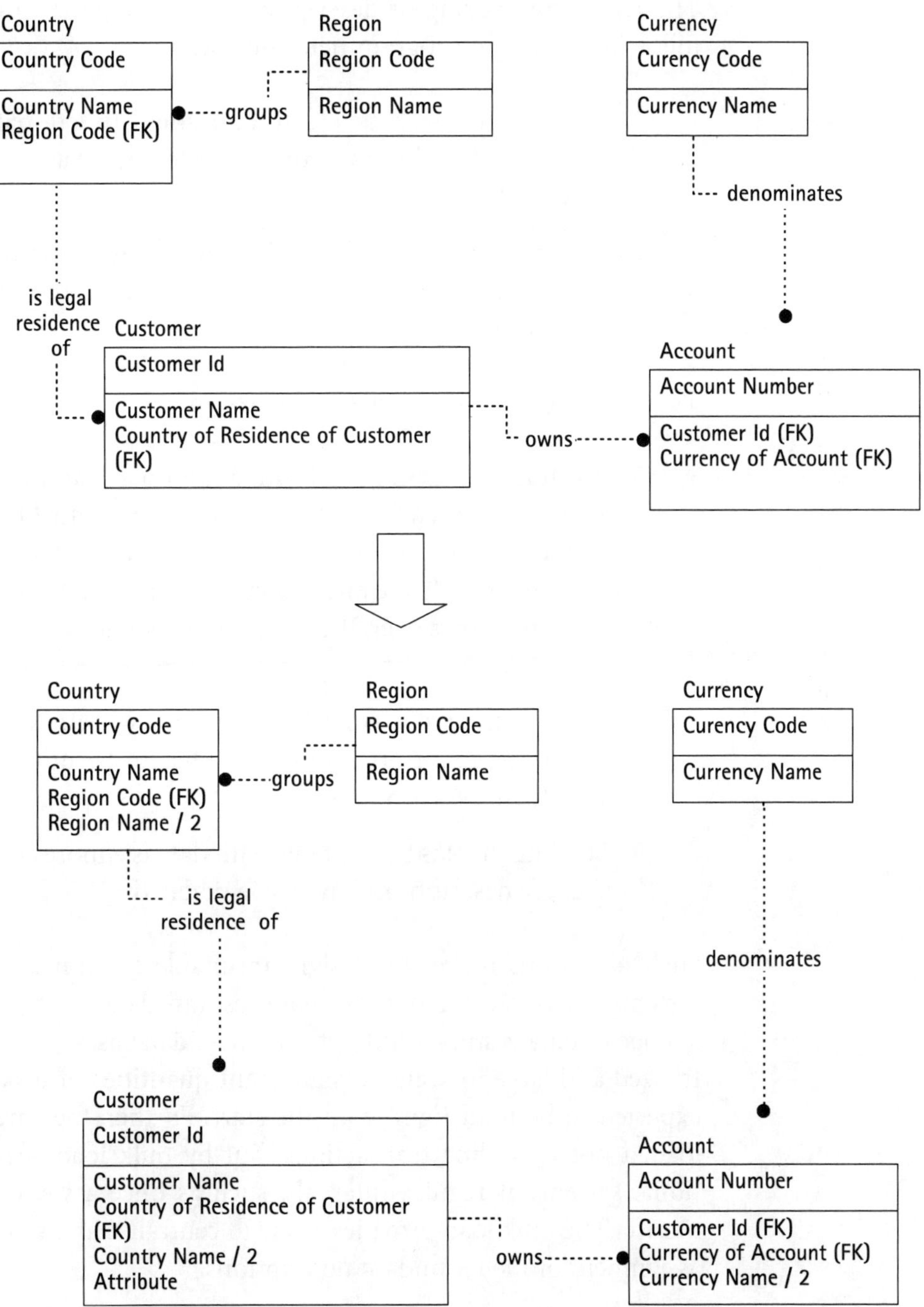

Figure 13.6 Controlled redundancy of descriptions.

The redundant storing of descriptions in this manner provides the following benefit to programmers and users:

- There is no need to create additional functionality to retrieve the descriptions from the reference data tables where they exist.
- There is no need to know how to navigate the database to get to the reference data tables in order to retrieve the descriptions.

There is of course a downside to the design:

- All those descriptions take up additional space. Descriptions are usually much larger than any other data attributes in a database, and incorporating them in many tables can cause both the overall size and growth rate of the database to multiply many times over. If disk space is an issue, this can be a big problem.
- There is the risk that the descriptions will no longer match the codes. Extra processing logic has to be implemented to keep them synchronized.
- Loading the `Customer` table with data is a more complex task because descriptions have to be updated.

Such objections make the design unsuitable for transaction-based systems. However, for data warehouses and data marts, redundant storage of data is still a valid option. These databases are usually centralized and large in scale, so significant quantities of disk space are expected to be used right from the start. Further, they are typically loaded not by online transactions, but by bulk loads from operational systems at regular intervals, such as once a week or once a month. The bulk load provides a way to centralize and so control the assignment of the redundant descriptions.

The kind of redundancy suggested here is *controlled redundancy.* This is an acceptable option in database design. Redundancy that is not controlled is completely unacceptable.

Again it should be noted that the reference data tables are not eliminated in this design. They continue to exist. The only thing that is being done is redundantly adding descriptions to those other tables where code values occur.

Fusing Codes and Descriptions

Another denormalized design that is sometimes implemented involves merging all code values and descriptions into a single table. This is an extreme variation of some of the denormalized designs discussed earlier in this chapter. However, it is not an uncommon solution. Figure 13.7 illustrates an example of this design. All codes and descriptions now exist in a single table, `Table of Codes.` However, as several tables have been merged, it is still necessary to distinguish among them. This is achieved by implementing an attribute called *Code Type*, which could have values of "REGION," "COUNTRY," and "CURRENCY."

With this design in place there are two main advantages:

- There is only one table that needs to be accessed in order to resolve codes to descriptions.
- Having all code values and descriptions in one table makes this kind of reference data a lot easier to administer in terms of the number of tables involved and the amount of program logic that has to be written and supported to update this single table.

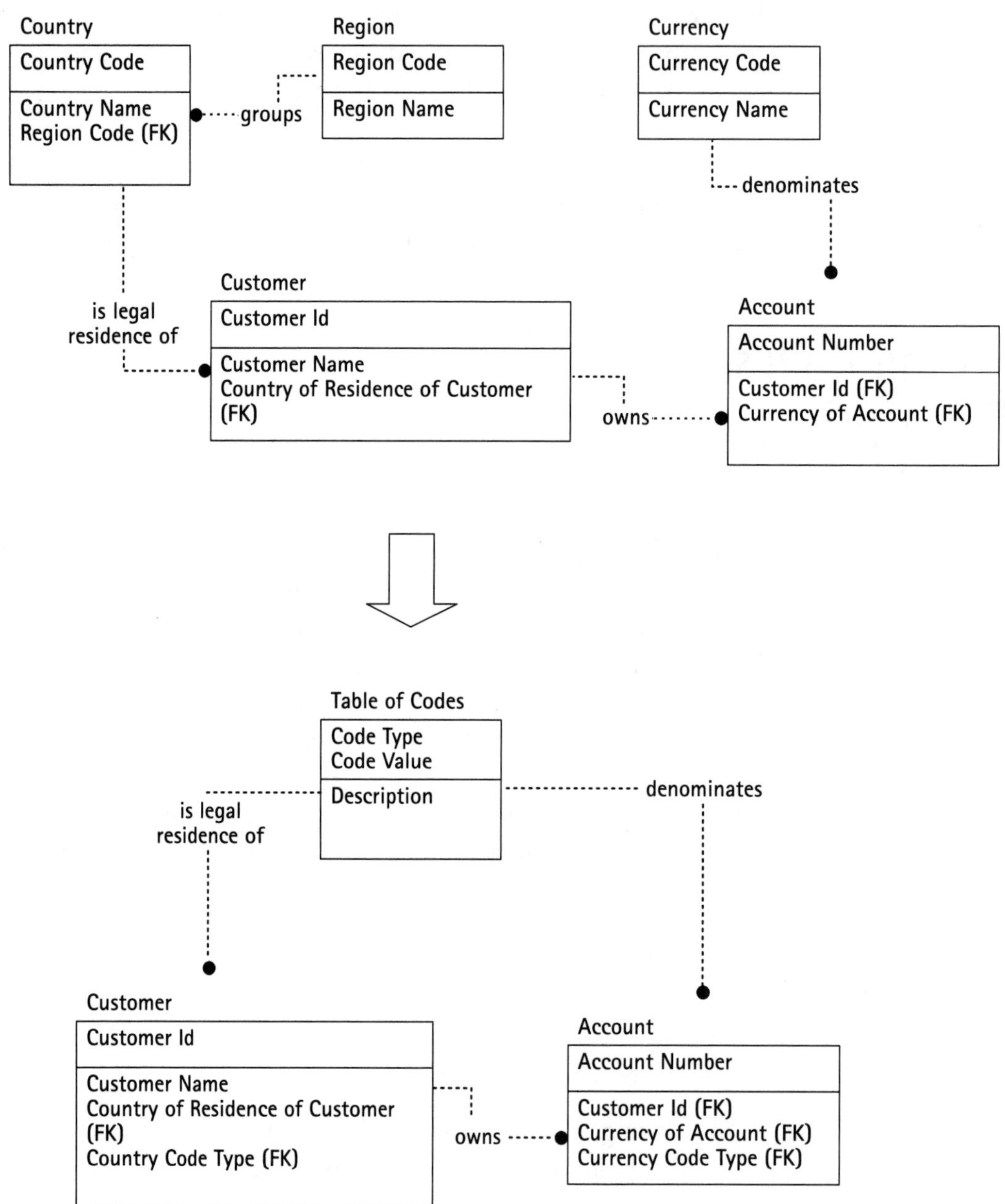

Figure 13.7 Implementing a single Table of Codes and Descriptions.

Likewise, however, there are considerable disadvantages:

- The programmer (or user) must know what *Code Type* to select to obtain the correct set of values in the `Table of Codes`. For instance, suppose the description of the *Customer Currency* is required, and the correct value of *Code Type* for Currency is "CURRENCY." If the value of *Customer Currency* is stored in a variable called "MyCurrency," the following SQL would be needed:

```
SELECT DESCRIPTION
            FROM TABLE_OF_CODES
            WHERE CODE_VALUE = MyCurrency
            AND CODE_TYPE = "CURRENCY"
```

  Knowing that "CURRENCY" is the correct value for *Code Type* in this instance is not obvious from the database design itself.

- The datatypes of the codes and descriptions must be the same if they are to be unified into a single table. For example, if the *Currency Code* was Character(3) and the *Country Code* was Character(4), the *Code Value* would have to be at least Character(4). This might cause problems in the program logic.
- There is a loss of metadata, making the overall design much harder to understand and use.
- If the original tables contained columns other than the *Code Value* and *Description*, these are lost. For instance, the fact that a `Country` belongs to a `Region` is completely lost in the above design. This is a major problem that always requires a solution in this design approach. Figure 13.8 shows a more complete design solution.

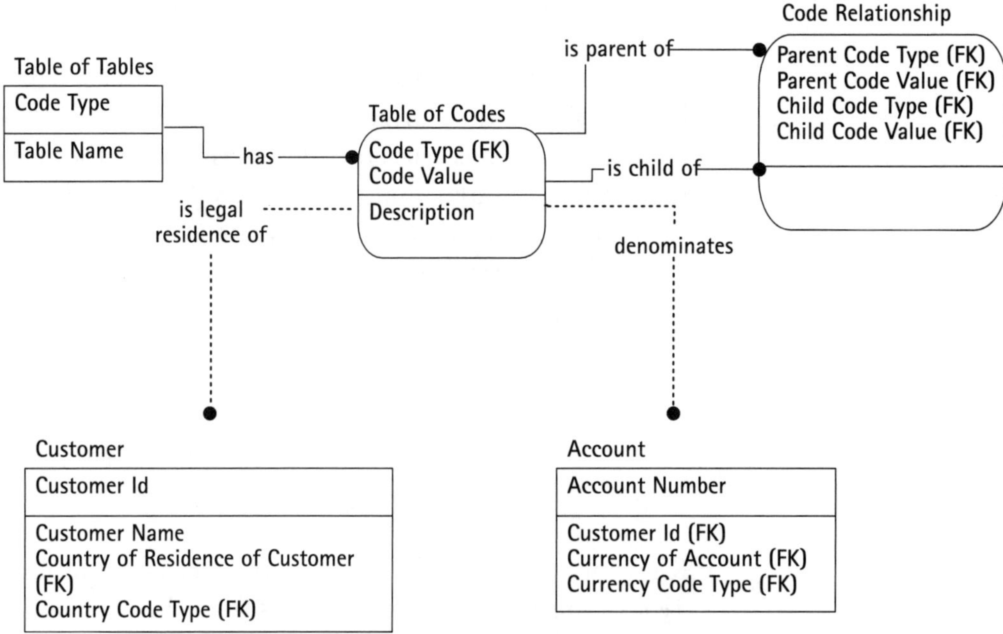

Figure 13.8 A more complete design for a single Table of Codes and Descriptions.

In Figure 13.8 there is a `Table of Tables` which has one row per reference data table in the normalized design. It contains the full name of the table in addition to the *Code Type* that represents the table. There is also a table of relationships that will allow relationships such as the one between `Country` and `Region` in the normalized design.

This design may be worth considering if a table of codes and descriptions is used in addition to the normalized reference data tables. Like the design discussed in the previous section where descriptions are added to all tables where codes occur, a single table of codes and descriptions represents controlled redundancy. It has an advantage over placing descriptions in all tables in that it requires a lot less disk space. However, it does require an additional join to retrieve descriptions.

A single table of all codes and descriptions is also worth considering if very high response times are needed from a transaction-based system. However, the complexity it adds to program logic, and the increased probability of introducing bugs—the costs of controlled redundancy—are usually too high a price to pay.

Reference Data in Data Warehouses and Data Marts

Operational systems are primarily oriented to automating business functions, whereas data warehouses and data marts are used for decision support. A normalized database design is always best for operational systems, designed as they are to process large numbers of individual transactions. However, when normalization is applied to data warehouses and data marts, it causes the disruption of two major requirements of decision support systems:

- Users need run queries that read large sets of records and return results in a short time.
- Users need to be able to understand the structure of the data they are dealing with so they can construct queries.

In response to these problems, *dimensional modeling* has been developed. This technique is used to build warehouses and marts containing fact tables and dimension tables. The fact tables hold the data to be analyzed, preferably at the lowest level of detail. The fact data is analyzed in terms of the data contained in the dimension tables (often this is reference data). Dimensional modeling emphasizes building fact and dimension tables that users need and want, so the first step in design is to determine exactly what kinds of analysis users want to perform. This is a little different from building tables that match a business process that exists autonomously, as is done for operational systems.

One of the most common design elements in a data warehouse or mart is the *star schema*. This consists of a fact table surrounded by the required dimension tables. Figure 13.9 shows a simple example of a star schema.

In this example the fact table, `Sales`, contains sales information for an enterprise. Users need to analyze `Sales` data by product, customer, date of sale, product type, and state in which the customer resides. These then become the dimension tables surrounding the fact table. `Product Type` and `State` are reference data tables, while

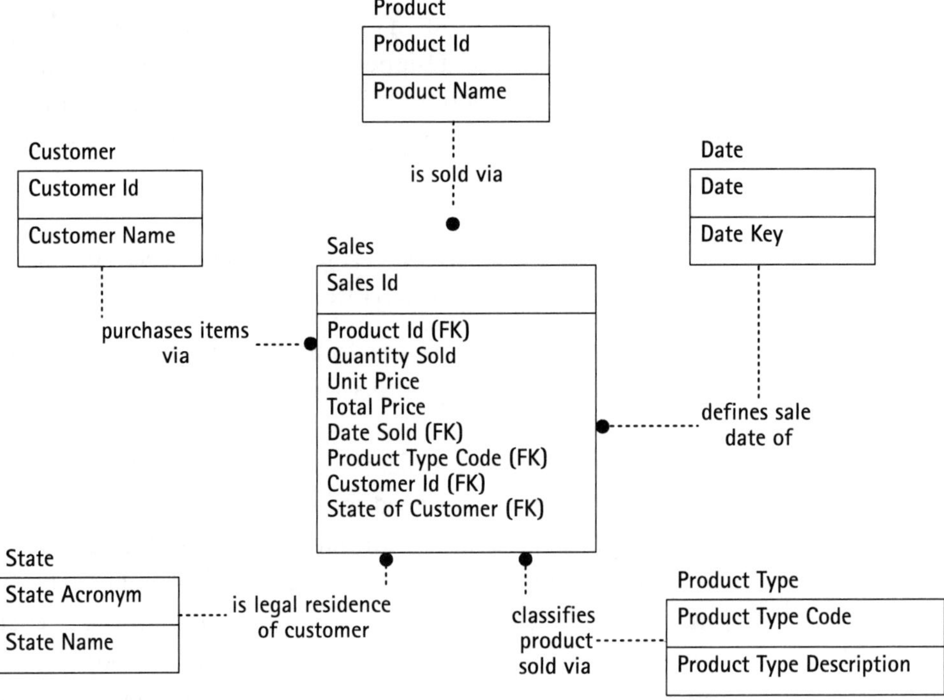

Figure 13.9 Example of a star schema.

`Customer` and `Product` are tables used to structure the enterprise's transactions (they describe real things within the context of the enterprise). The `Date` table represents the dimension of time, and is rather special, although it too can be considered as reference data.

There is another type of design also used in data warehouses, a variation on the star schema called the *snowflake schema.* In this design, the reference data tables that qualify other dimension tables are related directly to these dimension tables instead of to the fact table.

Figure 13.10 provides an example of a snowflake schema, based on Figure 13.9. The tables `Product Type` and `State` are now directly related to `Product` and `Customer`, instead of to the fact table. It is more logical to see reference data in these kinds of relationships, and it may speed up certain kinds of queries, such as analyzing `Sales` by *State of Customer.* However, it may slow down other kinds of query; for instance, a query analyzing `Sales` by both `Customer` and `Product Type` involves four tables and three relationships in Figure 13.10, but three tables and two relationships in Figure 13.9. Also, Figure 13.10 is a little more complex for users to understand than Figure 13.9.

The use of star versus snowflake schemas continues to be a topic of discussion in the data warehousing field. The best approach a designer can take is to carefully analyze all business requirements before creating a database design, rather than making some preconceived notion try to fit the business requirements.

Physical Implementation of Reference Data Tables

In developing a database, it is worthwhile involving the database administrator (DBA) in discussing the implementation of reference data as a distinct topic from the outset. One reason is that reference

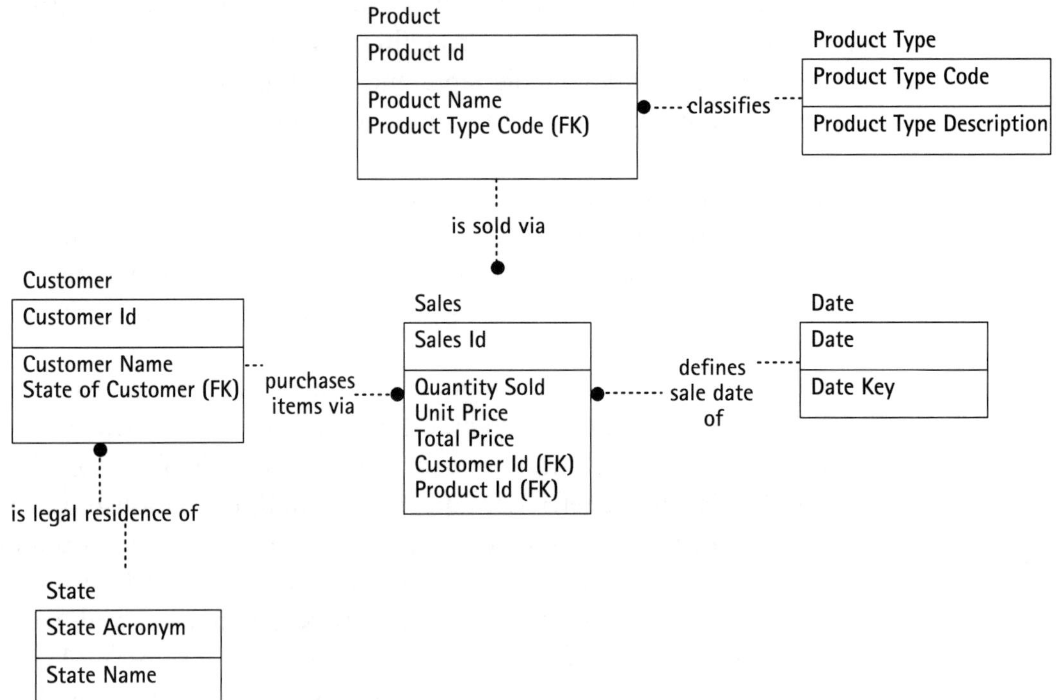

Figure 13.10 Example of a snowflake schema.

data tables usually have to be implemented and populated before other tables, and the DBA can be of great assistance in doing this.

An important feature of reference data tables is their relatively small size, and the fact that they are read frequently and updated rarely. These characteristics are ideal for improving performance by placing the tables in physical proximity on disk. That way, when one table is read, a great deal of reference data will be pulled into the cache and will be available when other reference data needs to be read. It is typically the DBA's responsibility to implement this kind of design.

Another important element of physical design is the creation of indexes. The reference data tables should be indexed on the primary key—that is, on the code value for codes and descriptions, or code value plus effective date for constant values. In several database management systems, there are different types of indexes. Some types of index permit faster data retrieval than others (e.g., clustered indexes in Microsoft SQL Server) but are less efficient for frequent update. This is ideal for reference data. Again, the active participation of the DBA is required here.

Conclusion

The implementation of reference data in a database design benefits greatly by the reference data tables being in third normal form. Many denormalization techniques result in a loss of places where metadata can be attached and a loss of dimensions available for analysis; they can also introduce the need for more complex programming, and make navigation of the database more difficult. Some denormalization techniques, such as controlled redundancy of descriptions, or star and snowflake schemas, do overcome some design problems and may even be required in certain circumstances. However, denormalized designs must be created for specific reasons and may require additional maintenance functions to be added to the information system concerned.

CHAPTER 14

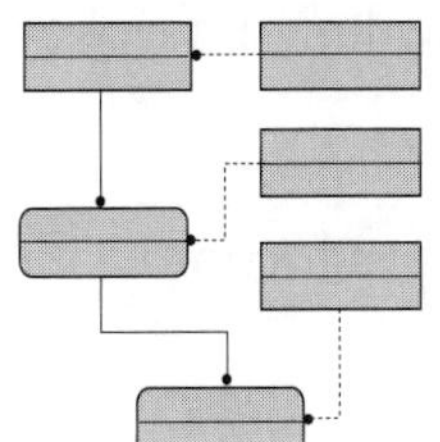

Populating Reference Data Tables

UNLIKE MANY OTHER DATA TABLES, reference data tables usually need to be populated with production data prior to the implementation of a system. This requirement presents developers with a number of issues that require careful management. In this chapter we shall explore these issues and other problems connected with the population of reference data tables.

Production versus Test Reference Data

When a system is being developed, it is important to distinguish between test reference data and production reference data. Test data is used purely for testing purposes—for establishing test cases and expected results. Production data is real data, and some is always needed in the reference data tables at the time a system goes live. Test reference data may include some production data, but it is very difficult to segregate the two in a test database.

One of the worst things that can happen is to have production data contaminated with test data when a system is implemented. Developers need to ensure that this does not happen. They can start by clearly defining production reference data during the design phase of a system. Two things need to be decided:

- which reference data tables will contain production data when the system is implemented
- what values will these tables be populated with

These design decisions should be recorded so that later, when the system goes live, there is no doubt about what data the tables will initially contain.

Managing test data is a little different. In theory it should be defined in written test plans, but often it is simply entered into data tables, either through the system's user interface or some other utility. This lack of control increases the danger that it will be mingled with what is intended to be production data, and the two will be inseparable at the point of implementation.

The entire problem could be avoided by somehow defining and capturing the production reference data needed for system start-up. Data modeling tools would be a good place to do this, but unfortunately they do not store data at the table record level (although they can store domain values for individual columns).

A more practical option is to delete all records in all tables at the point of implementation and use system data entry facilities, or database utilities, for development staff to enter the production data. There are a number of problems involved in loading each reference data table separately:

- Some of the reference data tables are unlikely to have user interfaces that allow them to be updated, such as type codes.

- There may be security concerns about allowing staff to freely update tables.
- If a large amount of reference data needs to be added, the chance of making an error during data entry are increased.
- Postponing tasks to the point of implementation of a system is unwise. There is always a tendency to push too many things along to this stage, turning the implementation into a nightmare.

Rather than relying on piecemeal updates to reference data tables, a better approach is to have a single process to load all production data into these tables. The process should take its input from a single source file where the data has been defined. Ideally this would be a text file. It need not be, but for the purposes of the discussion here, a text file format will be assumed. A text file is easy for users and systems personnel to review in order to agree that all necessary reference data has been included. Figure 14.1 illustrates this design approach.

An important item in the load process is to delete all existing data in the reference data tables prior to loading the data from the source text file. This is to ensure that no test data remains in the database.

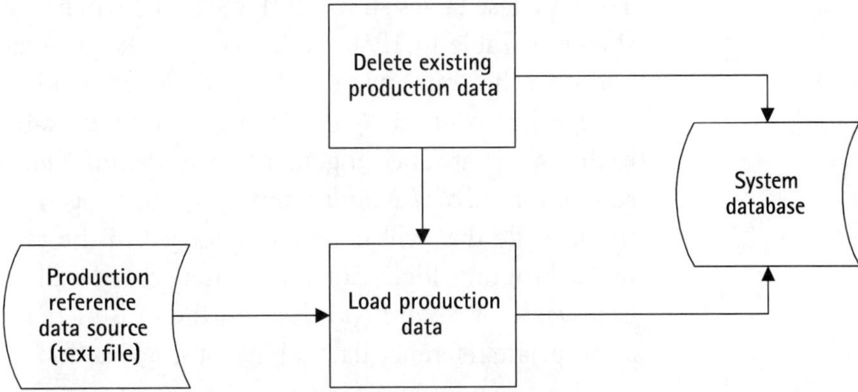

Figure 14.1 A single load process for production reference data.

When deleting reference data in this way, all the reference data tables should be cleaned out. Only then can there be certainty that nothing other than production data exists in these tables.

Another consideration in such a load is the order in which reference data tables should be loaded. Tables that have no foreign key columns but are parent tables of other tables should be loaded first. Then, tables that are child tables (i.e., have relationships to other reference tables) can be loaded. This is particularly necessary if referential integrity constraints (e.g., insert triggers) have been implemented in the database. For instance, a trigger might cause the load process to fail if an attempt is made to insert a record with a foreign key value that has not yet been established in its parent table. Of course some database products allow ways in which RI can be bypassed, especially during the bulk load of tables.

Foreign key relationships must be handled by the text file that is the source of the information for the load process. It is best to keep the design of this file as simple as possible. One option is shown in Table 14.1. Here each field is stored in a separate record in the text file and grouped by a record number for the target table. Each value of the record number corresponds to an individual record in the target file.

The database tables shown in Figure 14.2 will be loaded from the file shown in Table 14.1. As can be seen, the `Region` table is loaded first, and then the `Country` table. This sequence avoids problems with the foreign key column *RgnCode* in the `Country` table. Each record in each table is grouped together by the *Record Number* column in the source file. *Record Number* simply groups together those records in the text file that will update one record in the target reference data table. Program logic can be written to read all source records for each value of *Record Number* and then insert the new record in the appropriate reference data table in a single action.

Table 14.1 Sample production data source text file.

Record Number	Table Name	Column Name	Column Value
001	REGION	RGNCODE	EUR
001	REGION	RGNDESC	Europe
002	REGION	RGNCODE	LAC
002	REGION	RGNDESC	Latin America and Caribbean
003	COUNTRY	CTYCODE	SWE
003	COUNTRY	CTYDESC	Sweden
003	COUNTRY	RGNCODE	EUR
004	COUNTRY	CTYCODE	FRA
004	COUNTRY	CTYDESC	France
004	COUNTRY	RGNCODE	EUR
005	COUNTRY	CTYCODE	MEX
005	COUNTRY	CTYDESC	Mexico
005	COUNTRY	RGNCODE	LAC

One other advantage of this approach is that the source file, with some effort, can be sorted prior to being loaded so that the reference data records are loaded in a predefined sequence, such as alphabetically by code. Having records physically ordered in tables may improve performance for some database management systems.

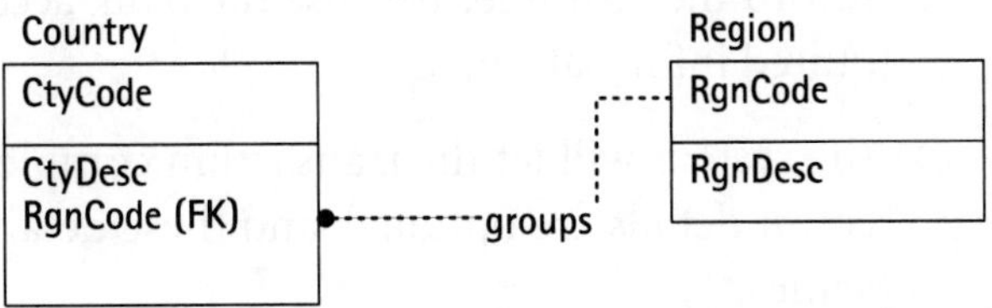

Figure 14.2 Database tables loaded by source text file.

An additional concern may be the translation of datatypes. This is particularly a problem for constant values, where a number or date is often involved. These are obviously expressed in character form in a text file but can easily be converted by a load program.

While this discussion has mainly focused on production data, it is possible to handle test data in a similar way. By definition, however, test data is irrelevant for reference data tables that have no interface to allow their update in production and are expected to be fully loaded with production data at system implementation. For the remaining reference data tables, testing their update features is usually the main testing task required, and using a single load process is not really helpful.

Avoidance of Null Values

After a system has gone into production, it is not always possible for users to enter certain transaction data because they simply do not know it. For instance, a user may wish to record customer information; when the system prompts for the data entry of the customer's bank account details, the user does not know them. Obviously the user cannot enter this information. One of two things will now happen:

- the system will not let the user complete the transaction to record the customer because the bank account details are required information, or
- the system will let the transaction complete, as the bank account details are optional, and these details will contain null values.

Null values are supported by many database management systems to indicate that no value has been stored. Some other (mostly older) software products do not support nulls and store spaces or zeroes instead. For the purposes of this discussion, the term *null values* also includes these situations.

Most modern database management systems will not permit a primary key to contain a null value under any circumstances. When populating reference data tables, null values should never be used for the non-key attributes, that is, for descriptions and constant values.

However, there can be temptations to use nulls. For instance, if a transaction table has always been used to record amounts in U.S. dollars, and there is suddenly a need to record other currencies, an additional column for *Currency Code* may be added to the table. The column will be set to null values immediately after it is added (unless a default value is assigned at the same time, which would be the correct thing to do). It is tempting to leave the column in this state, with null values essentially meaning "US Dollars," but this would be very poor design. Null values mean that data is unknown or not available, and they should not be used to indicate a real value of any kind. Furthermore, if a `Currency` reference data table is created with *Currency Code* and *Currency Description*, no database management system will allow *Currency Code*—the primary key—to have a null value. There can be other problems too. For instance, database management systems also tend to treat nulls in special ways; for instance, most of them will not even consider null values when performing SQL aggregate functions like SUM or AVERAGE. In short, null values should never be used to represent anything other than the absence of data.

While modern database management systems may prevent the usage of null values in primary keys, there are some older products that do not have this constraint, and "empty" values like spaces can still be used. Regrettably this allows the equivalent of null values to creep into primary keys and foreign keys that should be non-null. Significant problems can occur when these databases are converted to platforms that do not allow nulls in these columns.

The problem can be avoided by never permitting nulls (or their equivalent) for codes, descriptions, or constant values. Then when nulls are used in foreign key columns in transaction data tables, they really must mean that data is unknown or not available.

Specifying a Value for Unknown Data

While nulls can be used to record unavailable or unknown data, they should not be used to record the fact that data is known but cannot be entered for a transaction because it is not present in a reference data table. This problem can be overcome by including a record for an unknown value (meaning unknown to the table, not to the user) in every reference data table. Table 14.2 shows an example of this for a `Country` reference table.

A record has been added to the table with a code of *** and a description of *** Unknown Country ***. If a user is entering data in a transaction table and comes across a country that is not in the reference data table, they can select the value "Unknown."

The code and description of the record for "Unknown" in the reference data table can be chosen so that they will sort to the beginning or end of lists that appear on screens. They should be clearly distinguishable from other values.

Table 14.2 Using a value for unknown data.

Country Code	Country Description
***	*** Unknown Country ***
FRA	France
IRE	Ireland
SWE	Sweden

There needs to be some way of monitoring the use of "Unknown." The correct values will have to be added to the reference data table and the transaction data edited to change the value from "Unknown" to the correct value.

The advantages of this design are as follows:

- If the reference data is used in a transaction where a value must be entered, then the "Unknown" value can be selected. In this way the transaction can be completed.
- Users can be forced to select "Unknown" rather than simply avoiding entering a value.
- If a value is known but is missing from the parent reference data table, then it may be more valid to select "Unknown" than to have a null value recorded.

However, there are also disadvantages:

- The transaction data tables can end up with optional columns containing both nulls and "Unknown." Program logic then has to be written to treat both values appropriately, and it may be confusing on reports. Of course for mandatory fields, there should be no nulls entered, so this does not apply to them. However, having "Unknown" for a mandatory field may also cause problems.

- Additional work must be done to monitor the usage of "Unknown" and take appropriate actions.
- If processing has to occur based on specific values, the usage of "Unknown" may cause problems.

Overall this design option has to be examined carefully as there are distinct advantages and disadvantages.

Specifying a Value for "None"

Sometimes reference data is used for optional fields in transaction data. In such circumstances there will be a non-identifying relationship between the reference data table and the transaction data table, and nulls will be allowed. The user may wish to distinguish between a null value—where data is not available—and a value of "None."

Table 14.3 and Figure 14.3 show an example of this. A company wishes to maintain a *Delinquency Status* for each `Customer`, which it calculates using a complex formula based on past customer history, buying patterns, time of year, and so on. The value of "None" exists to apply to a `Customer` who has no *Delinquency Status.*

Table 14.3 Values for a Delinquency Status table.

Delinquency Status Code	Delinquency Status Description
01	None
02	Marginally Delinquent
03	Delinquent
04	Seriously Delinquent

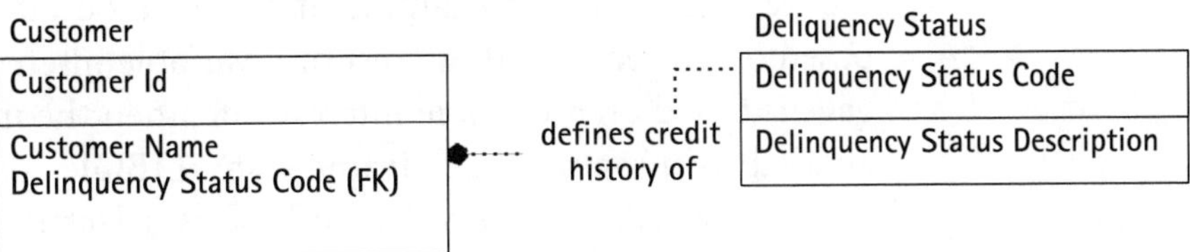

Figure 14.3 Database design for Customer Delinquency Status.

Specifying a Value for "Other"

A somewhat different approach to dealing with values that need to be entered at a transaction level but do not exist in a parent reference data table is to place a value of "Other" in the reference data table. When a value is encountered that is not in the reference data table, then "Other" can be selected. The implication is that the parent reference data table is not going to be updated to include additional values. If it is updated, then there may be records in transaction data tables with values of "Other" that are now represented by a discrete new value in the reference data table. This would be a major problem.

Specifying a Value for "Not Applicable"

Sometimes a value of "Not Applicable" may be usefully incorporated in a reference data table. Unfortunately it may be because it is required for a column in a database table that is denormalized. After all, if an attribute (column) is a property of an entity (table), how can it ever have a value of "Not Applicable"?

Figure 14.4 shows an example of a Mortgage table. Mortgages are based on either a fixed interest or a variable interest rate. If a mortgage is based on a variable interest rate, then the interest rate is calculated from some base (Prime Rate, LIBOR) plus an additional percentage called a *spread.* The base is selected from a reference data table.

Figure 14.5 shows a denormalized version of Figure 14.4, with the subtypes placed back in the Mortgage supertype.

In Figure 14.4 there should be no value for *Interest Rate Type Code* in Mortgage for a fixed rate mortgage. A value of null does not quite capture the situation, and a value of "Not Applicable" would be better.

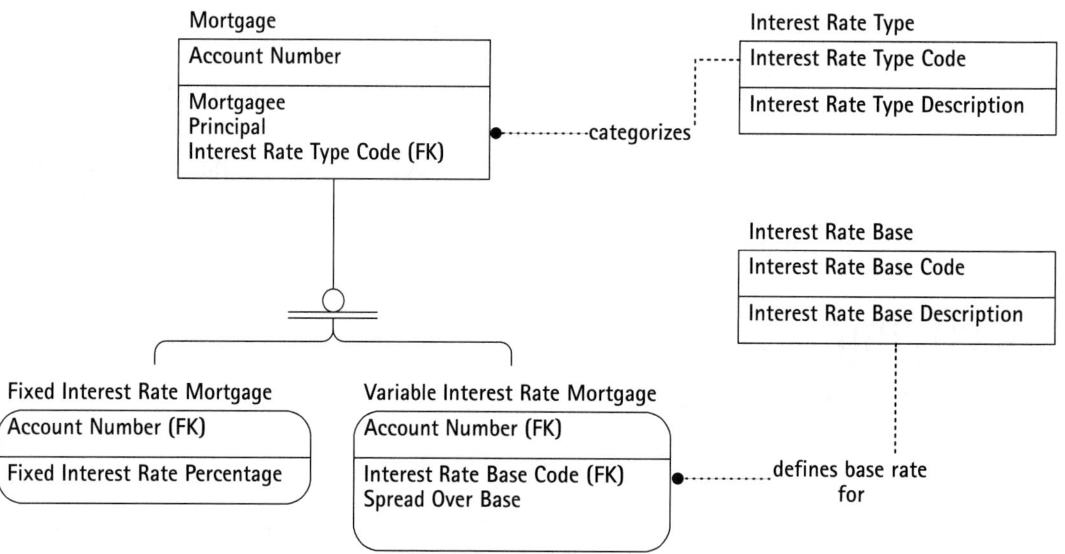

Figure 14.4 Normalized subtypes.

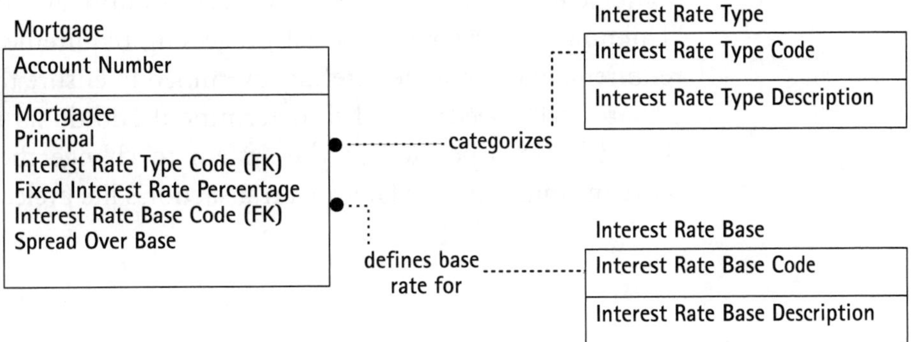

Figure 14.5 Denormalized design.

Specifying a Value for "All"

Because an instance of a column cannot have multiple values, it is not a good idea to have a value in a reference data table for "All." However, "All" is seen quite frequently in combo boxes on screens—usually to enter a selection criterion of some kind, where the selection of "All" simply bypasses whatever criterion is being selected, since all values will be accepted in the query. The concept does not carry over to database design and the population of reference data tables. It is only valid in the context of GUI design.

Conclusion

Reference data tables usually have to be populated at the point where a system goes into production. When this happens, these tables cannot be contaminated with test data. It is recommended that systems development teams create a strategy and tools to address the needs of production implementation of reference data.

Some reference data tables may need additional values such as "Unknown" to cater for special processing requirements. Business requirements should be carefully examined to ensure that these values are really needed, and to determine if additional functionality should be incorporated in the system to change these values to more meaningful ones later in a transaction's life cycle.

CHAPTER 15

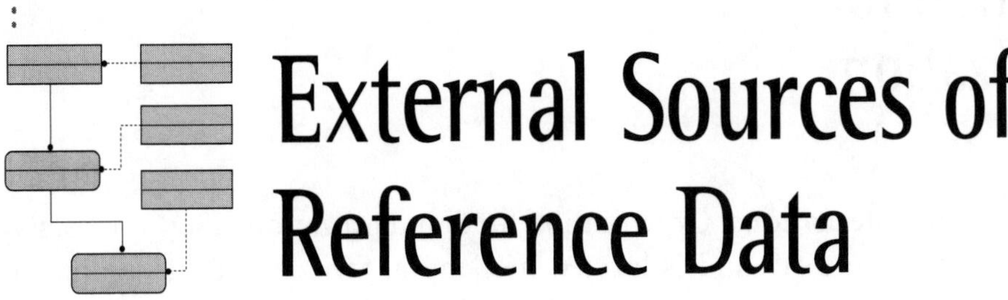

External Sources of Reference Data

AS NOTED IN CHAPTER 1, a great deal of reference data is created by parties outside the enterprise. Some of these parties may actually own the standard that contains the reference data. In most cases, however, there are no restrictions on the use of these standards.

We shall examine a few representative organizations and the standards they maintain. This is to provide an idea of how these organizations work, what can be expected of them, what issues may exist within the standards themselves, and what other problems an enterprise may encounter when it tries to adopt external standards for reference data.

ISO: The International Organization for Standardization

The International Organization for Standardization (ISO) was established in 1947 and is located in Geneva, Switzerland. It is a major standard setting organization that is a federation of national standards bodies from approximately 130 countries. Only one national standards body represents each member country.

Oddly, ISO is not an acronym (which would logically be "IOS") but a kind of short title derived from the Greek word *isos* meaning "equal." It was chosen to circumvent the need to translate the acronym into the different languages of member countries, and so in all languages the term ISO is used consistently. This is rather interesting from a reference data management viewpoint.

One of the main goals of ISO is to promote liberalization in global trade by helping remove technical barriers to trade. These can include standards that exist in one country for a particular product or service but that exist in a completely different form in another country. When standards are harmonized or, better yet, everyone agrees to a common standard, problems created by technical trade barriers are diminished. ISO defines a standard as follows:

> *Standards are documented agreements containing technical specifications or other precise criteria to be used consistently as rules, guidelines, or definitions of characteristics, to ensure that materials, products, processes and services are fit for their purpose.* [ISO00]

Some of the standards ISO has developed are for physical characteristics of things, such as the thickness of credit cards. Some are for management, such as the well-known ISO 9000 standard that provides a framework for quality management and quality assurance. However, ISO has been particularly successful in creating standards for information. ISO itself notes that

> *The ISO international codes for country names, currencies and languages help to eliminate duplication and incompatibilities in the collection, processing and dissemination of information. As resource-saving tools, universally understandable codes play an important role in both automated and manual documentation.* [ISO00]

New standards are being created by ISO all the time. National standards bodies tend to hear about needs for standardization from industry groups (typically associations of companies in the same industry) within their particular country. Once the national standards body is convinced there is a need, it brings the matter before ISO as a whole. If ISO agrees that a new standard is needed, the first phase is to create working groups to define the scope of the standard. Then the standard itself is created. This can be a complex process involving the participation of many national standards bodies. The final standard must be approved by ISO, through a voting process, and is then published by ISO.

After a standard is created, it is generally reviewed every five years. This task is carried out by an ISO Registration Authority. However, some standards, particularly those important for reference data, change too quickly for five-year revisions alone. They are handled by ISO maintenance agencies, and we will examine two such standards: ISO 4217 for currency codes and ISO 3166 for country codes.

ISO 4217: Currency Codes

The table of ISO currency codes is reproduced in Appendix 1. This table is actually the English version of Table A.1 of the standard. There are three tables in the standard; each is available in English and French:

- Table A.1, Currency and Funds Codes
- Table A.2, Funds Codes
- Table A.3, codes for historic denominations of currencies

There are only six Funds Codes listed in Tables A.1 and A.2 of the 1995 revision of the standard. They include entries such as "USS" for "US Dollar same day funds," and "USN" for "US Dollar next day funds." The majority of the entries in Table A.1 are for currencies, but in addition to Funds Codes, there are also several entries for precious metals.

From a data modeling perspective this is interesting. Table A.1 can be considered as a supertype entity, containing currencies, funds, and precious metals. There is no column in the table that indicates which of these three types each row belongs to. If an enterprise is interested only in currencies, it may not wish to store the codes for funds and precious metals in its databases.

This example has an important implication. If an enterprise wishes to use an external standard for reference data, it should understand the standard and use only those components of the standards that map properly to the data contained in its information systems. For instance, there is no guarantee that the standard, in the format it is made available to the enterprise, will be in third normal form. This issue can be seen in ISO 4217.

Another interesting feature of ISO 4217 is that the first column, called "Entity," is actually derived where possible from the ISO standard for country codes—ISO 3166. It is intended to represent the country that issues the currency. However, this correspondence does not always work. For the precious metals there is no issuing country. Some organizations, rather than countries, issue currencies, such as the International Monetary Fund (not found in ISO 3166) issues Special Drawing Rights—code "XDR"—which is considered to be a currency.

Some currencies are used in more than one country (as taken from ISO 3166). For example, the U.S. dollar is used in the British Virgin Islands, Federated States of Micronesia, Marshall Islands, U.S. Virgin Islands, and some other countries. In other words, there is a one-to-many relationship in this table.

Some countries use more than one currency. The Rand and the Namibian Dollar are listed as currencies for Namibia. Thus, Table A.1 actually contains a many-to-many relationship between country and currency.

There are some other points in Table A.1 that are interesting from a data modeling point of view:

- Antarctica has no universal currency.
- Code "XTS" is used only for testing purposes.
- Code "XXX" is reserved for transactions where no currency is involved.
- Poland has two currencies, both with the same name, "Zloty," but different codes, "PLZ" and "PLN."
- Two codes, "XFU" and "XFO," are assigned to a category called "Special Settlement Currencies"; these are the only alphabetic codes that do not have equivalent numeric codes.

The lesson in this for a data analyst is that the standard may need to be restructured to be input into reference data tables in a database. Furthermore, not all of the standard may be applicable to a given enterprise. For instance, the enterprise may only want true currencies and may only be interested in the alphabetic code and its corresponding description.

In addition to the content of the standard itself, the process by which it changes is important to understand.

As noted earlier, all ISO standards are revised every five years, but certain ones, like ISO 4271, are known to change more quickly and are assigned to maintenance agencies. The maintenance agency (MA) for ISO 4217 has a number of members. These members have a right to vote on decisions of the MA, although this is rare in practice. A secretariat which performs most of the actual work of the MA is located within the British Standards Institute (BSI) in London, England. The MA staff at BSI is responsible for effecting changes to the standard. In addition, the MA offers a subscription service that provides each subscriber with a set of tables and notification of changes within one business day. The cost of this service is 205 British pounds per annum.

On average there are about five changes to ISO 4217 every year, although this varies, with considerably more activity in certain years. Changes can come about because of new currencies being issued by new countries or other entities, or existing currencies being redenominated (that is, reformed to change their exchange rates relative to more stable currencies).

When a new currency arises or an existing one changes, the MA should be informed by representatives of the country (or other entity) involved. There is a procedure to inform the MA, involving submission of what is essentially a change request form. While this is normally what happens, it is not always the case. Sometimes the MA will hear about changes to currencies from subscribers to their service or other parties. In such cases the Chair of the Maintenance Agency—currently the World Bank—is consulted. The World Bank is usually in a position to confirm just how real the new or changed currency is, as they have contacts at national central banks all over the world.

If the MA is informed of a new currency, the first step is to assign a code. Generally, the first two characters of the alphabetic code are taken from the alpha-2 country codes of ISO 3166. The last letter is assigned based on the first letter of the currency name, where this is possible. Where it is not possible the best approximation is used. A three-digit numeric code is also assigned. The first time a currency is recorded for a country, the ISO 3166 three-digit country code is used. If the currency is redenominated, a completely new numeric code is assigned, outside the ranges used in ISO 3166. These seem to start with 900. Thus, the numeric codes can appear to jump around somewhat for countries that have changed their currencies. For instance, the Belarussian Ruble went from code "BYB," number 112, to code "BYR," number 974. Confusingly, the official name of "Belarussian Ruble" did not change.

Those currencies that are not associated with single issuing countries have codes assigned in a slightly different way. They begin with the letter "X," such as "XCD" for "Eastern Caribbean Dollar," and their numeric codes are beyond the ranges used for ISO 3166.

One recent exception to this scheme was the Euro, the regional currency introduced in Europe in 1999. This has a code of "EUR," which does not begin with an "X." The code was assigned to make life easier for financial institutions and with some thought that "EU" might be added to ISO 3166 in the future.

This brief description of the ISO 4217 standard and the way in which its maintenance agency functions has some important lessons for those wishing to use such standards in enterprise reference data maintenance:

- International standards require some understanding if they are to be used correctly.
- There is no guarantee that an international standard exists in a structure that is directly compatible with database designs in third normal form.
- An enterprise may not need all of the standard for its purposes.
- Even bodies that create standards are subject to information float (the time it takes from a relevant fact becoming known to the time the fact is incorporated in the published standard).

ISO 3166: Country Codes

ISO 3166 is a standard for representing counties and their subdivisions. The standard has become more well known recently because the alpha-2 (two-letter) codes are used as Internet country code top-level domain identifiers. Like the currency code standard, ISO 3166 has a maintenance agency (MA) to keep it up to date. In the case of ISO 3166, the MA staff is principally located at the Deutsches Institut für Normung (DIN) in Berlin, Germany.

ISO 3166 is actually a three-part standard:

- **ISO 3166-1.** Codes for the names of countries, dependencies, and other areas of geopolitical interest.
- **ISO 3166-2.** Codes for names of the principal administrative subdivisions of the countries coded in ISO 3166-1. This

is relatively new, having been first issued on 15 December 1998.

- **ISO 3166-3.** Codes for formerly used names of countries. These are countries that have been removed from ISO 3166-1 since its first publication in 1974.

ISO 3166-1 consists of the familiar alpha-2 codes (e.g., "DK" for "Denmark") and the country names (in English and French). For each entry there is also an alpha-3 country code (that is, an alphabetic code that is three characters long) and a three-digit numeric code, although these are more rarely used. The table of alpha-2 country codes and English names is shown in Appendix 2.

As can be seen from Appendix 2, some entries do not have assigned codes but are there to help in the use of the table—for example, "Vatican City State see HOLY SEE." Some of the names of the countries may be controversial for certain enterprises, rendering the codes as stated in the standard problematical to use, such as "TAIWAN, PROVINCE OF CHINA." These issues highlight the fact that an enterprise may need to think about how it uses an international standard, and that it may not be usable without some adaptation to the needs of the enterprise.

The tremendous growth of the Internet, and its use of the alpha-2 codes as top-level domain identifiers, has fueled interest in this standard. However, the standard is not intended to create new top-level domain identifiers. The scope of this standard is to provide codes that represent countries.

ISO 3166-2 consists of codes for the administrative subdivisions of a country created from the alpha-2 country code plus a separator, plus an alphanumeric code up to three characters long. This last component can be one, two, or three characters long. The effect is to make the overall codes variable in length with a minimum of four characters (e.g., "MG-T" for the province of Antananarivo in Madagascar) and a maximum of six characters (e.g., "DK-025" for the county of Roskilde in Denmark). Wherever possible the subdivision codes have been taken from meaningful national coding schemes in use in the countries concerned.

This is an example of a hierarchical code: the first part of the code comes from a separate but related standard. The codes are only unique as a whole. Different countries can use the same subdivision code (the part that follows the separator). No country can use the same subdivision code more than once.

Unlike many other instances of reference data, ISO 3166-2 is quite large. It contains several thousand entries. With this number of entries, the rate of change is also somewhat faster than would be expected for an international standard. ISO 3166-1, by contrast, has approximately 230 entries and changes much more slowly.

An Example of a Related Standard: Road Vehicle Distinguishing Signs

There is at least one other way of representing countries by using codes: the oval plates with letters on them that are sometimes seen on the backs of cars that cross international borders. A list of these codes is kept by the United Nations, in accordance with the 1968 Convention on Road Traffic (Article 45 (4)) and the 1949 Convention on Road Traffic (Appendix 4). The list is shown in Appendix 3; clearly there are differences from the ISO 3166 standard shown in Appendix 2.

Thus there may be alternative international standards for representing a particular kind of reference data. In this situation the enterprise needs to determine which standard it should use. This should be based on which standard is more widely recognized and generally adopted. For instance, it is fair to say that ISO 3166 is more widely used than the country codes for road vehicles shown in Appendix 3. However, there is a more important consideration: does the business of the enterprise dictate which standard should be used? An enterprise providing roadside assistance to international travelers might want to adopt the country codes shown in Appendix 3.

Some enterprises may need to have more than one international standard to represent reference data. An insurance company may wish to represent countries with both ISO 3166 and the road vehicle codes. In such cases the need usually arises for what is often termed a *crosswalk* between the two sets of reference data. A crosswalk table shows the correspondence between one set of codes and another. However, it is generally not possible to find crosswalk tables for international standards. The organizations responsible for each standard do not usually have any mandate to match their coding schemes with any other standard. It is then up to each enterprise using different coding schemes to create the crosswalk tables. An example for matching ISO 3166 alpha-2 codes with road vehicle codes is shown in Appendix 4. Even though this is based on international standards, it cannot itself be considered a standard, because it has been created in an ad hoc manner and has no official sanction by any of the standards bodies concerned.

Enterprises must be very careful about how they construct crosswalk tables. It is easy to see how errors can occur. For instance, it is quite possible that a crosswalk table created by one enterprise will differ from a crosswalk table created by another enterprise to match up the same reference data. This situation can lead to data quality problems if these enterprises have to exchange information.

Standard and Poor's Ratings

Not all standards are maintained by international organizations, or even governmental organizations. Standard and Poor's is a corporation that provides a variety of financial information and services. Among these services is the ratings of long-term issues—that is, the creditworthiness of an obligor with respect to a specific financial obligation, a class of financial obligations, or a specific financial program. *Long-term* is a relative term, and depends on the financial market concerned. In the U.S., it means obligations with maturities of 365 days or more. Table 15.1 shows the Standard and Poor's Long-Term Issue Rating Codes. Appendix 5 shows this table with its rating definitions.

These codes are well established and well known in the U.S. financial sector. They have not changed in very many years.

Standard and Poor's also rates the creditworthiness of issuers, that is, the overall financial capacity of an obligor to pay its financial obligations. Table 15.2 shows the codes used to represent creditworthiness of issuers over the long term. The full definitions of these codes are given in Appendix 6.

The codes used in Tables 15.1 and 15.2 are nearly identical, even though they are measuring different things: the codes in Table 15.1 are for issues (financial obligations like bonds), whereas the codes in Table 15.2 are for issuers (the corporations or other legal entities that issue financial obligations). Not only do the tables pertain to different things, but the definitions of the individual codes are quite different (see Appendices 5 and 6). There is one other difference. Some of the codes in Table 15.2 can be assigned a pi subscript. This

Table 15.1 Standard and Poor's Long-Term Issue Rating Codes.

Long-Term Issue Code
AAA
AA+
AA
AA-
A+
A
A-
BBB+
BBB
BBB-
BB+
BB
BB-
B+
B
B-
CCC+
CCC
CCC-
CC
C
D
r
N.R.

Table 15.2 Standard and Poor's Long-Term Issuer Rating Codes.

Long-Term Issuer Code
AAA
AA+
AA
AA-
A+
A
A-
BBB+
BBB
BBB-
BB+
BB
BB-
B+
B
B-
CCC+
CCC
CCC-
CC
C
SD
D
R
N.R.

means "public information" and represents ratings based on information generally in the public domain, rather than in-depth meetings with an issuer's management. Ratings with pi subscripts can never have + or - at the end of the code.

From a database design viewpoint Tables 15.1 and 15.2 are quite different. These tables describe different things, and the codes they contain have different definitions. However, to many users they are essentially the same, because there is so much overlap between the actual code values used in the tables. The lesson here is that database designers should pay more attention to the meaning behind the reference data than the actual values that are used to represent it in coded form.

An interesting fact about the Standard and Poor's long-term issue and issuer ratings is their stability. They have not changed in many years and are unlikely to do so, as they represent a complete classification scheme rather than physical or notional objects, which may be created or disappear over time. Because they are less vulnerable to issues of information float than, say, the country codes dealt with earlier in this chapter, the rating codes may be represented in reference data tables with the actual codes as the primary key, rather than using a surrogate key (see Chapter 5). This can simplify a great deal of system design and implementation, but it must still be regarded as a calculated risk because there is no guarantee that the rating codes will not change.

Another interesting fact about the Standard and Poor's ratings is that although they represent a well-known standard, they may be used and interpreted differently by different enterprises. For instance, some banks and securities companies recognize BBB– and better as the ratings for investment-grade financial obligations, while anything with a lower rating is considered "high yield" (a more polite term for "junk"). However, in other banks and securities companies, investment grade may be considered to be BBB and better.

This illustrates that the use of a common standard is not itself a guarantee that two enterprises will be able to exchange data related to this standard in a meaningful way.

Conclusion

External sources of reference data, particularly well-recognized standards, can be extremely useful to an enterprise. They make it much easier to share data with other enterprises and reduce the resources an enterprise would otherwise need for finding out about changes in whatever it is that the reference data represents. However, it cannot be expected that even the most popular reference data standards exist in a form that is immediately ready for inclusion in a database. There may be semantic, formatting, scope, usage, and other issues that an enterprise must clarify before the standard can be used. In the end the database structures that the enterprise uses to hold the reference data may look quite different from the way the standard is presented on paper. Simply deciding to use an external source of reference data is not enough. Analysis and design are still required if it is to be used successfully.

CHAPTER 16

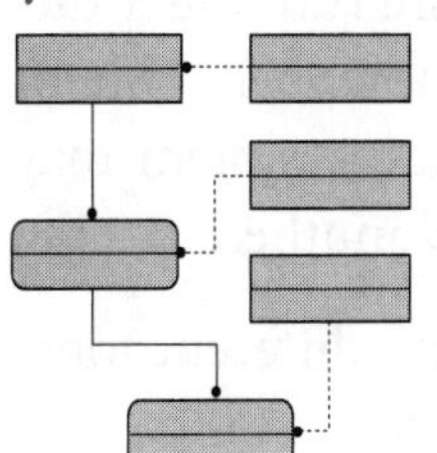

Multilingual Issues

THERE IS INCREASING INTEREST IN building computer systems that function in more than one language. Such systems help organizations to have an effective presence in countries with different working languages. Software developers are also focusing on multilingual applications because they can be marketed more widely than packages available only in English.

Codes and descriptions are very important for any multilingual system. The reason is that they often represent the great majority of data that needs to be translated. Before examining this role in detail, however, let us briefly review the components of a system that need special treatment when designing a multilingual system These are:

- **Text.** It is obvious that texts need to be translated.
- **Character representations.** English can be represented using the ANSI character set, but this is not true of other

languages, which may use diacritical marks (accents) and sometimes characters that are not part of the Latin alphabet.

- **Operating System.** When applications are run under different operating systems, strange things can happen. One of these is that a given character in one operating system may appear as a completely different character in another.
- **Font.** Even within a single operating system, different fonts may display the same text as different characters.
- **Patterns.** There are a number of other cultural characteristics that differ among languages, such as how a date is formatted (month before day or vice versa); what character represents a decimal point; what is the accepted sequence for sorting (not only for the same letter with different accents, but also for different letter combinations like "LL" and "CH" that may sometimes sort as if they are distinct letters).

A full discussion of all these topics is well beyond the scope of this book, but they are complex and wide-ranging enough to show that building a system for multilingual use is not for the faint-hearted. We will concentrate on the role of reference data and how it can be managed. In this context we will only be discussing codes and descriptions because they are central to the translation of texts.

Within a system, there are three kinds of text for which translations must be provided:

- Fixed pieces of text (prompts) that appear on screens and printed reports.
- The variable data that appears on screens and reports. Obviously, only character data is relevant.
- Written documentation that supports a system, including online help.

Reference data is relevant only for the variable data that appears on screens and reports. In most cases the bulk of this variable data is numeric and is taken from transaction data. However, when variable data is textual, it nearly always consists of descriptions from reference data tables. Sometimes there may be other types of textual data, but transactions typically contain very little text that is not reference data codes. When free-form text is found in transaction data, it is either impossible to translate or requires a great deal of effort to translate.

Consider the tables shown in Figure 16.1. Within the `Customer` table there are a number of text fields. Some of these fields cannot be translated because they only exist in one language:

Customer First Name
Customer Last Name
Customer Street Address Line 1
Customer Street Address Line 2

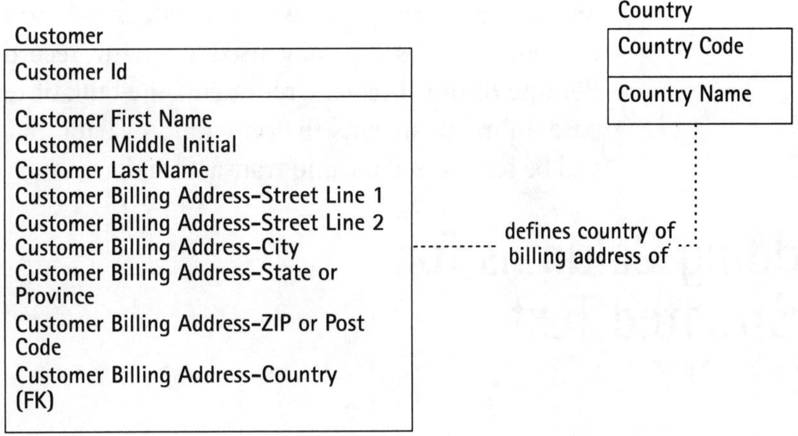

Figure 16.1 An example of text in transaction data.

There is only one *Customer First Name* and one *Customer Last Name*, and not French, German, or English versions of them. It is true that there might be a problem with character sets; for instance, for a Japanese corporation the name may need to be represented in the Latin alphabet as well as in Hiragana or Katakana or Kanji. However, this is a comparatively rare need.

An argument can be made for translating *Customer Billing Address-City*, because the names of cities vary from language to language—"London" in English is "Londres" in Spanish. However, if the *Customer Billing Address-City* is only to be used for mailings to the customer, there is little point.

When it comes to the *Customer Billing Address-Country*, however, the enterprise may not only wish to mail information to the customer, but may analyze customers by country. The persons reading the reports produced for this analysis may be working in several different languages, and so there may be a real need to have the name of the country in different languages.

Again the scope of reference data comes into play. A lot of data recorded for a single transaction applies only to that transaction, but reference data is typically used in many records and many tables. Because of this it usually represents the bulk of textual data in a database. In many systems the only kind of data that requires translation will be reference data, and transaction data can be left alone.

Adding Columns for Translated Text

If it is decided that a system needs to function in a multilingual environment, then reference data tables that hold codes and descriptions must have the descriptions available in more than one language. There are several ways to do this. One design option is to add columns for translated descriptions to reference data tables. Figure 16.2 shows how the `Country` table can be enhanced to contain additional columns where descriptions in other languages are stored.

This design has the advantage that for one code value, all translated descriptions are contained in one record in the `Country` table. However, it has the disadvantage that program, query, and reporting logic has to "know" the correct column name to get the description in the desired language. With a lot of reference data tables, keeping track of these names may be a problem. Of course standard naming conventions can be used to ease this problem. There is also the problem that translations may not be present for all records. The system should have a default language in which all descriptions are recorded (e.g., English). The English description could be used where the translations into the other languages have not yet been made.

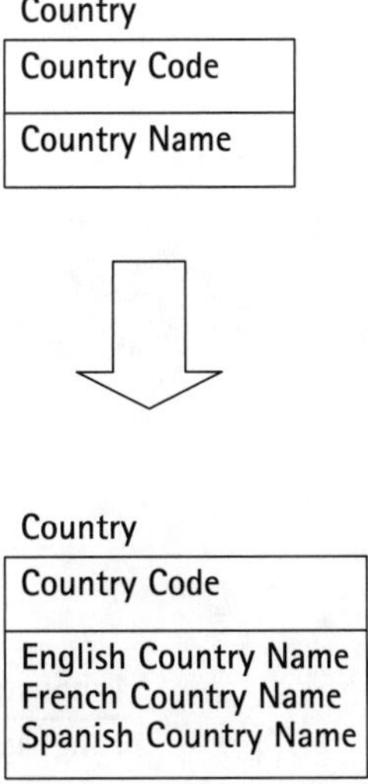

Figure 16.2 Adding columns to a table to contain descriptions in other languages.

Making Language Part of the Key

An alternative to adding columns to each table is to include a language code as part of the key of each reference table. Figure 16.3 illustrates this approach. The reference data table now has *Language Code* as part of its primary key.

A `Language` table has been implemented to hold details of every language used in the system. For simplicity the design in Figure 16.3 only allows languages to be specified in one language in the `Language` table.

Every reference data table holding codes and descriptions will have *Language Code* as part of the primary key. Records are found by searching for a combination of a code value and a *Language Code* value.

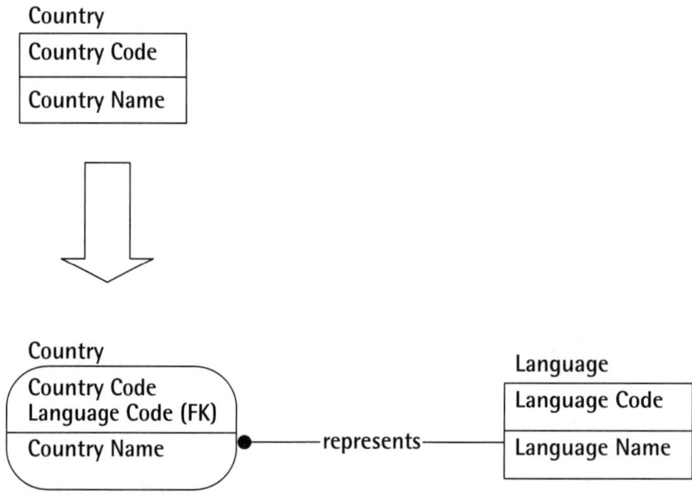

Figure 16.3 Adding language code to the key of the reference data table.

There are some major disadvantages to the scheme illustrated in Figure 16.3. There are now two attributes that form the primary key of the `Country` table. This makes populating transaction data tables more difficult. Furthermore, what happens if we want to include other non-key attributes like *Capital City* or *Current Population*? Clearly the same information would have to be put into multiple records, violating third normal form. Figure 16.4 shows a better-modeled version.

In Figure 16.4 there is a new table that holds country names in all the languages in the `Language` table. If an additional language is

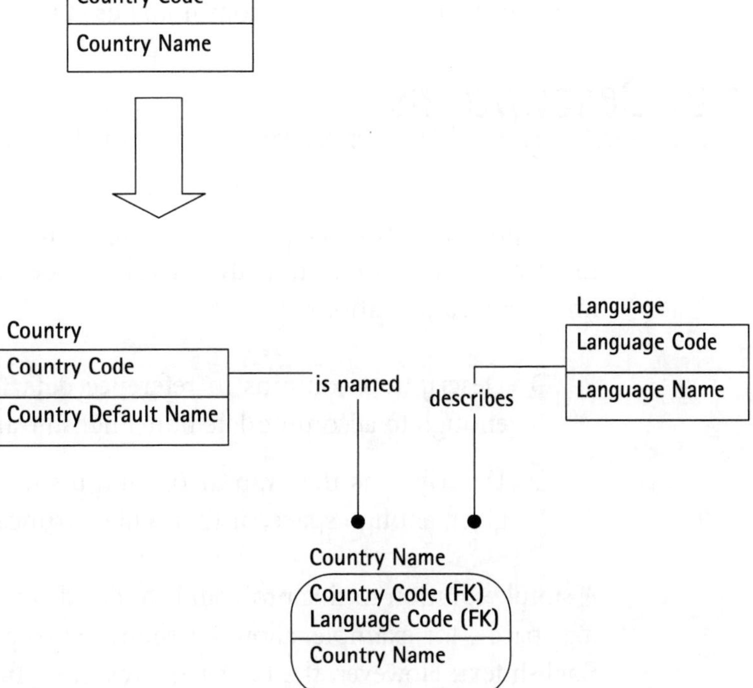

Figure 16.4 Creating a new table to hold country names.

required for the system, a new record is added to the `Language` table. No tables have to be restructured, which is a disadvantage of the approach of adding columns to reference tables (see Figure 16.2). Furthermore, the program, query, and reporting logic does not have to "know" the appropriate column name to get a description from a table in a given language. Instead it has to know the value of *Language Code* for the language currently being used (one value instead of many column names). In addition, there are none of the problems about violating third normal form that exist in Figure 16.3. However, programming is more complex. There is now another table that has to be included in SQL statements that obtain the name of a country. As a concession to efficiency, a denormalized *Country Default Name* has been included in the `Country` table. This can enable a program to pick up the country name from the `Country` table for the language most commonly used in the system.

Sizes of Descriptions

Descriptions in most languages are longer than their equivalents in English. This point is not always fully understood but has some important ramifications:

- Description columns in reference data tables must be long enough to accommodate non-English translations.
- Descriptions that appear on outputs of the system must be given enough space, or they will be truncated.

A simple solution to this problem is to decide on a factor for increasing space—for example, allow 1.5 times the length of the maximum English text. However, the longer the text, the smaller the increase in length when it is translated from English to another language. Designers must carefully consider the context of the data and languages they are dealing with when working to solve this problem.

Missing Translations

Multilingual descriptions tend to have problems when translations are missing. For instance, suppose a new record is added to the `Country` table in a system that operates in English, French, and Spanish, but only the English *Country Name* is known. At a minimum, users working in French and Spanish will not see the new country on their system outputs. The inconsistent state of the data may also cause other problems—bugs—in the system. How can these problems be overcome?

The first step is to design the system to have a default language (usually English). No matter what language the user is working in, the system will guarantee to have an English translation for any piece of text.

Program logic can then be constructed so that if a translation cannot be found in a given language, the system obtains the translation in the default language. This differs from the design of the reference data tables in the following ways:

- Where different columns are used, as in Figure 16.2, if the system finds a null value in the appropriate description column, then it will return the value in the description column for the default language.
- If *Language Code* is part of the key, as in Figure 16.4, and the system does not find a particular record, then it can search for the record with the same code value for the default language. Alternatively, an attribute for the default country name can be set up, as in the `Country` table in Figure 16.4.

The result of this design is that no matter what language a user is working in, the system will always retrieve a description from the reference data, even though it may be in the default language.

Constructing retrieval logic like this can be time consuming, and there is an alternative worth considering. The logic that updates reference data can be changed so that when a new record is added, all translated descriptions are first populated with the default language version. Tables 16.1 and 16.2 illustrate how this approach is used in a `Country` table with primary keys of *Country Code* and *Language Code*. The table has to maintain descriptions in three languages—English, French, and Spanish—designated by the language codes "EN," "FR," and "SP," respectively. When the table has "USA" added to it, three records are added, as shown in Table 16.1. Thus the system can always find a record for any of the three languages it is designed to operate in. This makes retrieval program logic easier to implement compared with first trying to find a record for the user's preferred language, and if this is not found, retrieving the record for the default language.

When translations become available for the descriptions, the records can be updated, as shown in Table 16.2. A similar approach can be taken for the design in which additional columns are added to reference data tables for descriptions each time the system is enhanced to include a new language.

Table 16.1 Adding "USA" to a Country table.

Country Code	Language Code	Country Name
USA	EN	United States of America
USA	FR	United States of America
USA	SP	United States of America

Table 16.2 Updating Translations for "USA" in a Country table.

Country Code	Language Code	Country Name
USA	EN	United States of America
USA	FR	États Unis d'Amerique
USA	SP	Estados Unidos de America

Translating Acronyms

Unfortunately acronyms sometimes take different forms in different languages. Table 16.3 shows the acronyms for the North Atlantic Treaty Organization in English, French, and Spanish.

Users will expect to see acronyms in the language they are using, which means that translations must be stored in reference data tables.

If the design of storing translated descriptions on a single record were followed, then acronym columns would have to be added to the table involved. For instance, an `Institution` table could be changed to have the design shown in Figure 16.5.

Table 16.3 Acronyms and descriptions for NATO.

Language	Acronym	Description
English	NATO	North Atlantic Treaty Organization
French	OTAN	Organisation du Traité D'Atlantique Nord
Spanish	OTAN	Organización del Tratado de Atlántico Norte

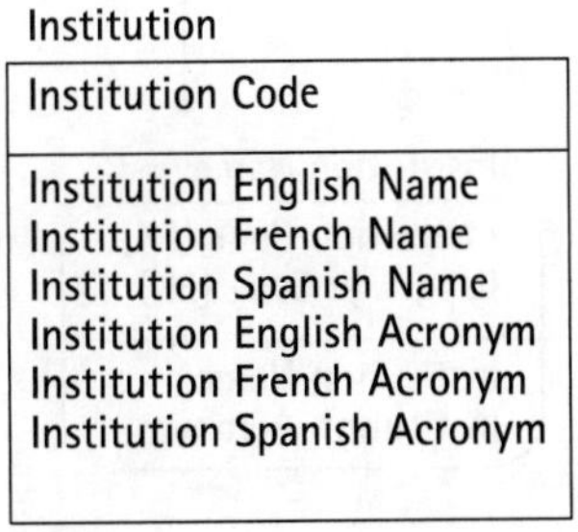

Institution

Institution Code
Institution English Name Institution French Name Institution Spanish Name Institution English Acronym Institution French Acronym Institution Spanish Acronym

Figure 16.5 Institution table holding translated descriptions and acronyms.

The design that added *Language Code* to the primary key of all reference code and description tables, as illustrated in Figure 16.4, could have a single extra column to hold translated acronyms, as shown in Figure 16.6.

The design in Figure 16.6 has a single column for all acronyms, whereas the design in Figure 16.5 has a different column for each language version of the acronym. On the other hand, all the reference data for a single country resides in one record in Figure 16.5, whereas it is spread across several records in Figure 16.6. The designer can choose between these two approaches depending on the requirements of the system being built.

There is one other problem associated with translating acronyms. When an acronym is used as a primary key code value in reference data, it must be always be in one language. If this is not done, and acronyms from different languages are used, then data integrity will be compromised. It is particularly important when codes are used as foreign keys in transaction tables. Programmers who build

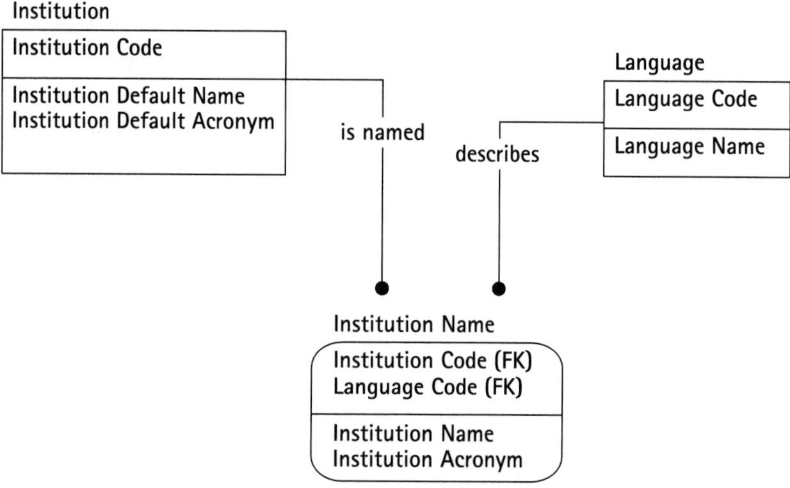

Figure 16.6 Institution Name table with language code modified to hold translated acronyms.

update screens must understand that they use the acronym in the system's default language to update transaction tables, even though the user may see acronyms and descriptions in a different language on the screen.

An alternative that overcomes this problem is to use a sequence number to represent the code value that is the primary key of the table. This option is described more fully in Chapter 5.

Tables of Texts and Messages

In multilingual systems there is a need to store translated texts and messages. *Texts* are words or phrases that have to appear as fixed text on screens or reports. Messages are longer texts that the system uses to communicate with the user, such as in the standard Windows message box. Messages can contain parameters that are resolved to other pieces of text when displayed. For example, the message "You entered the value <parameter 1> which is incorrect," displays <parameter 1> as some value that the user entered.

Texts and messages can be stored in tables. These tables look somewhat like reference data but are really not—they contain system, not business, data. The issues in the design of these tables are similar to those already discussed in this chapter.

The table of `Texts` can have a primary key that is the text in the default language (preferably English). The table can either have one column for each additional language or can have the language code also included in the key and therefore have one record for each translation of a given text in each additional language.

The table of `Messages` should have a key of a message number. The message text may be too long to store in a character field, and the designer should consider utilizing a datatype capable of storing a large number of characters (e.g., *memo* in Microsoft Access, *text* in Microsoft SQL Server). The message will have to include some tags that can be substituted with actual values when it is displayed to the user.

Getting Text Translated

Designing a system to be multilingual is not easy. Actually obtaining translated texts is also difficult and can be very time consuming. Qualified translators must be used—preferably people who understand the business area that the system is being built for. It is often quite difficult to find good translators.

Translators need to know the context in which the pieces of text they are translating are to be used. For reference data this may be tricky. It is best to have a business analyst who knows both the detailed requirements of the system and the reference data work with the translators to ensure the final product is accurate.

Translation also takes time, which is another reason why the designs discussed above call for the addition of descriptions in a default language and their later replacement with proper translations. It is important that as few dependencies as possible be created between obtaining translations and building a system.

Managing the translation process is not easy. When reference data will be translated piecemeal, the designer may wish to add columns to the reference data tables to indicate that a translated description has been approved for use. This could be a Boolean datatype or a date.

Conclusion

Reference data is very important in any effort to make a system multilingual. It comprises most of the data stored in a database that will need translation. However, creating additional structures to hold translations in other languages increases the complexity of any system, particularly the programming. In addition, the effort to get reference data translated can be long and difficult.

CHAPTER 17

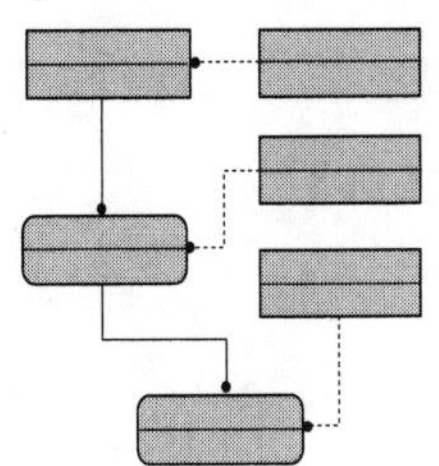

How Is Reference Data Different from Other Data?

THE CHARACTERISTICS AND BEHAVIOR of reference data have been examined in detail in earlier chapters. If an enterprise is to make a commitment to managing reference data as a distinct class of data, it is necessary to show that it really is different from the other kinds of data that the enterprise deals with. In Chapters 3 and 4 we discussed what makes reference data unique, based on the definition given in Chapter 1:

> *Reference data is any kind of data that is used solely to categorize other data found in a database, or solely for relating data in a database to information beyond the boundaries of the enterprise.*

In this chapter we attempt to set reference data in the context of the other kinds of data that an organization manages.

Figure 17.1 categorizes the kinds of data that can be found in a database. They are arranged in layers, from the most general and least frequently occurring, to the most specific with the highest volume.

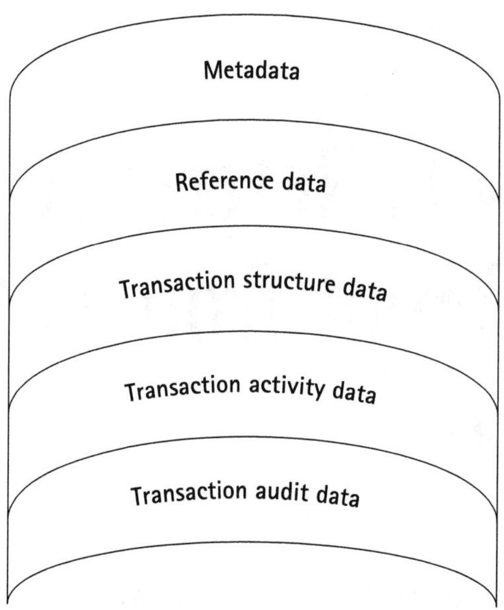

Figure 17.1 Different classes of data that occur in a database.

Let us examine these layers one by one.

- **Metadata** is, roughly speaking, data about data. Most commonly it comprises the business and technical definitions of tables and columns, although it may sometimes include a wealth of other information. Unfortunately although metadata exists, it is rarely implemented in a live database. It is true that the physical structures of tables and datatypes of columns can easily be determined via functions embedded in program logic in most applications, but the more important business definitions are rarely present. Ideally every database should contain tables with these definitions, although sometimes they are included in help files or other forms of documentation.

  Obviously, metadata has a wide scope, applying to the entire design of the database, and it typically changes relatively slowly—about as fast as the database design changes. This is not always true; for example, metadata about when data was last updated can change quite frequently. The volume of metadata is typically not high, although this is not always the case. While metadata can play a role in the transactions the system processes, it usually has a much larger role in providing information to users about what is contained in the database and how to use it. Because metadata is associated with database design, it can apply across the enterprise to a number of physical database implementations.

- **Reference data** also has a wide scope, as it is used to categorize, classify, or otherwise qualify or constrain transaction data. Constant values achieve this via business rules, whereas coded values achieve it though relationships between tables. Reference data is typically, though not always, present in low volume. It does not change very frequently, although again there may be exceptions. The things that reference data represents are not controlled or owned by the business activities of the organization—they are external to it. This includes reference data used to classify transaction data. Like metadata, some reference data may be used in a number of different database implementations within an enterprise.
- **Transaction structure data** represents data required to create a framework within which transactions occur. For instance, an application designed to sell something would need to record `Product` and `Customer` information before an `Order` could be processed. Transaction structure data has the scope of the types of transactions to which it pertains, although some tables may apply to several types of transaction. Transaction structure data typically has a much higher volume and update rate than reference data. More importantly it is created and changed as a result of the enterprise's activities—that is, the enterprise "owns" it.

- **Transaction activity data** is what an operational system is built to record. This is often referred to more simply as the *transaction* data—without clearly distinguishing *structure* and *activity*. For example, in an order processing system it will be the orders themselves, along with payment and accounting information. The scope of transaction activity data is only to transactions, and it typically has a very high volume and high frequency of update.
- **Transaction audit data** records audit information about individual transactions that are performed in an application. Very often this data is not recorded in a database, or a database management system takes care of it by automated logging. If it is recorded, it applies only to single instances of transactions and may present a very high volume (with several audit records per transaction) and a very high frequency of creation.

The characteristics of these different kinds of data are summarized in Table 17.1. The special nature of reference data, and its differences from other types of data, are good reasons to manage it in a distinct way, and it is therefore reasonable for an enterprise to invest resources in managing it separately from the other kinds of data.

Table 17.1 Summary of characteristics of different classes of data.

Class of data	Scope	Volume	Frequency of update
Metadata	Enterprise-wide	Low	Very low
Reference data	Multiple databases	Low	Low
Transaction structure data	One to several transaction types	Medium	Medium
Transaction activity data	One transaction type	High	High
Transaction audit data	Instances of transactions	High	High

As noted earlier, there may be a gradation from reference data to transaction structure data. One way to distinguish between the two is that reference data consists of codes and descriptions, or constant values, perhaps with some relationships to other reference data. Transaction structure data is typically much more complex, with many non-key fields that are not foreign keys, such as names of people and institutions, addresses, and the like.

If reference data is considered a distinct class of data, is it closer in nature to metadata or to transaction structure data? Metadata is used to convey understanding of the database design and how to use the database. Because reference data is so important in categorizing transaction data, and therefore in analyzing transaction data, it is necessary to understand it. In this regard it resembles metadata. Sometimes, however, reference data may have limited scope, such as a type code that applies to only one database table. However, type codes are bound up in database design in an important way: they determine the subtypes that a parent table can be broken into. Thus type codes even more closely resemble metadata in that they carry information concerning database design.

Occasionally a reference data table may be updated more frequently than may seem usual. An interest rate or a foreign exchange rate may be updated even on an intraday basis. These must be regarded as special cases, even though they still have the wide scope typical of reference data. They do not resemble metadata so much as operational transaction data.

Given the resemblance between metadata and reference data, it is a pity that metadata is not addressed in many implemented applications of databases. Were this the case, there would probably be a more generally accepted model for how an enterprise treats reference data. As it is, reference data is generally not treated in a distinct manner, which increases the chances of incurring problems with it.

Why Treat Reference Data Differently?

The arguments made above support the idea that reference data is a special class of data, different from other classes of data in a database. It might well be asked if this is just an academic point or if there are any real-world implications.

Reference data has always been treated as something of a backwater in database design and application development. Yet every system contains reference data, and if not handled properly it can cause severe problems. If we accept reference data as being a distinct "layer" in a database, it may be possible to "peel" it away from a given database design or system architecture within an enterprise and manage it in a way that corresponds to its unique character. In theory it could be separately maintained and be made available for any particular database or system. "Available" in this context could mean primarily at a design level. Thus, if a new database needed to be designed, a design would already exist for reference data—and if something new came up as a result of the new database, it could be added to the common design for reference data. Alternatively there could be a distinct database containing only reference data tables, available as a service to other databases in the enterprise.

Going beyond this, it might be possible to encapsulate navigation within reference data, particularly for users who perform complex analyses of data but do not have the time to understand how to navigate the database. The users could pick a particular column, and any reference data related to this column could be automatically available as analysis dimensions.

Conclusion

There is good reason to view reference data as distinct from other classes of data managed by an enterprise. Treating reference data as a distinct class of data can help an enterprise to administer it effectively and reduce the chances of incurring any of the problems to which reference data is so prone and which can have such wide-ranging effects.

CHAPTER 18

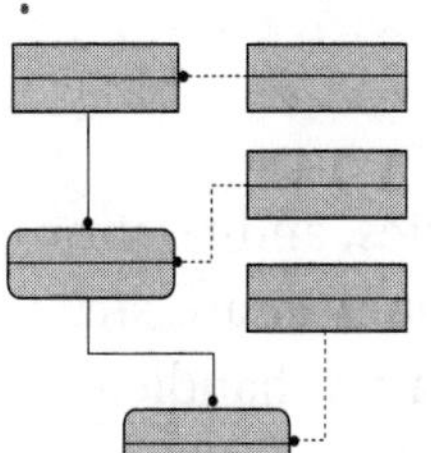

Using Reference Data for Queries

IN CHAPTER 13 WE DISCUSSED THE IMPORTANCE of reference data in queries, especially its role as dimension tables in data warehouses and data marts. Several of the unique features of reference data combine to affect the way it is used in queries. These features include

- the wide scope of reference data
- the metadata associated with the meaning of individual values of reference data
- the fact that reference data predominantly contains terms that have linguistic meaning in a database—namely, descriptions.

These unique features tend to make reference data important in those queries that are somewhat unstructured, as opposed to the more structured "traditional" ways of querying data that use SQL so well.

Traditional Database Queries

A relational database design contains tables, attributes, and relationships, and this tends to drive the ways in which queries are structured. Queries against relational databases are mainly handled by SQL. When programmers or systems analysts assist users to structure a query, they tend to ask the users to define what entities they want to query, and then what attributes within these entities they want use, and then what values they wish to search for against these queries. It should be put to the users in business and not technical terms, but this information is what is required to build the query. There is thus a hierarchy to building queries:

- select tables to be searched and the relationships among them
- select attributes that will be used to query information
- define values for search attributes
- select tables from which the query will construct the results set
- select attributes that will appear in the results set
- define sorting and grouping

The other way in which queries are conducted today is by keyword search. This method has become immensely popular with the advent of the Internet. In these queries, one or more keywords are entered, and links to Web pages containing those words are returned—ideally sorted by relevance.

Queries Using Reference Data

The traditional way of structuring and executing queries based on SQL is very effective. However, there is a need for handling reference data in a different way. The unique features of reference data discussed earlier make it likely that a user will want to query for reference data based on one or more *values*, without any reference to a relational database design. For instance, a user may ask for an answer to a question such as

> *"Tell me everything our company is doing in Jamaica."*

Indeed, senior managers tend to ask more general questions like this and become frustrated that they cannot be answered quickly. Information technology personnel also become frustrated because they see such questions as superficial. They typically see a mismatch between an unstructured query and structured data and immediately start trying to get to something much more specific such as

> *"Exactly what sort of things do you want to know about our business in Jamaica—who works for us, what our sales are . . . ?"*

This kind of response essentially places the responsibility for understanding what the database contains and how to navigate it back on senior management. Now it is their turn to become frustrated.

The properties of reference data do, however, permit unstructured queries to be answered at various levels. We will now examine how this can be done. There are several levels in the resolution of the query.

Level 1: Identify Reference Tables

Take the question,

> *"Tell me everything our company is doing in Jamaica."*

In this particular example we can immediately recognize that Jamaica is a description of a country. Descriptions may not always be so easy to categorize, and so it may not always be so easy to find the reference data tables where they are housed.

If it were possible to scan all descriptions in all reference data tables to search for "Jamaica," then we could obtain a results set that would indicate which reference data tables contain the term. We would then know which reference data tables we are dealing with. This information might be quite useful in the cases where an uncommon term was searched for.

Another valid result might be that the term is not found at all. If our organization manages reference data correctly, then the answer to the question would be

> *"Our company does no business in Jamaica."*

Level 2: Identify Related Transaction Structure Tables

Suppose that we did find an entry for "Jamaica" in the reference data tables—say, in the `Country` data table. The next step would be to identify which other tables utilize `Country` data. These are likely to be other reference data tables and tables containing data used to structure transactions (customers, suppliers, products, etc.). Simply obtaining a list of these tables can be a partial answer; certainly this information is worth knowing because it helps to define how the database will be navigated.

At this point, one can return to the user who has requested this information and provide a list of tables that may contain information about "Jamaica" and ask if the user wants all of these tables to be searched or just some. Of course a simple list of tables is inadequate. The user needs proper business definitions for all of these tables so he or she can understand the decisions being made.

Level 3: Identify Where the Value Is Used

The list of related tables—tables in which `Country` is used in our example—does not go far enough. We need to identify those that have rows where the *Country Code* for "Jamaica" has been used. Having identified the row for "Jamaica" in the `Country` reference table, and knowing the code for it, the related tables can be scanned to at least count the rows that contain values for "Jamaica."

When this is complete, we can go back to the user and say that we have a certain number of "hits" for the following tables. It is also important to inform the user of the tables where no value was found for "Jamaica." This implies that the business transactions these tables support are not carried out in Jamaica.

The user now has a reasonable idea of the types of business done in Jamaica and their relative importance. From now on the user must specify more complex queries to deal with individual transactions. These will be the more traditional types of database query.

How Can It Be Done?

Information technology professionals will ask how such a scenario as presented here can be implemented. There are really only two things needed:

- A repository of reference data—a single place where all descriptions can be searched.
- A repository that accurately represents how reference data is utilized in an enterprise's databases. Data models can provide this.

Even if the tools are available, it takes a commitment to actually use them and have the metadata they contain match the reality of what is implemented. However, the example we have just worked through illustrates the power that this approach can have.

Conclusion

The role that reference data plays in queries is often heavily influenced by the fact that individual reference data values have special meaning and wide scope. Queries using reference data may be less structured as a result. It is possible to handle these queries if there is an enterprise-wide strategy for handling reference data and metadata is also properly managed by the enterprise.

CHAPTER 19

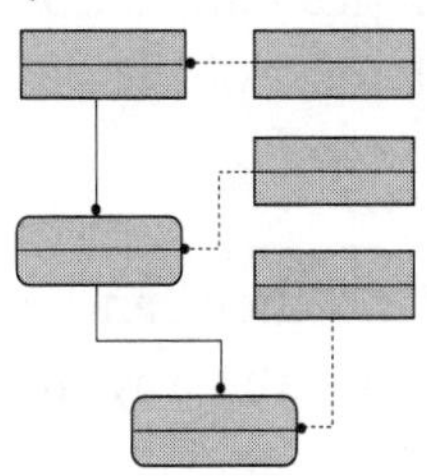

Implementing the Management of Reference Data

EVEN THOUGH THE IMPORTANCE OF reference data is widely acknowledged, relatively few enterprises make a serious attempt to manage it. Most enterprises have an information architecture that has evolved as a result of many self-contained projects that have delivered systems solutions over time. They often have poorly developed concepts regarding shared data and other systems components and are even today trying to deal with automating business processes rather than using data as a strategic resource.

However, in all organizations, the potential exists for reference data to do harm if something goes wrong with it. This alone should be a sufficient motivation to devote some resources to the management of reference data. There are also positive benefits to consider, such as improved data quality and the reduction of costs in developing and maintaining components of the information architecture.

Consideration of the wide scope of reference data quickly leads to the following conclusions:

- There should be one unit within an enterprise responsible for the administration of all reference data.
- There should be one database in which reference data is updated and from which it is disseminated to the rest of the organization's information systems.

Although these conclusions are somewhat self-evident, they can be rather difficult to put into practice. This chapter explores the ways in which an enterprise can attain the goal of successfully managing its reference data. The first step is to assign responsibility for the administration of reference data.

Data Ownership and Data Stewardship

Data ownership and *data stewardship* are terms that are increasingly being heard in the context of information systems. Data ownership refers to the persons or organizations that have legal proprietary rights over data. It does apply to reference data, but not in the way most information systems professionals use the term. Much reference data is actually produced by official standards-setting organizations, and these organizations are the owners of their standards. For instance, ISO is the International Organization for Standardization located in Geneva, Switzerland. It owns certain standards, including ISO 4217 which defines codes that represent currencies, and ISO 3166 which defines codes that represent countries. Everyone is free to *use* these standards, but ISO *owns* them. Nevertheless it is interesting that so much reference data has clearly defined owners (at least for the standard that defines the data). This contrasts with the other kinds of data found in an enterprise's database, which belongs to whoever owns the enterprise. In the case of a public company, the owners are the company's shareholders.

Owners do not necessarily look after their property. They may employ other people to perform this task, and such people are stewards. *Stewardship* is an ancient concept, and there are many biblical references to it. The royal Scottish clan Stewart, also spelled Stuart, descend from Walter, the third High Steward of Scotland (d. A.D. 1241). He was Keeper of the Household for the Scottish monarchs and gave himself the surname of his office. Perhaps because the term *stewardship* has such a long lineage, it embodies a number of important concepts like trust and accountability.

Data stewardship is therefore a much better term than *data ownership* to describe the role of individuals in an enterprise responsible for data integrity and quality. The role of the data steward has the following characteristics:

- A data steward does not own the data for which he or she is responsible.
- A data steward is responsible for ensuring that the data for which he or she is responsible meets the needs of the enterprise that employs the steward in that role.
- A data steward is accountable to the owners of the enterprise because they also own its information systems. However, the data steward is also accountable to all other stakeholders who need or rely on (but do not own) the data administered by the data steward.
- The data steward has the authority to do anything with the data that he or she administers in order to carry out the stewardship role.

Reference Data and Data Stewardship

Because reference data is not generated by the transactions that flow through an enterprise, it is very unlikely there will be any business person (i.e., someone outside the information systems department of the enterprise) who will feel any responsibility for reference data. This may not be true for other classes of data, where some business persons or units may feel that they own the data, even though, as pointed out in the previous section, they have no legal title to it.

Such lack of interest concerning reference data may be both a benefit and a liability. It is a benefit because there are unlikely to be turf wars about reference data. The liability is that it may be difficult to get the enterprise to devote resources to maintaining reference data, and we shall return to this issue later.

The fact that generally no one is interested in reference data means that responsible staff within the information systems department will usually have to play the role of data stewards for reference data. In a strange way this seems to fit the notion of service that is implied in the term *stewardship* better than situations involving the administration of more popular classes of data found in an enterprise.

The Role of the Data Steward for Reference Data

If a data steward is to look after reference data, what functions will this person or persons have to carry out? A list is presented below that is strongly influenced by the unique characteristics of reference data. It is also assumed that the data steward will administer a single central repository of reference data, something that is explored in greater detail in subsequent sections.

- The data steward will maintain a list of all data that is considered centrally administered reference data for the enterprise.

  This will define what reference data is in scope or out of scope for the data steward. Remember that some classification schemes, while they can be considered reference data, are highly personal and/or highly transient in nature and thus are irrelevant in terms of central administration.

- The data steward will be responsible for maintaining links with external bodies that define standards used as reference data by the enterprise.

  Active links with these external bodies are needed so the enterprise can become aware of changes in the reference data standard. There are, for example, several changes per year to ISO Currency Codes, and for approximately $300 per year the enterprise can purchase a subscription to the ISO maintenance agency to be advised of these changes by fax. If reference data is critical to the enterprise, the enterprise must be aware of changes to it as quickly as possible.

- The data steward will be responsible for all metadata concerning reference data.

  This is particularly critical for reference data, where individual values can have distinct meanings. The data steward may not be able to assign metadata to reference data because he or she lacks the specialist knowledge required. However, the steward must be responsible for collecting it, having it verified, and making sure it is up to date. The data steward must also make sure that reference data stakeholders, or any interested party, can get access to this metadata. Metadata may also include policies for the usage of reference data.

- The data steward will maintain a single central repository of all reference data, which will be the corporate standard.

  At a minimum the repository can comprise electronic documents containing reference data values. Ideally it will be a lot more. The repository is discussed in subsequent sections.

  The data steward will probably have to check acronyms, descriptions, and the like with experts on the data before updating the repository. Assuring the quality of data in the repository is very important.

- The data steward will be responsible for assigning coded values to represent descriptions and acronyms in reference data.

  This is necessary to ensure that the same reference data is not represented by more than one coded value throughout the enterprise.

- The data steward will be responsible for managing the life cycles of reference data.

  This means that the data steward will determine the time periods within which individual reference data values apply for the enterprise, and how these values are succeeded by other values.

- The data steward will be responsible for disseminating changes in reference data throughout the enterprise.

  This can be quite a daunting task. It means that the data steward must be aware of all changes to reference data, whether they come from within the enterprise or from outside. Structural and metadata changes must be communicated to all affected stakeholders. In most cases that will mean the staff responsible for the databases that contain the affected reference data, but it may sometimes be a wider group. Changes in data values must be communicated to the information systems—optimally by some automated means, but perhaps by manual processes.

- The data steward must be responsible for resolving conflicts that arise from the use of reference data.

  The most frequent conflicts that arise with reference data are usually concerned with the elimination of redundancy and the mapping of codes.

- The data steward must maintain the enterprise's strategy for handling reference data.

  As time goes by, the ways in which an enterprise maintains its reference data may have to change—for instance, if the enterprise grows considerably. The data steward has the knowledge of how the enterprise uses reference data and the current means by which it is managed. If the enterprise's strategy for maintaining reference data no longer matches the needs of the enterprise (or this can be predicted with some certainty), the data steward must devise a change in the strategy and bring the situation to the attention of those responsible for information systems planning.

- The data steward(s) must be recognized as the sole point of contact for reference data issues.

  Coordination implies a single point to which issues can be addressed. There may be more than one person involved in the tasks associated with the stewardship of reference data, although they do not have to be located in the same place. It is preferable that these persons are all in the same unit. If this is not the case, they should at least be part of a single working group for reference data administration.

As can be seen there are quite a number of functions that call for a variety of skills. Some technical skills are required because database design is involved, but significant interpersonal skills are also needed. For instance, the steward may need to explain to systems development teams that they cannot implement redundant reference data. The steward will also have to interact with business experts to validate codes, descriptions, and the business usage of reference data. Simply finding the right business experts and getting their time to discuss these issues can be quite a task.

The number of people functioning as data stewards for reference data will vary with the size of the enterprise, the commitment to information quality, resource issues, and other factors. However, it may not always be easy to find individuals who want to play this role.

Who Wants To Be a Reference Data Steward?

Reference data is not the most popular topic in information systems. It does not have the appeal of new technology, nor does it represent a single business process or a set of information from which a business can derive important knowledge. Thus there is usually no single group of business users to whom success and value can be clearly demonstrated in terms of their mainline functions. Reference data more closely resembles infrastructure that provides general support for everyone who deals with information in the enterprise.

For these reasons it may be difficult to find staff who want to become reference data stewards. Of course senior management commitment can make an enormous difference; this is discussed later in this chapter

What can be said is that for individuals who are interested in reference data, there are many opportunities to make a difference. Someone who tries to become involved with reference data is unlikely to encounter many competitors in this area and can quickly and easily become a recognized expert. The wide scope of reference data provides a good reason, or excuse, to become involved in many different organizational units and projects, where assistance with reference data will very likely be welcome—as most information technology professionals do not want to be bothered with it. The use of reference data as dimensions to analyze transaction data ensures that end users of data will need support also.

However, data stewardship is only one necessary component for successfully managing reference data. Another is a central repository, and that is discussed next.

A Reference Data Repository

Because reference data is shared by many, and because it is important in categorizing other data, it must be of the highest quality. In fact, it must be free of defects. This is a daunting challenge for the reference data stewards. However, their task may be impossible if they have to deal with many different databases in the enterprise as the database of record for different kinds of reference data.

The only real way to solve this issue, and to make reference data stewardship work, is to have one single point where all authoritative information about reference data is stored. This is something more than what is commonly called a database, since it contains data and metadata, so it is termed a *reference data repository* (RDR).

The RDR can be implemented in a number of ways. At its most simple it could be a set of electronic documents. It should be implemented using a relational database management system. It must be built to support the functions of the reference data stewards described in the previous section. These functions require the management of significant amounts of metadata in addition to the data that constitutes the reference data itself.

Ideally the RDR should be available to everyone in the enterprise. Obviously only the data stewards should be able to change information in the RDR, but everyone else should be allowed to view it.

Unfortunately there do not seem to be any commercial products available to perform this task. However, building a repository is not that difficult, as most reference data tables have rather simple structures with only one primary key column and one or a few nonprimary key columns.

Building an RDR may not be a very difficult technical task, but distributing reference data across an enterprise is far from easy, and that is the task we will consider next.

Distributing Reference Data

Reference data can generally be found in many information systems within an enterprise. These systems may have databases implemented in a variety of hardware and software platforms. Keeping reference data consistent among these systems involves getting updated reference data into these systems on a timely basis. This requires a single central RDR as discussed in the previous section, which is actively maintained by a reference data stewardship function. However, the RDR is just the starting point in the distribution process for reference data.

Building a distribution network for reference data can bring significant benefits to the enterprise. These include increased information quality, the elimination of expenditures required to maintain many redundant reference data update facilities, improved ability to communicate data between different systems and databases, and a known, controllable component of information architecture instead of an undocumented set of processes implemented at undocumented points within the enterprise.

This section discusses the issues involved in implementing a distribution mechanism for reference data, and how they can be overcome or at least mitigated. Also discussed are the ways in which the distribution mechanism can be designed, built, and deployed.

Legacy Systems

Whenever an initiative to distribute reference data across an enterprise is considered, one of the first issues raised is what to do about legacy systems. This problem can seem so daunting to so many people that it must be tackled early on if the initiative is to retain credibility.

The term *legacy systems* refers to systems and databases usually developed years ago using combinations of software and hardware that are no longer used to build new systems. Many young enterprises with no legacy systems tend to focus their energies solely on growth and create information systems infrastructure in an unplanned way. In so doing, they are building the legacy systems of the future. Whatever their origin, legacy systems are usually difficult to change because of the odd combinations of software and hardware they run on, the lack of documentation, and frequently poor design. It is not unusual to find that the information systems staff who have knowledge about the legacy systems have left the enterprise (perhaps even through retirement). It is also not uncommon to find that the business users who rely on these systems are very reluctant to permit any changes to be made to them. The users are well aware that legacy systems receive little support from the information systems department and that any tinkering with them may cause problems that could take a long time to fix.

Unfortunately legacy systems are often at the core of an enterprise's information systems architecture. They were the first systems to be built, and often automated a vital part of the enterprise's business (and consequently tend to process transactions rather than manage information).

If a distribution strategy from reference data is to be successful, it must address legacy systems. There are several alternatives that can be considered.

- **Ignore legacy systems.** Surprisingly this is not uncommon. Legacy systems are simply not included in the strategy because they are too difficult to deal with. This is not a good approach. Indeed, it is irresponsible because legacy systems often exist to automate important business functions.
- **Delay dealing with legacy systems.** In this approach the legacy systems are at least acknowledged. The strategy consists of first distributing reference data to information systems that are more up to date, and then addressing legacy systems. Of course everyone suspects the legacy systems will never actually be addressed. If an analysis of the reference data content of legacy systems is not undertaken, however, there is little difference from ignoring the issue altogether.
- **Wait for the rewrite.** This is a variation on the previous option of delaying any action with respect to the legacy system. If a legacy system is scheduled for a rewrite, or replacement, or significant reengineering, the reference data steward is likely to be involved. Therefore it makes sense, unless there is some very urgent need, to wait for this effort rather than expend resources on what is clearly going to be a

short-lived solution. However, if the rewrite of the legacy system is not a plan but a vague wish, then waiting for the rewrite is simply a way of avoiding the issue.

- **Utilize the existing update facilities in legacy systems.** It is quite probable that the legacy systems have some way of manually updating reference data, such as a set of screens where this information can be entered or some kind of batch update facility. A valid approach is to use these facilities. This means that whenever reference data changes in the RDR, the changes are communicated to the person(s) responsible for updating the legacy system. These persons then use the existing update facilities to enter the changes into the legacy system. With this approach the data stewards can be reasonably sure the legacy systems are up to date in terms of reference data.

- **Utilize existing infrastructure to electronically update reference data in legacy systems.** Some legacy systems exist in hardware/software combinations that are "open" in some way—for instance, they may be accessible via a LAN or via the Internet. In addition, their databases may support a common access standard like ODBC (Open Database Connectivity) through which programs outside the legacy system can update the database. There may be an opportunity to create programs that can use these features to update the reference data tables in the legacy system. At a minimum this requires understanding the structure, content, meaning, and use of the reference data in the legacy system. A somewhat safer approach may be not to distribute deletions or changes to primary keys to legacy systems, but only to propagate additions and changes to non-key attributes into their reference data.

- **Reengineer legacy systems.** Sometimes there is a pressing need to change the way in which a legacy system manages reference data, and yet its database is not easily accessible. In these cases some reengineering of the system may need to be done in order for reference data to be propagated into it from the central repository. The previous option of using any openness that is available is always a simpler solution, but it may not be available.

Systems that are not legacy systems are more likely to have more accessible architectures, better documentation, and support staff with extensive knowledge of how they work. They should be much better candidates for accepting distributed reference data than legacy systems, although they may still have their problems.

Understanding the Target Systems

If an enterprise decides to use the concept of an RDR from which reference data is distributed, then the chain of distribution must be understood. A necessary first step is to understand the systems and databases (legacy and modern) to which reference data updates will be supplied.

The following information needs to be gathered:

- which databases in which systems are to be supplied with reference data
- the structures of the tables in these databases that hold reference data, and how these tables map to the reference data held in the RDR
- any constraints on what reference data may be added to these databases and systems
- timing considerations about when these databases may be updated
- the physical location of the systems and their databases (both geographical and network locations)

- contact persons who work with the target systems and databases, including information systems staff who maintain the systems, and operational staff who schedule tasks or manually update the target systems

This is the minimum amount of information that needs to be gathered to formulate a distribution strategy. The data stewards should collect it and retain it in the RDR. It may yield some surprising results, such as classes of reference data that were unknown to the data stewards prior to collecting the information. It will also probably highlight other potential problems concerning data quality issues, redundancies, and incompatibilities between reference data in different systems and databases.

How can the information be collected? It is not that easy to do. In very small enterprises it may be enough to ask individuals in the information systems department. They can provide the relevant documentation to the data stewards and answer questions. In larger enterprises collecting this kind of data is a more daunting task. A good source of information may be a central data administration unit that has knowledge about many of the databases implemented in the enterprise. Ideally they will have data models of these databases in some electronic form, and some way of easily recognizing reference data tables within these models.

However, not all enterprises have data administration units, and even if they do, these units may not have all the information that is needed. The only real alternative is to survey the information systems department as a whole to find out about the use of reference data in as many systems as possible. People generally do not like having to participate in surveys, so it is a good idea to limit the number of questions asked to what is absolutely necessary. It is also a good idea to send the survey to high-level staff who are known to have responsibilities for several systems. In that way the survey will be better targeted to the people who can really answer it. Follow-up will nearly always be required, so the survey can be considered successful if it results in the identification of many relevant systems, good contact persons for these systems, and some basic understanding of the reference data in these systems.

At this point it may be obvious that a reference data distribution mechanism cannot be built for all systems and databases in the enterprise. It may be impossible to find out about all of these systems and databases, or to gather the minimum required information about each of them. There may be additional problems, like geographical dispersion or organizational conflicts that present limits to what can be achieved. However, it is a valid strategy to first build a reference data distribution mechanism for a representative sample of systems and databases in the enterprise. If that is successful, then it should be extensible to other systems and databases later on.

Such a phased approach is also helpful in reducing the demands on budgetary allocations and staff time. It is almost certain that the staff who function as reference data stewards have other tasks they must perform and that they cannot neglect. Senior management is also likely to be happier with an initial demonstration project that can give them an idea of the costs and difficulty involved and that measures the benefits to be gained.

Nevertheless some organizations, especially in the financial sector, really want to take control of their reference data, and they may opt for very large-scale projects that address the entire enterprise. Naturally such projects will have the resources and management commitment to succeed.

Let us suppose that the reference data stewards can gather enough information about a sufficient number of target systems and databases to formulate a strategy for distributing reference data. The next step is to create the means of distributing the reference data.

Manual Distribution of Reference Data

Once information has been gathered about a sufficient number of target systems and databases, it is possible to design a mechanism to distribute reference data. The best strategy is one that leads to a general mechanism, rather than a series of specialized ones. However, as noted in the discussion of legacy systems, automated distribution of reference data may not always be possible. If this is the case, the strategy should consider two distinct components:

- a manual way of distributing reference data
- a generalized automated way of distributing reference data

The manual way will involve informing staff responsible for data entry into target systems that a change in reference data has occurred. These staff can then enter the changes into the system or database for which they are responsible, perhaps via a screen or a batch process.

The manual distribution channel can work as follows:

1. When the data stewards become aware of a change to an item of reference data, they make the change in the central RDR.
2. The RDR contains a list of target systems and databases where the reference data in question is used.
3. Those target systems and databases that must be updated manually are identified as such in the RDR. They are associated with the email addresses of contact persons.
4. The data stewards email the staff associated with the affected systems and databases informing them of the changes required. For each system and database this is (a) the person who operationally makes the change, and

(b) the person who has overall responsibility for the operation of the system or database. In this way a safeguard against staff turnover is built into the distribution mechanism.

5. The data stewards can send out these emails immediately if the changes are urgent. If the changes are not urgent, they can batch all changes into one email to each person and send this on a periodic basis, such as at the end of the month.

6. Ideally the RDR should be accessible to the individuals who receive the emails. They should be able to view a list of all reference data changes that pertain to their system or database. They should be able to update the RDR to indicate that they have updated their system or database and be able to enter notes and comments about the actions they have taken into the RDR. This argues that the RDR should be accessible over the enterprise's intranet or the Internet.

Electronic Distribution of Reference Data

While manual distribution of reference data may be needed in some cases, electronic distribution is the ideal. And although no system or database should have its own special management capabilities for updating reference data, this may not always be fully achievable; for instance, a database may contain unique reference data not maintained in the RDR. However, the benefits of electronic distribution of reference data are significant. The remainder of this section explores the characteristics needed by a successful electronic distribution mechanism.

Perhaps the first item that should be identified is the channel by which reference data from the RDR will reach the target databases that must be updated. The alternatives are as follows:

- **Direct read.** If the target databases are on the same physical infrastructure as the RDR, they may be able to read its database directly. This is rather unlikely to be the case in real life, so it is not a good candidate for a general approach. It is good in that it is a *pull* solution—the target database obtains reference data as it needs it.
- **Using the Internet.** Although LANs (local area networks) and WANs (wide area networks) have been successfully used for a number of years, the Internet is really supplanting them (often in the guise of an intranet). The Internet offers a near perfect channel for distributing data. It is global in reach, supports high bandwidth, and has a huge array of supporting software. The Internet can function in both pull and push modes. That is, it can be used to actively distribute reference data or as a channel through which reference data is requested and then delivered.
- **Magnetic media.** Sending files on diskettes (or even CDs) is becoming less frequent with the advent of the Internet. It always involves a time delay, is more expensive because it involves shipping physical objects, and is more prone to failures from physical damage. It should only be used as a last resort, and it is a push solution—the RDR sends out data without any requests from the target systems.

From this analysis, it can be seen that the best distribution channel is clearly the Internet.

How can reference data be moved around the Internet and be used to update the target database? Here are the alternatives:

- **Database replication.** A number of relational database packages on the market support replication, meaning that several instances of a database in different locations can have their data synchronized from time to time. What is available depends on the actual package being considered. However, this is not an ideal choice for reference data because it is very specific to individual database products. Within an enterprise reference data nearly always exists in a variety of software platforms, so a more general solution is required.

- **Remote database access.** It is now possible to access databases remotely across the Internet. However, this is still at a somewhat early stage and appears to be product-specific. There are also security concerns about direct access to a database. In the future it may be possible to access the RDR directly. This may even mean that target databases do not have to contain any reference data at all. Instead they could use the RDR as a service for it (assuming performance is adequate).

- **An Internet-based interface to the RDR.** It is now possible to build an Internet server application that directly accesses the RDR's database. This application could receive requests for reference data from a remote Web-based application and could return reference data as directed by these requests. This kind of application could make use of XML to deliver the reference data. XML stands for "eXtensible Markup Language" and is a set of rules for creating self-describing data.

  It is possible that target databases could use this approach to eliminate the need to hold their own reference data. However, it is questionable (at the moment) if high-performance systems could be successful without holding their own reference data. The remote server application that accessed the RDR could quite easily be too slow to provide reference data on a transaction by transaction basis. If the target database did store reference data, this general approach could be good as a mechanism for synchronizing the target's reference data tables with the RDR.

This scenario assumes a Web server-based application at the target database end. In the future new systems will probably look like this. Current systems and legacy systems are generally not associated with Web server-based applications, so it will not work for them.

- **Extract files sent to target systems.** It may be possible to generate extract files from the RDR and send them to the locations where the target databases reside. Special batch jobs could then be run to update the target databases. The files could be sent via email or downloaded directly to the target. Interfaces would need to be written to get the data from the interface files into the target databases. This could involve a lot of work. Furthermore it would be difficult to manage many different interface update applications. The idea of creating one special interface per target database should be avoided at all costs.

- **Use the browser.** Rather than relying on building Web server–based applications to communicate with the server application that accesses the RDR, it is possible to use the browser, just like a regular Internet application does. The browser can be used to download both data and executable programs from the RDR site. The executable programs could then be run to update the local target database with reference data.

  This approach is particularly attractive if the reference data tables in the target database conform to an enterprise-wide standard—that is, when the names of the tables and columns are what are used in the RDR, as are the columns used for primary keys, the datatypes of all columns, and the coding schemes. This approach becomes even easier if the target database can be reached via an ODBC connection from the PC where the browser is located. If this is the case, then no special routines have to be created to update the target database.

> This option is better than the previous one of sending extract files to the target, because the operator can manage all tasks through one session of the browser.

There are thus several design alternatives available for using the Internet to update reference data in target databases. The next design consideration is whether *all* reference data, or just *changes*, should be communicated to the targets.

The so-called *delta* approach to keeping different databases synchronized involves sending to the target only data that has changed since the last time the RDR and the target were synchronized. This is a very useful approach for situations in which there is a lot of data. However, it is much more difficult to manage. It is especially prone to failure if the target does not signal back to the RDR what data it has successfully updated. Problems can occur such as updating the target with the same data multiple times, or somehow not sending changed data to the target. These issues make the program logic more complex in the interface to update the target.

The other alternative is a *complete replace* approach. Here the RDR always sends a complete set of data to the target. The corresponding data at the target is deleted and then reinserted. With this approach entire tables can be dropped and then recreated at the target, which is very useful if reference data tables have structure changes such as new columns. Structure changes are not easy to deal with in the delta approach. The only drawback to the complete replace is that if large numbers of records are involved, it can be very time consuming. However, it is rare that reference data is very voluminous. The complete replace approach is therefore recommended for updating reference data in target databases.

With both the delta and complete replace approaches there are problems associated with managing deletions of records and changes in primary keys. Deletions and primary key value changes will likely affect records in tables that store transaction data. This problem can be completely avoided if the central maintenance of reference data does not involve deleting records or changing primary key values, as was described in the management of the reference data life cycle in Chapter 8. Fortunately deletions and primary key value changes are comparatively rare in reference data. If they do occur they may have to be treated outside the reference data distribution mechanism if it is impossible to predict what effect they will have on each target system. Getting control of this problem is one of the reasons for establishing an enterprise-wide reference data management strategy.

The complete replace approach does not have to be blindly executed at regular intervals. It may be possible for target systems to determine which tables need to be updated by comparing the date/time/time zone of last update in their database with the corresponding information for the same tables in the RDR. That way complete replaces need to be run only for tables that have been updated in the RDR since they were updated in the target system.

To summarize, we have seen that electronic distribution of reference data to target databases is possible, and there are a number of design options possible. The better options tend to rely on a common structure for reference data tables in the target databases and a degree of openness in these databases. This may not always be true, especially for legacy systems that may hold the same reference data as the RDR, but in a different format, and may not be accessible via facilities like ODBC. If manual update is not possible for these databases, the special update routines will have to be created.

Managing an Electronic Reference Data Distribution Project

A project to implement the electronic distribution of reference data to the information systems of an enterprise is not a light task. It is multidisciplinary by nature, involving systems development staff and network communications specialists. This may not be a project that appeals to data stewards because the nature of the work is quite different from what they normally do. However, a project of this kind will never be initiated without significant backing from senior management, and it is likely they will set up project management structures that will ensure success. Data stewards should embrace such a project and try to become involved in all of its aspects, even if they are not running it.

The Goals for Reference Data Administration

We have now examined the role of the reference data steward, the need for a central reference data repository, and how reference data may be distributed within an enterprise, both manually and electronically.

It was argued at the beginning of this chapter that all this infrastructure and activity should be housed within a single central unit responsible for the administration of the enterprise's reference data. In reality such a reference data administration unit will most likely be a function, consisting of a few data stewards charged with responsibility for reference data. These data stewards could have primary responsibilities in some other area and could have job titles that have nothing to do with reference data. Indeed, given the generally slow nature of changes to reference data, this should be expected. Perhaps only in the largest enterprises might there be a sufficient ongoing set of activities concerning reference data that any data steward could be occupied with full time. However, for the purposes of the present discussion, we will continue to refer to a reference data administration unit.

It is important that once a commitment to managing reference data has been made, there is no gradual loss of this commitment. One way to prevent this is to have a clearly articulated mission statement or charter for the group responsible for reference data administration. This could include elements such as the following:

- a commitment to zero defects in the reference data of the enterprise
- a commitment to providing knowledge about reference data to all individuals who need this knowledge in the enterprise
- a commitment to assisting all systems development projects with their reference data needs
- a commitment to building and maintaining the infrastructure to distribute reference data throughout the enterprise in a timely and accurate way

In addition to this mission statement there should be some kind of periodic activity that the data stewards perform. After the initial burst of activity to set up a unit responsible for reference data administration, the slowly changing nature of reference data could have a dampening effect on the vigilance required of the data stewards. Another problem may arise from the fact that although the data stewards work together, they may be geographically dispersed, perhaps even located in different countries. There is a need for data stewards to share knowledge and to retain or build their cohesion and commitment to managing reference data. Periodic meetings, say once a month, could help with all of these issues. An agenda could be constructed with certain items that would always have to be discussed, for instance,

- the need to create any new reference data tables
- changes in reference data communicated from external authorities
- issues with the reference data repository

- assigning data stewards to cover new systems development projects
- ideas for improving the quality of reference data and its use in the enterprise

The reference data administration unit should also report back to senior management at least once a year. This report should include some measurements of the unit's effectiveness and efficiency. Broadly speaking, *effectiveness* is the degree to which the goals of the unit have been reached, and *efficiency* refers to the resources taken to reach this level of effectiveness. The measurements should be clearly understandable to senior management and should be something that can be used to justify any budgetary allocation to the reference data administration unit.

We have now reviewed what is required for an enterprise to successfully maintain its reference data. However, before any of this can happen there has to be a commitment by senior management. Without such a commitment the necessary resources will not be made available, and the political support will be lacking to bring order to the uncontrolled, redundant maintenance of poor-quality reference data typical of so many enterprises.

Senior Management Commitment

Reference data does not generally have any champions in the community of business users in an enterprise—unless there has been some massive data quality problem. Unfortunately it rarely has any supporters within information systems departments either. This situation is beginning to change, as enterprises mature in terms of the use of the information as a strategic resource, the need to have greater integration between their information systems, the need to be more adaptable in rapidly evolving business environments, and drives to reduce costs. The importance of information quality is certainly gaining recognition, even though reference data may not be recognized as a distinct class of data with its own unique management needs.

Even so, there will never be a central administration of reference data within an enterprise unless senior management is committed to it. The lack of strong natural champions for reference data is mirrored by the need to manage the way it is handled across the entire enterprise. For instance, individual systems and database development projects cannot be allowed to build their own reference data maintenance facilities and to populate their reference data tables with inaccurate, incomplete, inconsistent, and untimely reference data.

The good news is that those individuals who understand the need to effectively manage reference data within their enterprise should be able to build a case to present to senior management without too much difficulty. If senior management is to devote financial and political resources to the maintenance of reference data, they will want to know why they should do it, how much of an investment is required, and what the likely return on this investment will be.

Any proposal to senior management should contain an estimate of the costs required to redundantly maintain reference data in different systems and databases, including the following:

- The costs to build the systems infrastructure (add, delete, update, and report functionality) to administer reference data in all these different systems. This can be obtained by finding the overall costs to implement each system and then estimating the percentage of the system devoted to reference data maintenance. Senior management may be particularly interested in this as a guide to the future annual outlays involved in building these components into new systems.
- The annual costs of maintaining redundant reference data functionality across the enterprise. This can be roughly estimated for each system by taking the annual cost of maintenance

for that system and then multiplying by the estimated percentage of the system devoted to reference data maintenance.

- The cost of staff to separately update the reference data in each of these systems and databases every year. The work hours involved should be estimated and an average cost per work-hour used. This estimate should not only include the time taken for data entry, but also the effort required to research and verify changes to reference data, assign codes, and complete any other administrative tasks that may be involved.

Data quality issues pertaining to reference data should be quantified, in particular the following:

- The cost of errors that arise from inaccurate, untimely, incomplete, or otherwise defective reference data in an enterprise's databases. This information may not be easy to gather, even though it covers a broad set of problems. It covers both the systems side, such as processing problems, and the business use side, such as making faulty business decisions based on incorrect information. It may require asking knowledgeable systems and business staff for their estimates.
- The cost of mapping different coding schemes for the same reference data when data is exchanged between different databases of the enterprise or is sent outside the enterprise. Information systems staff should know about the interfaces that pertain to the databases they look after. The cost to build and maintain these mapping functions should be estimated.

Risk is another area that is important to senior management. There should be an estimate of the following:

- The risk of systems failures caused by problems with reference data and the potential costs of these risks. This can involve gathering information about the costs of actual problems that have arisen and then estimating the probabilities of progressively worse scenarios and their costs.

- The risks of producing incorrect information from the enterprise's databases that is then used to make incorrect business decisions or is used in reporting to parties outside the enterprise. Again, a set of scenarios with different probabilities and associated costs should be developed.

The benefits of central reference data administration should be quantified, including those derived from

- the reduction of duplication of effort to maintain reference data across the enterprise
- an improvement of data quality
- the mitigation of risk
- the creation of a center of knowledge about reference data
- an improvement in the enterprise's ability to react to changes in reference data

Lastly, there should be a clear articulation of the structure of the proposed reference data administration unit (or function) and its associated costs. At a minimum the following should be estimated:

- the staff costs of reference data stewardship in terms of number of persons, work hours required per year, and annual financial cost
- additional infrastructure and operating costs needed to support the data stewardship function
- the costs to create and maintain a reference data repository (building costs and annual maintenance costs)
- the costs to create and maintain a reference data distribution facility (building costs and annual maintenance costs)

There may be additional special needs that have to be presented to senior management for particular enterprises, but the outlines given above represent a minimum amount of information required.

When making such a presentation, it is very helpful to have business users who articulate the need for improvements in reference data. Business users may be well aware of data quality issues that involve reference data, and their views are likely to be highly regarded.

By contrast, it is not helpful to confuse the need to manage reference data with the problems associated with common data and external data. These kinds of data were briefly examined in Chapter 1. Their management needs are detailed below to show just how different they are from reference data.

Common Data

Common data is any data that is widely shared among the information systems of an enterprise. It includes reference data but also typically includes data used to structure the transactions of an enterprise (e.g., customer and product data). This latter kind of data is termed *transaction structure data* and differs from reference data in the following ways:

- Transaction structure data changes much more frequently than reference data. Thus its distribution is more complex than that of reference data.
- It is needed to complete transactions. This may also be true of reference data, but there is more of a chance that reference data can be added to the transaction later. More importantly, there tends to be a great redundancy of update facilities for transaction structure data across an enterprise. Furthermore there is often a tendency for each of these update facilities to capture only the minimum amount of data

required to complete the transactions they deal with. All of this typically leads to data quality problems.

- The volume of data concerned is usually much higher than for reference data. This may mean that delta updates are the only option for distributing this data across the enterprise, whereas for reference data complete replacement of local copies of the data is often possible. There may also be issues with historical or archived data.
- The tables concerned have much greater numbers of non-key attributes than reference data—meaning more places where data quality issues can arise. Any initiative to manage transaction structure data can expect to spend a great deal of time dealing with data quality issues.
- Security may be an issue. Reference data is usually in the public domain, but transaction structure data is often not something an enterprise wants other parties to see. There may also be privacy issues, including legal regulations about confidentiality.

It is quite legitimate for an enterprise to want to take control of its transaction structure data. However, the issues involved are different from those of managing reference data, and the resources required for such a project can be expected to be much greater. If an enterprise does decide to manage common data centrally, it is better to separate reference data from transaction structure data in such an initiative.

External Data

External data was defined in Chapter 1 as any data that is imported into an enterprise's information systems from a source outside the enterprise. While this can include reference data, it is more likely to be transaction activity data (i.e., the transactions themselves, and not just the information to structure them). It differs from reference data in several ways:

- There is a need to deal with external data providers. This may involve complex business arrangements; for instance, the data in question may be purchased, or the enterprise may be performing a service for the external data provider. When data quality issues arise with external data, the data provider usually needs to be included in the resolution process.
- External data is much more heterogeneous as a class of data than either reference data or transaction structuring data. Therefore fewer generalizations apply to it.
- External data is typically less shared. It is usually intended for only one information system. There may be a need for an enterprise-wide mechanism to receive this data centrally, make sure it is from a known external party, and distribute it to the appropriate point for further processing in the enterprise. Sometimes, however, redundancy can be found in reference data. A data provider will quite happily sell the same data many times to one enterprise.
- There are special data quality problems associated with external data, such as changes in format from the receipt of one set of data to the next, or gaps in the data. These are different from issues found in reference data.

If there is a need to manage external data, then this should be done separately from reference data. It is important that senior management understand the difference between the two types of data.

Attempting to manage reference data in combination with either transaction structure data or external data is likely to create incompatible goals within any project or function established for this purpose. Senior management commitment to the central management of reference data in an enterprise should not be obtained by suggesting that anything other than reference data will be included.

Conclusion

This chapter has shown that the central management of reference data within an enterprise is possible and can bring tangible benefits. It does not require a great deal of resources, but it does need the backing of senior management. A road map has been laid out showing the infrastructure that needs to be created, although the details of what is possible will vary from enterprise to enterprise. Because reference data typically has few champions within an enterprise, it is unclear where the stimulus for the required effort will originate. However, as more enterprises use information as a strategic business resource and become concerned with the quality of this information, the topic of managing reference data is likely to become increasingly more visible.

Conclusion

APPENDIX 1

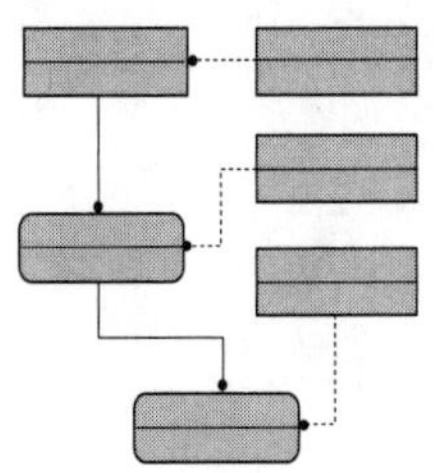

ISO 4217 Currency Codes

THIS TABLE IS REPRINTED, with permission, from Table A.1 (E) of the ISO 4217 standard as published in 1995 (the year of the last published major revision). More information, and more current information, can be found on the Web site for the International Organization for Standardization (ISO) at *www.iso.ch.*

Entity	Currency	Alphabetic Code	Numeric Code
AFGHANISTAN	Afghani	AFA	004
ALBANIA	Lek	ALL	008
ALGERIA	Algerian Dinar	DZD	012
AMERICAN SAMOA	US Dollar	USD	840
ANDORRA	Spanish Peseta	ESP	724
	French Franc	FRF	250
	Andorran Peseta	ADP	020
ANGOLIA	New Kwanza	AON	024
ANGUILLA	East Caribbean Dollar	XCD	951

Entity	Currency	Alphabetic Code	Numeric Code
ANTARCTICA	No Universal Currency		
ANTIGUA AND BARBUDA	East Caribbean Dollar	XCD	951
ARGENTINA	Argentine Peso	ARS	032
ARMENIA	Armenian Dram	AMD	051
ARUBA	Aruban Guilder	AWG	533
AUSTRALIA	Australian Dollar	AUD	036
AUSTRIA	Schilling	ATS	040
AZERBAIJAN	Azerbaijanian Manat	AZM	031
BAHAMAS	Bahamian Dollar	BSD	044
BAHRAIN	Bahraini Dinar	BHD	048
BANGLADESH	Taka	BDT	050
BARBADOS	Barbados Dollar	BBD	052
BELARUS	Belarussian Ruble	BYB	112
BELGIUM	Belgian Franc	BEF	056
BELIZE	Belize Dollar	BZD	084
BENIN	CFA Franc BCEAO+	XOF	952
BERMUDA	Bermudian Dollar (customarily known as Bermuda Dollar)	BMD	060
BHUTAN	Indian Rupee	INR	356
	Ngultrum	BTN	064
BOLIVIA	Boliviano	BOB	068
	Mvdol*	BOV	984
BOTSWANA	Pula	BWP	072
BOUVET ISLAND	Norwegian Krone	NOK	578
BRAZIL	Brazilian Real	BRL	986

Entity	Currency	Alphabetic Code	Numeric Code
BRITISH INDIAN OCEAN TERRITORY	US Dollar	USD	840
BRUNEI DARUSSALAM	Brunei Dollar	BND	096
BULGARIA	Lev	BGL	100
BURKINA FASO	CFA Franc BCEAO+	XOF	952
BURUNDI	Burundi Franc	BIF	108
CAMBODIA	Riel	KHR	116
CAMEROON	CFA Franc BEAC++	XAF	950
CANADA	Canadian Dollar	CAD	124
CAPE VERDE	Cape Verde Escudo	CVE	132
CAYMAN ISLANDS	Cayman Islands Dollar	KYD	136
CENTRAL AFRICAN REPUBLIC	CFA Franc BEAC++	XAF	950
CHAD	CFA Franc BEAC++	XAF	950
CHILE	Chilean Peso	CLP	152
	Unidades de formento*	CLF	990
CHINA	Yuan Renminbi	CNY	156
CHRISTMAS ISLAND	Australian Dollar	AUD	036
COCOS (KEELING) ISLANDS	Australian Dollar	AUD	036
COLOMBIA	Colombian Peso	COP	170
COMOROS	Comoro Franc	KMF	174
CONGO	CFA Franc BEAC++	XAF	950
COOK ISLANDS	New Zealand Dollar	NZD	554
COSTA RICA	Costa Rica Colon	CRC	188
COTE D'IVOIRE	CFA Franc BCEAO+	XOF	952
CROATIA	Croatian Kuna	HRK	191
CUBA	Cuban Peso	CUP	192

Entity	Currency	Alphabetic Code	Numeric Code
CYPRUS	Cyprus Pound	CYP	196
CZECH REPUBLIC	Czech Koruna	CZK	203
DENMARK	Danish Krone	DKK	208
DJIBOUTI	Djibouti Franc	DJF	262
DOMINICA	East Caribbean Dollar	XCD	951
DOMINICAN REPUBLIC	Dominican Peso	DOP	214
EAST TIMOR	Timor Escudo	TPE	626
	Rupiah	IDR	360
ECUADOR	Sucre	ECS	218
	Unidad de Valor Constante (UVC)*	ECV	983
EGYPT	Egyptian Pound	EGP	818
EL SALVADOR	El Salvador Colon	SVC	222
EQUATORIAL GUINEA	CFA Franc BEAC++	XAF	950
ESTONIA	Kroon	EEK	233
ETHIOPIA	Ethiopian Birr	ETB	230
EUROPEAN MONETARY CORPORATION FUND (E.M.C.F.)**	European Currency Unit (E.C.U.)	XEU	954
FAEROE ISLANDS	Danish Krone	DKK	208
FALKLAND ISLANDS (MALVINAS)	Falkland Islands Pound	FKP	238
FIJI	Fiji Dollar	FJD	242
FINLAND	Markka	FIM	246
FRANCE	French Franc	FRF	250
FRENCH GUIANA	French Franc	FRF	250
FRENCH POLYNESIA	CFP Franc	XPF	953

Entity	Currency	Alphabetic Code	Numeric Code
FRENCH SOUTHERN TERRITORIES	French Franc	FRF	250
GABON	CFA Franc BEAC++	XAF	950
GAMBIA	Dalasi	GMD	270
GERMANY	Deutsche Mark	DEM	280
GHANA	Cedi	GHC	288
GIBRALTAR	Gibraltar Pound	GIP	292
GREECE	Drachma	GRD	300
GREENLAND	Danish Krone	DKK	208
GRENADA	East Caribbean Dollar	XCD	951
GUADELOUPE	French Franc	FRF	250
GUAM	US Dollar	USD	840
GUATEMALA	Quetzal	GTQ	320
GUINEA	Guinea Franc	GNF	324
GUINEA-BISSAU	Guinea-Bissau Peso	GWP	624
GUYANA	Guyana Dollar	GYD	328
HAITI	Gourde	HTG	332
	US Dollar	USD	840
HEARD ISLAND AND McDONALD ISLANDS	Australian Dollar	AUD	036
HONDURAS	Lempira	HNL	340
HONG KONG	Hong Kong Dollar	HKD	344
HUNGARY	Forint	HUF	348
ICELAND	Iceland Krona	ISK	352
INDIA	Indian Rupee	INR	356
INDONESIA	Rupiah	IDR	360
INTERNATIONAL MONETARY FUND (I.M.F.)**	SDR	XDR	960

Entity	Currency	Alphabetic Code	Numeric Code
IRAN (ISLAMIC REPUBLIC OF)	Iranian Rial	IRR	364
IRAQ	Iraqi Dinar	IQD	368
IRELAND	Irish Pound	IEP	372
ISRAEL	Shekel	ILS	376
ITALY	Italian Lira	ITL	380
JAMAICA	Jamaican Dollar	JMD	388
JAPAN	Yen	JPY	392
JORDAN	Jordanian Dinar	JOD	400
KAZAKHSTAN	Tenge	KZT	398
KENYA	Kenyan Shilling	KES	404
KIRIBATI	Australian Dollar	AUD	036
KOREA, DEMOCRATIC PEOPLE'S REPUBLIC OF	North Korean Won	KPW	408
KOREA, REPUBLIC OF	Won	KRW	410
KUWAIT	Kuwaiti Dinar	KWD	414
KYRGYZSTAN	Som	KGS	417
LAO PEOPLE'S DEMOCRATIC REPUBLIC	Kip	LAK	418
LATVIA	Latvian Lats	LVL	428
LEBANON	Lebanese Pound	LBP	422
LESOTHO	Rand	ZAR	710
	(financial Rand)*	ZAL	991
	Loti	LSL	426
LIBERIA	Liberian Dollar	LRD	430
LIBYAN ARAB JAMAHIRIYA	Libyan Dinar	LYD	434

Entity	Currency	Alphabetic Code	Numeric Code
LIECHTENSTEIN	Swiss Franc	CHF	756
LITHUANIA	Lithuanian Litus	LTL	440
LUXEMBOURG	Luxembourg Franc	LUF	442
MACAU	Pataca	MOP	446
MACEDONIA, THE FORMER YUGOSLAV REPUBLIC OF	Denar	MKD	807
MADAGASCAR	Malagasy Franc	MGF	450
MALAWI	Kwacha	MWK	454
MALAYSIA	Malaysian Ringgit	MYR	458
MALDIVES	Rufiyaa	MVR	462
MALI	CFA Franc BCEAO+	XOF	952
MALTA	Maltese Lira	MTL	470
MARSHALL ISLANDS	US Dollar	USD	840
MARTINIQUE	French Franc	FRF	250
MAURITANIA	Ouguiya	MRO	478
MAURITIUS	Mauritius Rupee	MUR	480
MEXICO	Mexican Nuevo Peso	MXN	484
MICRONESIA (FEDERATED STATES OF)	US Dollar	USD	840
MOLDOVA, REPUBLIC OF	Moldovan Leu	MDL	498
MONACO	French Franc	FRF	250
MONGOLIA	Tugrik	MNT	496
MONTSERRAT	East Caribbean Dollar	XCD	951
MOROCCO	Moroccan Dirham	MAD	504
MOZAMBIQUE	Metical	MZM	508
MYANMAR	Kyat	MMK	104

Entity	Currency	Alphabetic Code	Numeric Code
NAMIBIA	Rand	ZAR	710
	Namibia Dollar	NAD	516
NAURU	Australian Dollar	AUD	036
NEPAL	Nepalese Rupee	NPR	524
NETHERLANDS	Netherlands Guilder	NLG	528
NETHERLANDS ANTILLES	Netherlands Antillian Guilder	ANG	532
NEW CALEDONIA	CFP Franc	XPF	953
NEW ZEALAND	New Zealand Dollar	NZD	554
NICARAGUA	Cordoba Oro	NIO	558
NIGER	CFA Franc BCEAO+	XOF	952
NIGERIA	Naira	NGN	566
NIUE	New Zealand Dollar	NZD	554
NORFOLK ISLAND	Australian Dollar	AUD	036
NORTHERN MARIANA ISLANDS	US Dollar	USD	840
NORWAY	Norwegian Krone	NOK	578
OMAN	Rial Omani	OMR	512
PAKISTAN	Pakistan Rupee	PKR	586
PALAU	US Dollar	USD	840
PANAMA	Balboa	PAB	590
	US Dollar	USD	840
PAPUA NEW GUINEA	Kina	PGK	598
PARAGUAY	Guarani	PYG	600
PERU	Nuevo Sol	PEN	604
PHILIPPINES	Philippine Peso	PHP	608
PITCAIRN	New Zealand Dollar	NZD	554
POLAND	Zloty	PLZ	616
	Zloty	PLN	985

Entity	Currency	Alphabetic Code	Numeric Code
PORTUGAL	Portuguese Escudo	PTE	620
PUERTO RICO	US Dollar	USD	840
QATAR	Qatar Rial	QAR	634
REUNION	French Franc	FRF	250
ROMANIA	Leu	ROL	642
RUSSIAN FEDERATION	Russian Ruble	RUR	810
RWANDA	Rwanda Franc	RWF	646
SAINT HELENA	Saint Helena Pound	SHP	654
SAINT KITTS AND NEVIS	East Caribbean Dollar	XCD	951
SAINT LUCIA	East Caribbean Dollar	XCD	951
SAINT PIERRE AND MIQUELON	French Franc	FRF	250
SAINT VINCENT AND THE GRENADINES	East Caribbean Dollar	XCD	250
SAMOA	Tala	WST	882
SAN MARINO	Italian Lira	ITL	380
SAO TOME AND PRINCIPE	Dobra	STD	678
SAUDI ARABIA	Saudi Riyal	SAR	682
SENEGAL	CFA Franc BCEAO+	XOF	952
SEYCHELLES	Seychelles Rupee	SCR	690
SIERRA LEONE	Leone	SLL	694
SINGAPORE	Singapore Dollar	SGD	702
SLOVAKIA	Slovak Koruna	SKK	703
SLOVENIA	Tolar	SIT	705
SOLOMON ISLANDS	Solomon Islands Dollar	SBD	090
SOMALIA	Somalia Shilling	SOS	706
SOUTH AFRICA	Rand	ZAR	710

Entity	Currency	Alphabetic Code	Numeric Code
SPAIN	Spanish Peseta	ESP	724
SRI LANKA	Sri Lanka Rupee	LKR	144
SUDAN	Sudanese Pound#	SDP	736
	Sudanese Dinar	SDD	736
SURINAME	Suriname Guilder	SRG	740
SVALBARD AND JAN MAYEN	Norwegian Krone	NOK	578
SWAZILAND	Lilangeni	SZL	748
SWEDEN	Swedish Krona	SEK	752
SWITZERLAND	Swiss Franc	CHF	756
SYRIAN ARAB REPUBLIC	Syrian Pound	SYP	760
TAIWAN, PROVINCE OF CHINA	New Taiwan Dollar	TWD	901
TAJIKISTAN	Tajik Ruble	TJR	762
TANZANIA, UNITED REPUBLIC OF	Tanzanian Shilling	TZS	834
THAILAND	Baht	THB	764
TOGO	CFA Franc BCEAO+	XOF	952
TOKELAU	New Zealand Dollar	NZD	554
TONGA	Pa'anga	TOP	776
TRINIDAD AND TOBAGO	Trinidad and Tobago Dollar	TTD	780
TUNISIA	Tunisian Dinar	TND	788
TURKEY	Turkish Lira	TRL	792
TURKMENISTAN	Manat	TMM	795
TURKS AND CAICOS ISLANDS	US Dollar	USD	840
TUVALU	Australian Dollar	AUD	036
UGANDA	Uganda Shilling	UGX	800

Entity	Currency	Alphabetic Code	Numeric Code
UKRAINE	Karbovanet	UAK	804
UNITED ARAB EMIRATES	UAE Dirham	AED	784
UNITED KINGDOM	Pound Sterling	GBP	826
UNITED STATES	US Dollar	USD	840
	(Same day)*	USS	998
	(Next Day)*	USN	997
UNITED STATES MINOR OUTLYING ISLANDS	US Dollar	USD	840
URUGUAY	Peso Uruguayo	UYU	858
UZBEKISTAN	Uzbekistan Sum	UZS	860
VANUATU	Vatu	VUV	548
VATICAN CITY (HOLY SEE)	Italian Lira	ITL	380
VENEZUELA	Bolivar	VEB	862
VIET NAM	Dong	VND	704
VIRGIN ISLANDS (BRITISH)	US Dollar	USD	840
VIRGIN ISLANDS (US)	US Dollar	USD	840
WALLIS AND FUTUNA ISLANDS	CFP Franc	XPF	953
WESTERN SAHARA	Moroccan Dirham	MAD	504
YEMEN	Yemeni Rial	YER	886
YUGOSLAVIA	Yugoslavian Dinar	YUN	890
ZAIRE	New Zaire	ZRN	180
ZAMBIA	Kwacha	ZMK	894
ZIMBABWE	Zimbabwe Dollar	ZWD	716
Entry Not Applicable	Gold	XAU	959

Entity	Currency	Alphabetic Code	Numeric Code
Entry Not Applicable	Bond Markets Unit: European Composite Unit (EUROC)	XBA	955
Entry Not Applicable	Bond Markets Unit: European Monetary Unit (E.M.U.-6)	XBB	956
Entry Not Applicable	Bond Markets Unit: European Unit of Account 9 (E.U.A.-9)	XBC	957
Entry Not Applicable	Bond Markets Unit: European Unit of Account 17 (E.U.A.-17)	XB5	958
Entry Not Applicable	Palladium	XPD	964
Entry Not Applicable	Platinum	XPT	962
Entry Not Applicable	Silver	XAG	961
Entry Not Applicable	Special Settlement Currencies: UIC-Franc	XFU	
Entry Not Applicable	Special Settlement Currencies: Gold-Franc	XFO	
Entry Not Applicable	Codes specifically reserved for testing purposes	XTS	963
Entry Not Applicable	The codes assigned for transactions where no currency is involved	XXX	999

+ CFA Franc BCEAO; Responsible Authority: Banque Central des États de l'Afrique de l'Ouest.

++ CFA Franc BEAC; Responsible Authority: Banque Central des États de l'Afrique Centrale.

* Funds code.

** This entry is not derived from ISO 3166 but is included here in alphabetic sequence for convenience.

Being phased out.

APPENDIX 2

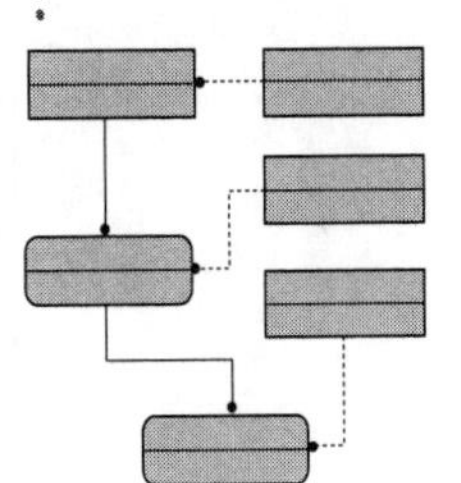

ISO 3166 Country Codes

THIS TABLE IS PRINTED, with permission, from the ISO 3166-1 standard. More information, and more current information, can be found on the Web site of the International Organization for Standardization (ISO) at *www.iso.ch.*

Country Name	Country Code
AFGHANISTAN	AF
ALBANIA	AL
ALGERIA	DZ
AMERICAN SAMOA	AS
ANDORRA	AD
ANGOLA	AO
ANGUILLA	AI
ANTARCTICA	AQ
ANTIGUA AND BARBUDA	AG
ARGENTINA	AR

Country Name	Country Code
ARMENIA	AM
ARUBA	AW
AUSTRALIA	AU
AUSTRIA	AT
AZERBAIJAN	AZ
BAHAMAS	BS
BAHRAIN	BH
BANGLADESH	BD
BARBADOS	BB
BELARUS	BY
BELGIUM	BE
BELIZE	BZ
BENIN	BJ
BERMUDA	BM
BHUTAN	BT
BOLIVIA	BO
BOSNIA AND HERZEGOVINA	BA
BOTSWANA	BW
BOUVET ISLAND	BV
BRAZIL	BR
BRITISH INDIAN OCEAN TERRITORY	IO
BRUNEI DARUSSALAM	BN
BULGARIA	BG
BURKINA FASO	BF
BURUNDI	BI
CAMBODIA	KH
CAMEROON	CM
CANADA	CA

Country Name	Country Code
CAPE VERDE	CV
CAYMAN ISLANDS	KY
CENTRAL AFRICAN REPUBLIC	CF
CHAD	TD
CHILE	CL
CHINA	CN
CHRISTMAS ISLAND	CX
COCOS (KEELING) ISLANDS	CC
COLOMBIA	CO
COMOROS	KM
CONGO	CG
"CONGO, THE DEMOCRATIC REPUBLIC OF THE"	CD
COOK ISLANDS	CK
COSTA RICA	CR
CÔTE D'IVOIRE	CI
CROATIA	HR
CUBA	CU
CYPRUS	CY
CZECH REPUBLIC	CZ
DENMARK	DK
DJIBOUTI	DJ
DOMINICA	DM
DOMINICAN REPUBLIC	DO
EAST TIMOR	TP
ECUADOR	EC
EGYPT	EG
EL SALVADOR	SV
EQUATORIAL GUINEA	GQ

Country Name	Country Code
ERITREA	ER
ESTONIA	EE
ETHIOPIA	ET
FALKLAND ISLANDS (MALVINAS)	FK
FAROE ISLANDS	FO
FIJI	FJ
FINLAND	FI
FRANCE	FR
FRENCH GUIANA	GF
FRENCH POLYNESIA	PF
FRENCH SOUTHERN TERRITORIES	TF
GABON	GA
GAMBIA	GM
GEORGIA	GE
GERMANY	DE
GHANA	GH
GIBRALTAR	GI
GREECE	GR
GREENLAND	GL
GRENADA	GD
GUADELOUPE	GP
GUAM	GU
GUATEMALA	GT
GUINEA	GN
GUINEA-BISSAU	GW
GUYANA	GY
HAITI	HT
HEARD ISLAND AND MCDONALD ISLANDS	HM

Country Name	Country Code
HOLY SEE (VATICAN CITY STATE)	VA
HONDURAS	HN
HONG KONG	HK
HUNGARY	HU
ICELAND	IS
INDIA	IN
INDONESIA	ID
"IRAN, ISLAMIC REPUBLIC OF"	IR
IRAQ	IQ
IRELAND	IE
ISRAEL	IL
ITALY	IT
JAMAICA	JM
JAPAN	JP
JORDAN	JO
KAZAKSTAN	KZ
KENYA	KE
KIRIBATI	KI
"KOREA, DEMOCRATIC PEOPLE'S REPUBLIC OF"	KP
"KOREA, REPUBLIC OF"	KR
KUWAIT	KW
KYRGYZSTAN	KG
LAO PEOPLE'S DEMOCRATIC REPUBLIC	LA
LATVIA	LV
LEBANON	LB
LESOTHO	LS
LIBERIA	LR
LIBYAN ARAB JAMAHIRIYA	LY

Country Name	Country Code
LIECHTENSTEIN	LI
LITHUANIA	LT
LUXEMBOURG	LU
MACAU	MO
"MACEDONIA, THE FORMER YUGOSLAV REPUBLIC OF"	MK
MADAGASCAR	MG
MALAWI	MW
MALAYSIA	MY
MALDIVES	MV
MALI	ML
MALTA	MT
MARSHALL ISLANDS	MH
MARTINIQUE	MQ
MAURITANIA	MR
MAURITIUS	MU
MAYOTTE	YT
MEXICO	MX
"MICRONESIA, FEDERATED STATES OF"	FM
"MOLDOVA, REPUBLIC OF"	MD
MONACO	MC
MONGOLIA	MN
MONTSERRAT	MS
MOROCCO	MA
MOZAMBIQUE	MZ
MYANMAR	MM
NAMIBIA	NA
NAURU	NR
NEPAL	NP

Country Name	Country Code
NETHERLANDS	NL
NETHERLANDS ANTILLES	AN
NEW CALEDONIA	NC
NEW ZEALAND	NZ
NICARAGUA	NI
NIGER	NE
NIGERIA	NG
NIUE	NU
NORFOLK ISLAND	NF
NORTHERN MARIANA ISLANDS	MP
NORWAY	NO
OMAN	OM
PAKISTAN	PK
PALAU	PW
"PALESTINIAN TERRITORY, OCCUPIED"	PS
PANAMA	PA
PAPUA NEW GUINEA	PG
PARAGUAY	PY
PERU	PE
PHILIPPINES	PH
PITCAIRN	PN
POLAND	PL
PORTUGAL	PT
PUERTO RICO	PR
QATAR	QA
RÉUNION	RE
ROMANIA	RO
RUSSIAN FEDERATION	RU

Country Name	Country Code
RWANDA	RW
SAINT HELENA	SH
SAINT KITTS AND NEVIS	KN
SAINT LUCIA	LC
SAINT PIERRE AND MIQUELON	PM
SAINT VINCENT AND THE GRENADINES	VC
SAMOA	WS
SAN MARINO	SM
SAO TOME AND PRINCIPE	ST
SAUDI ARABIA	SA
SENEGAL	SN
SEYCHELLES	SC
SIERRA LEONE	SL
SINGAPORE	SG
SLOVAKIA	SK
SLOVENIA	SI
SOLOMON ISLANDS	SB
SOMALIA	SO
SOUTH AFRICA	ZA
SOUTH GEORGIA AND THE SOUTH SANDWICH ISLANDS	GS
SPAIN	ES
SRI LANKA	LK
SUDAN	SD
SURINAME	SR
SVALBARD AND JAN MAYEN	SJ
SWAZILAND	SZ
SWEDEN	SE
SWITZERLAND	CH

Country Name	Country Code
SYRIAN ARAB REPUBLIC	SY
"TAIWAN, PROVINCE OF CHINA"	TW
TAJIKISTAN	TJ
"TANZANIA, UNITED REPUBLIC OF"	TZ
THAILAND	TH
TOGO	TG
TOKELAU	TK
TONGA	TO
TRINIDAD AND TOBAGO	TT
TUNISIA	TN
TURKEY	TR
TURKMENISTAN	TM
TURKS AND CAICOS ISLANDS	TC
TUVALU	TV
UGANDA	UG
UKRAINE	UA
UNITED ARAB EMIRATES	AE
UNITED KINGDOM	GB
UNITED STATES	US
UNITED STATES MINOR OUTLYING ISLANDS	UM
URUGUAY	UY
UZBEKISTAN	UZ
VANUATU	VU
Vatican City State see HOLY SEE	
VENEZUELA	VE
VIETNAM	VN
"VIRGIN ISLANDS, BRITISH"	VG
"VIRGIN ISLANDS, U.S."	VI

Country Name	Country Code
WALLIS AND FUTUNA	WF
WESTERN SAHARA	EH
YEMEN	YE
YUGOSLAVIA	YU
"Zaire see CONGO, THE DEMOCRATIC REPUBLIC OF THE"	
ZAMBIA	ZM
ZIMBABWE	ZW

APPENDIX 3

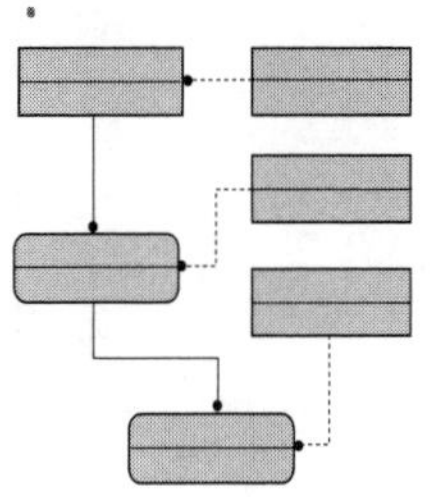

Distinguishing Signs of Vehicles in International Traffic

THIS TABLE IS TAKEN from the information provided by the International Telecommunication Union (ITU). More information, and more current information, can be found on the ITU's Web site at *www.itu.int//itudoc/un/editrans/unedipro/dissig.html.*

Country	Country Code
Albania	AL
Alderney	GBA
Algeria	DZ
Andorra	AND
Argentina	RA
Australia	AUS
Austria	A
Bahamas	BS
Bahrain	BRN
Bangladesh	BD

Country	Country Code
Barbados	BDS
Belarus	[SU] */
Belgium	B
Benin	DY
Bosnia and Herzegovina	BIH
Botswana	RB
Brazil	BR
British Honduras	BH
Brunei	BRU
Bulgaria	BG
Cambodia	K
Canada	CDN
Central African Republic	RCA
Chile	RCH
China	RC
Congo	RCB
Costa Rica	CR
Côte d'Ivoire	CI
Croatia	HR
Cyprus	CY
Czech Republic	CZ
Denmark	DK
Dominican Republic	DOM
Ecuador	EC
Egypt	ET
Estonia	EST
Faroe Islands	FO
Fiji	FJI

Country	Country Code
Finland	FIN
France	F
Gambia	WAG
Georgia	GE
Germany	D
Ghana	GH
Gibraltar	GBZ
Greece	GR
Grenada	WG
Guatemala	GCA
Guernsey	GBG
Guyana	GUY
Haiti	RH
Holy See	V
Hong Kong	HK
Hungary	H
Iceland	IS
Indonesia	RI
India	IND
Iran (Islamic Republic of)	IR
Ireland	IRL
Isle of Man	GBM
Israel	IL
Italy	I
Jamaica	JA
Japan	J
Jersey	GBJ
Jordan	HKJ

Country	Country Code
Kazakstan	KZ
Kenya	EAK
Kuwait	KWT
Kyrgyzstan	KS
Lao People's Democratic Republic	LAO
Latvia	LV
Lebanon	RL
Lesotho	LS
Lithuania	LT
Luxembourg	L
Madagascar	RM
Malawi	MW
Malaysia	MAL
Mali	RMM
Malta	M
Mauritius	MS
Mexico	MEX
Monaco	MC
Morocco	MA
Myanmar	BUR
Namibia	NAM
Netherlands	NL
Netherlands Antilles	NA
Surinam	SME
New Zealand	NZ
Nicaragua	NIC
Nigeria	WAN
Niger	RN

Country	Country Code
Norway	N
Pakistan	PK
Papua New Guinea	PNG
Paraguay	PY
Peru	PE
Philippines	RP
Poland	PL
Portugal	P
Republic of Korea	ROK
Romania	RO
Russian Federation	RUS
Rwanda	RWA
Samoa	WS
San Marino	RSM
Senegal	SN
Seychelles	SY
Sierra Leone	WAL
Singapore	SGP
Slovakia	SK
Slovenia	SLO
South Africa	ZA
Spain (including African localities and provinces)	E
Sri Lanka	CL
St. Lucia	WL
St. Vincent	WV
Swaziland	SD
Sweden	S
Switzerland	CH

Country	Country Code
Syrian Arab Republic	SYR
Tajikistan	TJ
Thailand	T
The former Yugoslav Republic of Macedonia	MK
Togo	TG
Trinidad and Tobago	TT
Tunisia	TN
Turkey	TR
Turkmenistan	TM
Uganda	EAU
Ukraine	UA
United Kingdom	GB
United Republic of Tanzania	EAT
United States of America	USA
Uruguay	ROU
Uzbekistan	UZ
Venezuela	YV
Yugoslavia	YU
Zaire	ZRE
Zambia	RNR
Zanzibar	EAZ
Zimbabwe	ZW

*/ Belarus has not yet provided its new distinguishing sign; therefore the sign "SU" still appears on this list. "SU" stands for "Soviet Union."

APPENDIX 4

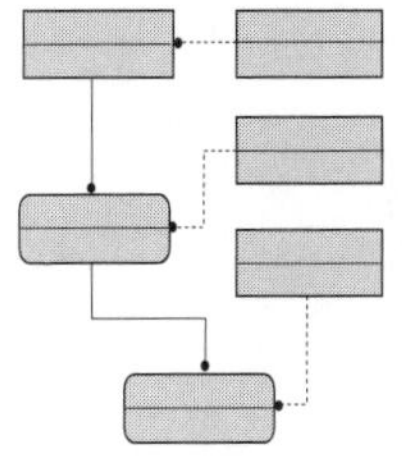

Crosswalk Table for ISO 3166 Country Codes and Distinguishing Signs of Vehicles in International Traffic

THIS TABLE HAS BEEN CONSTRUCTED from the information in Appendices 2 and 3. It is *not* a standard of any kind. Instead it illustrates how a crosswalk table can be constructed to map values in one international standard to another.

A missing value in the column "Vehicle Sign Code" means there is no corresponding value in the standard for Distinguishing Signs of Vehicles in International Traffic.

ISO 3166 Country Name	ISO 3166 Country Code	Vehicle Sign Code
AFGHANISTAN	AF	
ALBANIA	AL	AL
ALGERIA	DZ	DZ
AMERICAN SAMOA	AS	
ANDORRA	AD	AND
ANGOLA	AO	

ISO 3166 Country Name	ISO 3166 Country Code	Vehicle Sign Code
ANGUILLA	AI	
ANTARCTICA	AQ	
ANTIGUA AND BARBUDA	AG	
ARGENTINA	AR	RA
ARMENIA	AM	
ARUBA	AW	
AUSTRALIA	AU	AUS
AUSTRIA	AT	A
AZERBAIJAN	AZ	
BAHAMAS	BS	BS
BAHRAIN	BH	BRN
BANGLADESH	BD	BD
BARBADOS	BB	BDS
BELARUS	BY	SU
BELGIUM	BE	B
BELIZE	BZ	
BENIN	BJ	DY
BERMUDA	BM	
BHUTAN	BT	
BOLIVIA	BO	
BOSNIA AND HERZEGOVINA	BA	BIH
BOTSWANA	BW	RB
BOUVET ISLAND	BV	
BRAZIL	BR	BR
BRITISH INDIAN OCEAN TERRITORY	IO	
BRUNEI DARUSSALAM	BN	BRU

ISO 3166 Country Name	ISO 3166 Country Code	Vehicle Sign Code
BULGARIA	BG	BG
BURKINA FASO	BF	
BURUNDI	BI	
CAMBODIA	KH	K
CAMEROON	CM	
CANADA	CA	CDN
CAPE VERDE	CV	
CAYMAN ISLANDS	KY	
CENTRAL AFRICAN REPUBLIC	CF	RCA
CHAD	TD	
CHILE	CL	RCH
CHINA	CN	
CHRISTMAS ISLAND	CX	
COCOS (KEELING) ISLANDS	CC	
COLOMBIA	CO	
COMOROS	KM	
CONGO	CG	RCB
"CONGO, THE DEMOCRATIC REPUBLIC OF THE"	CD	
COOK ISLANDS	CK	
COSTA RICA	CR	CR
CÔTE D'IVOIRE	CI	CI
CROATIA	HR	HR
CUBA	CU	
CYPRUS	CY	CY
CZECH REPUBLIC	CZ	CZ

ISO 3166 Country Name	ISO 3166 Country Code	Vehicle Sign Code
DENMARK	DK	DK
DJIBOUTI	DJ	
DOMINICA	DM	
DOMINICAN REPUBLIC	DO	DOM
EAST TIMOR	TP	
ECUADOR	EC	EC
EGYPT	EG	ET
EL SALVADOR	SV	
EQUATORIAL GUINEA	GQ	
ERITREA	ER	
ESTONIA	EE	EST
ETHIOPIA	ET	
FALKLAND ISLANDS (MALVINAS)	FK	
FAROE ISLANDS	FO	FO
FIJI	FJ	FJI
FINLAND	FI	FIN
FRANCE	FR	F
FRENCH GUIANA	GF	
FRENCH POLYNESIA	PF	
FRENCH SOUTHERN TERRITORIES	TF	
GABON	GA	
GAMBIA	GM	WAG
GEORGIA	GE	GE
GERMANY	DE	D
GHANA	GH	GH
GIBRALTAR	GI	GBZ

ISO 3166 Country Name	ISO 3166 Country Code	Vehicle Sign Code
GREECE	GR	GR
GREENLAND	GL	
GRENADA	GD	WG
GUADELOUPE	GP	
GUAM	GU	
GUATEMALA	GT	GCA
GUINEA	GN	
GUINEA-BISSAU	GW	
GUYANA	GY	GUY
HAITI	HT	RH
HEARD ISLAND AND MCDONALD ISLANDS	HM	
HOLY SEE (VATICAN CITY STATE)	VA	V
HONDURAS	HN	
HONG KONG	HK	HK
HUNGARY	HU	H
ICELAND	IS	IS
INDIA	IN	IND
INDONESIA	ID	RI
"IRAN, ISLAMIC REPUBLIC OF"	IR	IR
IRAQ	IQ	
IRELAND	IE	IRL
ISRAEL	IL	IL
ITALY	IT	I
JAMAICA	JM	JA
JAPAN	JP	J

ISO 3166 Country Name	ISO 3166 Country Code	Vehicle Sign Code
JORDAN	JO	HKJ
KAZAKSTAN	KZ	KZ
KENYA	KE	EAK
KIRIBATI	KI	
"KOREA, DEMOCRATIC PEOPLE'S REPUBLIC OF"	KP	
"KOREA, REPUBLIC OF"	KR	ROK
KUWAIT	KW	KWT
KYRGYZSTAN	KG	KS
LAO PEOPLE'S DEMOCRATIC REPUBLIC	LA	LAO
LATVIA	LV	LV
LEBANON	LB	RL
LESOTHO	LS	LS
LIBERIA	LR	
LIBYAN ARAB JAMAHIRIYA	LY	
LIECHTENSTEIN	LI	
LITHUANIA	LT	LT
LUXEMBOURG	LU	L
MACAU	MO	
"MACEDONIA, THE FORMER YUGOSLAV REPUBLIC OF"	MK	MK
MADAGASCAR	MG	RM
MALAWI	MW	MW
MALAYSIA	MY	MAL
MALDIVES	MV	
MALI	ML	RMM
MALTA	MT	M

ISO 3166 Country Name	ISO 3166 Country Code	Vehicle Sign Code
MARSHALL ISLANDS	MH	
MARTINIQUE	MQ	
MAURITANIA	MR	
MAURITIUS	MU	MS
MAYOTTE	YT	
MEXICO	MX	MEX
"MICRONESIA, FEDERATED STATES OF"	FM	
"MOLDOVA, REPUBLIC OF"	MD	
MONACO	MC	MC
MONGOLIA	MN	
MONTSERRAT	MS	
MOROCCO	MA	MA
MOZAMBIQUE	MZ	
MYANMAR	MM	BUR
NAMIBIA	NA	NAM
NAURU	NR	
NEPAL	NP	
NETHERLANDS	NL	NL
NETHERLANDS ANTILLES	AN	NA
NEW CALEDONIA	NC	
NEW ZEALAND	NZ	NZ
NICARAGUA	NI	NIC
NIGER	NE	RN
NIGERIA	NG	WAN
NIUE	NU	
NORFOLK ISLAND	NF	

ISO 3166 Country Name	ISO 3166 Country Code	Vehicle Sign Code
NORTHERN MARIANA ISLANDS	MP	
NORWAY	NO	N
OMAN	OM	
PAKISTAN	PK	PK
PALAU	PW	
"PALESTINIAN TERRITORY, OCCUPIED"	PS	
PANAMA	PA	
PAPUA NEW GUINEA	PG	PNG
PARAGUAY	PY	PY
PERU	PE	PE
PHILIPPINES	PH	RP
PITCAIRN	PN	
POLAND	PL	PL
PORTUGAL	PT	P
PUERTO RICO	PR	
QATAR	QA	
RÉUNION	RE	
ROMANIA	RO	RO
RUSSIAN FEDERATION	RU	RUS
RWANDA	RW	RWA
SAINT HELENA	SH	
SAINT KITTS AND NEVIS	KN	
SAINT LUCIA	LC	WL
SAINT PIERRE AND MIQUELON	PM	
SAINT VINCENT AND THE GRENADINES	VC	WV

ISO 3166 Country Name	ISO 3166 Country Code	Vehicle Sign Code
SAMOA	WS	WS
SAN MARINO	SM	RSM
SAO TOME AND PRINCIPE	ST	
SAUDI ARABIA	SA	
SENEGAL	SN	SN
SEYCHELLES	SC	SY
SIERRA LEONE	SL	WAL
SINGAPORE	SG	SGP
SLOVAKIA	SK	SK
SLOVENIA	SI	SLO
SOLOMON ISLANDS	SB	
SOMALIA	SO	
SOUTH AFRICA	ZA	ZA
SOUTH GEORGIA AND THE SOUTH SANDWICH ISLANDS	GS	
SPAIN	ES	E
SRI LANKA	LK	CL
SUDAN	SD	
SURINAME	SR	SME
SVALBARD AND JAN MAYEN	SJ	
SWAZILAND	SZ	SD
SWEDEN	SE	S
SWITZERLAND	CH	CH
SYRIAN ARAB REPUBLIC	SY	SYR
"TAIWAN, PROVINCE OF CHINA"	TW	
TAJIKISTAN	TJ	TJ

ISO 3166 Country Name	ISO 3166 Country Code	Vehicle Sign Code
"TANZANIA, UNITED REPUBLIC OF"	TZ	EAT
THAILAND	TH	T
TOGO	TG	TG
TOKELAU	TK	
TONGA	TO	
TRINIDAD AND TOBAGO	TT	TT
TUNISIA	TN	TN
TURKEY	TR	TR
TURKMENISTAN	TM	TM
TURKS AND CAICOS ISLANDS	TC	
TUVALU	TV	
UGANDA	UG	EAU
UKRAINE	UA	UA
UNITED ARAB EMIRATES	AE	
UNITED KINGDOM	GB	GB
UNITED STATES	US	USA
UNITED STATES MINOR OUTLYING ISLANDS	UM	
URUGUAY	UY	ROU
UZBEKISTAN	UZ	UZ
VANUATU	VU	
Vatican City State see HOLY SEE		
VENEZUELA	VE	YV
VIETNAM	VN	
"VIRGIN ISLANDS, BRITISH"	VG	
"VIRGIN ISLANDS, U.S."	VI	

ISO 3166 Country Name	ISO 3166 Country Code	Vehicle Sign Code
WALLIS AND FUTUNA	WF	
WESTERN SAHARA	EH	
YEMEN	YE	
YUGOSLAVIA	YU	YU
"Zaire see CONGO, THE DEMOCRATIC REPUBLIC OF THE"		ZRE
ZAMBIA	ZM	RNR
ZIMBABWE	ZW	ZW

Note: The following entries appear in the standard for Distinguishing Signs of Vehicles in International Traffic but have no equivalent in ISO 3166:

Alderney

British Honduras

Guernsey

Isle of Man

Jersey

Zanzibar

APPENDIX 5

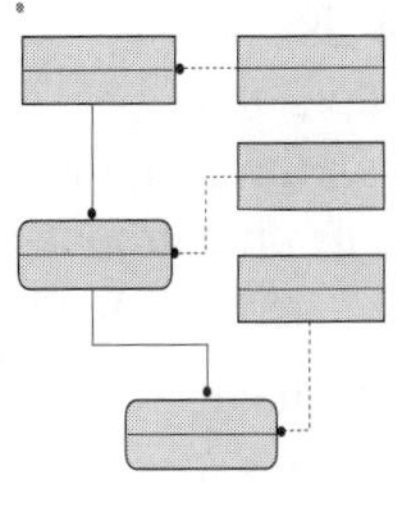

Standard and Poor's Long-Term Issue Credit Ratings

THE FOLLOWING INFORMATION is reprinted, with permission, from Standard and Poor's Web site at *www.standardandpoors.com/ratings/corporates/index.htm.*

Plus (+) or minus(-): The ratings from AA to CCC may be modified by the addition of a plus or minus sign to show relative standing within the major rating categories.

Rating	Definition
AAA	An obligation rated 'AAA' has the highest rating assigned by Standard & Poor's. The obligor's capacity to meet its financial commitment on the obligation is extremely strong.
AA	An obligation rated 'AA' differs from the highest rated obligations only in small degree. The obligor's capacity to meet its financial commitment on the obligation is very strong.

Rating	Definition
A	An obligation rated 'A' is somewhat more susceptible to the adverse effects of changes in circumstances and economic conditions than obligations in higher-rated categories. However, the obligor's capacity to meet its financial commitment on the obligation is still strong.
BBB	An obligation rated 'BBB' exhibits adequate protection parameters. However, adverse economic conditions or changing circumstances are more likely to lead to a weakened capacity of the obligor to meet its financial commitment on the obligation. Obligations rated 'BB', 'B', 'CCC', 'CC', and 'C' are regarded as having significant speculative characteristics. 'BB' indicates the least degree of speculation and 'C' the highest. While such obligations will likely have some quality and protective characteristics, these may be outweighed by large uncertainties or major exposures to adverse conditions.
BB	An obligation rated 'BB' is less vulnerable to nonpayment than other speculative issues. However, it faces major ongoing uncertainties or exposure to adverse business, financial, or economic conditions which could lead to the obligor's inadequate capacity to meet its financial commitment on the obligation.
B	An obligation rated 'B' is more vulnerable to nonpayment than obligations rated 'BB', but the obligor currently has the capacity to meet its financial commitment on the obligation. Adverse business, financial, or economic conditions will likely impair the obligor's capacity or willingness to meet its financial commitment on the obligation.

Rating	Definition
CCC	An obligation rated 'CCC' is currently vulnerable to nonpayment and is dependent upon favorable business, financial, and economic conditions for the obligor to meet its financial commitment on the obligation. In the event of adverse business, financial, or economic conditions, the obligor is not likely to have the capacity to meet its financial commitment on the obligation
CC	An obligation rated 'CC' is currently highly vulnerable to nonpayment.
C	A subordinated debt or preferred stock obligation rated 'C' is CURRENTLY HIGHLY VULNERABLE to nonpayment. The 'C' rating may be used to cover a situation where a bankruptcy petition has been filed or similar action taken, but payments on this obligation are being continued. A 'C' also will be assigned to a preferred stock issue in arrears on dividends or sinking fund payments, but that is currently paying.
D	An obligation rated 'D' is in payment default. The 'D' rating category is used when payments on an obligation are not made on the date due even if the applicable grace period has not expired, unless Standard & Poor's believes that such payments will be made during such grace period. The 'D' rating also will be used upon the filing of a bankruptcy petition or the taking of a similar action if payments on an obligation are jeopardized. Plus (+) or minus (-): The ratings from 'AA' to 'CCC' may be modified by the addition of a plus or minus sign to show relative standing within the major rating categories.

Rating	Definition
r	This symbol is attached to the ratings of instruments with significant noncredit risks. It highlights risks to principal or volatility of expected returns which are not addressed in the credit rating. Examples include: obligations linked or indexed to equities, currencies, or commodities; obligations exposed to severe prepayment risk–such as interest-only or principal-only mortgage securities; and obligations with unusually risky interest terms, such as inverse floaters.
N.R.	This indicates that no rating has been requested, that there is insufficient information on which to base a rating, or that Standard & Poor's does not rate a particular obligation as a matter of policy.

APPENDIX 6

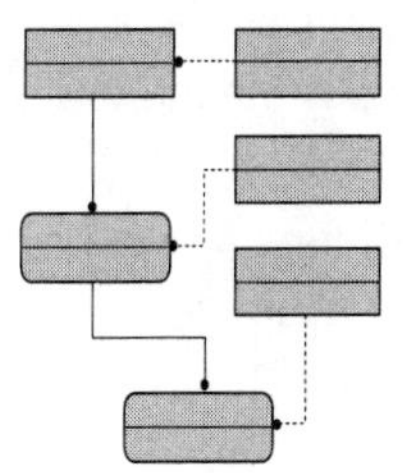

Standard and Poor's Long-Term Issuer Credit Ratings

THE FOLLOWING INFORMATION is reprinted, with permission from Standard and Poor's Web site at *www.standardandpoors.com/ratings/corporates/index.htm.*

Ratings from 'AA' to 'CCC' may be modified by the addition of a plus or minus sign to show relative standing within the major rating categories.

Ratings with a "pi" subscript are based on an analysis of an issuer's published financial information, as well as additional information in the public domain. They do not, however, reflect in-depth meetings with an issuer's management and are therefore based on less comprehensive information than ratings without a pi subscript. Ratings with a pi subscript are reviewed annually based on a new year's financial statements, but may be reviewed on an interim basis if a major event that may affect an issuer's credit quality occurs. Ratings with a pi subscript are not modified with + or – designations. Outlooks are not provided for ratings with a pi subscript, nor are they subject to potential CreditWatch listings.

Rating	Definition
AAA	An obligor rated 'AAA' has EXTREMELY STRONG capacity to meet its financial commitments. 'AAA' is the highest Issuer Credit Rating assigned by Standard & Poor's.
AA	An obligor rated 'AA' has VERY STRONG capacity to meet its financial commitments. It differs from the highest rated obligors only in small degree.
A	An obligor rated 'A' has STRONG capacity to meet its financial commitments but is somewhat more susceptible to the adverse effects of changes in circumstances and economic conditions than obligors in higher-rated categories.
BBB	An obligor rated 'BBB' has ADEQUATE capacity to meet its financial commitments. However, adverse economic conditions or changing circumstances are more likely to lead to a weakened capacity of the obligor to meet its financial commitments.
	Obligors rated 'BB', 'B', 'CCC', and 'CC' are regarded as having significant speculative characteristics. 'BB' indicates the least degree of speculation and 'CC' the highest. While such obligors will likely have some quality and protective characteristics, these may be outweighed by large uncertainties or major exposures to adverse conditions.
BB	An obligor rated 'BB' is LESS VULNERABLE in the near term than other lower-rated obligors. However, it faces major ongoing uncertainties and exposure to adverse business, financial, or economic conditions which could lead to the obligor's inadequate capacity to meet its financial commitments.
B	An obligor rated 'B' is MORE VULNERABLE than the obligors rated 'BB', but the obligor currently has the capacity to meet its financial commitments. Adverse business, financial, or economic conditions will likely impair the obligor's capacity or willingness to meet its financial commitments.

Rating	Definition
CCC	An obligor rated 'CCC' is CURRENTLY VULNERABLE and is dependent upon favorable business, financial, and economic conditions to meet its financial commitments.
CC	An obligor rated 'CC' is CURRENTLY HIGHLY VULNERABLE.
R	An obligor rated 'R' is under regulatory supervision owing to its financial condition. During the pendency of the regulatory supervision the regulators may have the power to favor one class of obligations over others or pay some obligations and not others. Please see Standard & Poor's issue credit ratings for a more detailed description of the effects of regulatory supervision on specific issues or classes of obligations.
SD	An obligor rated 'SD' (Selective Default) or 'D' has failed to pay one or more of its financial obligations (rated or unrated) when it came due. An 'SD' rating is assigned when Standard & Poor's believes that the obligor has selectively defaulted on a specific issue or class of obligations but it will continue to meet its payment obligations on other issues or classes of obligations in a timely manner.
D	An obligor rated 'SD' (Selective Default) or 'D' has failed to pay one or more of its financial obligations (rated or unrated) when it came due. A 'D' rating is assigned when Standard & Poor's believes that the default will be a general default and that the obligor will fail to pay all or substantially all of its obligations as they come due.
N.R.	An issuer designated N.R. is not rated.

APPENDIX 7

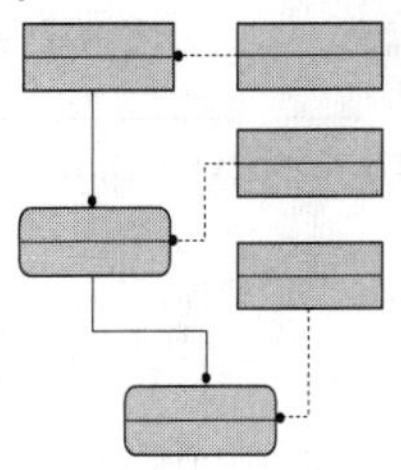

Matrices for Evaluating Reference Data Management within an Enterprise

LISTED BELOW ARE SEVERAL MATRICES for evaluating how well reference data is managed within an enterprise. Each consists of a set of questions, and each question has a Yes/No (Y/N) answer.

Some matrices have questions that are independent. These have letters (A, B, C, . . .) as question numbers. In these matrices all questions should be answered sequentially.

Other matrices have related questions. These have numbers (1, 2, 3, . . .) as question numbers. With related questions, an answer to one question will either result in an observation or a direction to go to another question.

Table A7.1 Criteria for assessing an enterprise's reference data strategy.

No.	Question	Ans.	Go to Question / Observation
	Section 1: Enterprise Level		
A	Does the enterprise recognize reference data as a separate class of data that needs to be managed in a distinct manner?	Y	The enterprise has, or is willing to develop, a strategy for reference data.
		N	The enterprise has no strategy for reference data.
B	Does the enterprise have a central reference database or repository?	Y	The enterprise has the first key element for implementing a reference data strategy.
		N	The enterprise is unlikely to be able to successfully implement a reference data strategy.
C	Does the enterprise have a clearly identified group responsible for updating/ managing the central reference database?	Y	The enterprise has the second key element for implementing a reference data strategy.
		N	The enterprise is unlikely to be able to successfully implement a reference data strategy.
	Section 2: For Each System in the Enterprise		
1	Does the system's database have its own reference data tables versus accessing a central reference data repository?	Y	2
		N	The system accesses a central reference database and is insulated against having reference data that differs from the corporate standard.

No.	Question	Ans.	Go to Question / Observation
2	Does the system have its own independent way of updating its reference data tables versus importing/synchronizing data with a central reference data repository?	Y	These reference data tables may be designed differently from the corporate standard and may contain data values differing from the corporate standard.
		N	Data is imported/synchronized with the central reference data repository. Thus there is a much reduced risk that these reference data tables are designed differently from the corporate standard and contain data values differing from the corporate standard. This also depends on the "intelligence" built into the interface.
	Section 3: Metadata across the Enterprise		
A	Does the enterprise have a strategy for managing metadata?	Y	The enterprise is in a position to manage reference data effectively.
		N	The enterprise will not be able to manage reference data effectively.
B	Does the organization have a mechanism for publishing metadata?	Y	Business users and developers are in a position to use reference data effectively.
		N	Business users and developers will not be able to use reference data effectively.
C	Does the organization recognize that metadata exists at the record level for reference data tables with codes and descriptions?	Y	Business users and developers are in a better position to use reference data effectively.
		N	Business users and developers will not be able to use reference data effectively.

No.	Question	Ans.	Go to Question / Observation
D	Does the organization record and publish business rules?	Y	Business users and developers are in a better position to use certain types of reference data effectively (particularly status codes and constant values).
		N	Business users and developers will not be able to use all types reference data effectively (particularly status codes and constant values).

Table A7.2 How to decide if a database table is a reference data table.

No.	Question	Ans.	Go to Question / Observation
1	Does the table have a coded value as part of the primary key?	Y	2
		N	6
2	Does the table consist of a single key field and a single non-key field that is a descriptive text? Descriptive text should be a name of an instance of the entity represented by the table.	Y	Table is a reference data table.
		N	3
3	Does the table have a primary key consisting of a coded value and an effective date, and a single non-key field that is a descriptive text? Descriptive text should be a name of an instance of the entity represented by the table.	Y	Table is a reference data table.
		N	4

No.	Question	Ans.	Go to Question / Observation
4	Is the coded value an "intelligent key" consisting of a concatenation of different pieces of information?	Y	Table is probably used to record transaction structure or activity, and not reference data.
		N	5
5	Does the table have a primary key consisting of a coded value from a known reference table and an effective date, and one or more non-key fields that are dates and quantities? Table contains no non-key field that is a descriptive text.	Y	Table is a reference data table for holding constant values.
		N	6
6	Are there a lot of non-key attributes that are not foreign keys of other reference data tables? These should not be computed or derived attributes, but ones that are data entered.	Y	Table is probably used to record transaction structure or activity, and not reference data.
		N	7
7	Does the key consist only of an effective date?	Y	This is probably a reference data table holding global constants.
		N	8
8	Is there only one record in the table?	Y	This is probably a reference data table holding global constants.
		N	Not possible to determine nature of table, but probably not a reference data table.

Table A7.3 Criteria for assessing life cycle management in a reference data table.

No.	Question	Ans.	Go to Question / Observation
1	Does the enterprise consider all reference data to be current, without life-cycle management?	Y	2
		N	There is no life-cycle management for the reference data table under consideration.
2	Does the reference data table have an effective date?	Y	3
		N	Problem: Only current values can be recorded in the table.
3	Does the reference data table hold constant values?	Y	4
		N	5
4	Is the effective date part of the primary key?	Y	Constant values can be updated gracefully over time.
		N	Problem: Only one version of constant values can be held. If updated, it may be impossible to reconstruct calculated values in transaction data that used old constant values.
5	Do transactions have a reference date that can be used to obtain a correct version of the reference data?	Y	7
		N	6
6	Does program logic use a default reference date to obtain a correct version of the reference data?	Y	7
		N	Problem: Transactions may not be able to distinguish among different versions of reference data.

No.	Question	Ans.	Go to Question / Observation
7	Does program logic actually have rules implemented to match transaction reference dates to reference data effective dates?	Y	Life-cycle management should be successful for the table under consideration.
		N	Problem: Transactions may not be able to distinguish between different versions of reference data.

Note: for this table "effective date" can include effective date, time, and time zone. "Versions" refers to the way in which succession of code values occurs.

Table A7.4 Criteria for examining columns in a non-reference data database table.

No.	Question	Ans.	Go to Question / Observation
1	Does column contain codes?	Y	2
		N	10
2	Is column a foreign key?	Y	3
		N	Problem: There is no parent reference data table for the code values in this column. Look for them hard-coded in programs, screens, and reports.
3	Is column a type code?	Y	4
		N	6
4	Is column a record type?	Y	Possible problem: Strong indication that two or more tables (perhaps not even closely related tables) are merged into the current one.
		N	5

No.	Question	Ans.	Go to Question / Observation
5	Do the type code values each identify a different subtype table?	Y	Type codes are well implemented
		N	Possible problem: There must be two or more subtype tables merged into the table under review.
6	Is column a status code?	Y	7
		N	9
7	Is there a date associated with each status value?	Y	8
		N	Possible problem: Possibly only the latest status is recorded. May be impossible to derive status as of a prior date.
8	Are business rules to derive status recorded?	Y	Status codes are well implemented.
		N	Possible problem: Status code may be inconsistently updated as there are different views of how it is derived.
9	Is column a code representing a classification scheme?	Y	Code represents a classification scheme.
		N	Code usually represents an entity external to the enterprise (e.g., Country, Currency).
10	Is column an indicator (flag)?	Y	11
		N	Column is not associated with reference data.
11	Does column represent presence and absence of a character (this is not the same thing as two different states)?	Y	Column truly functions as an indicator.
		N	Column may really be used to contain reference data, and may need to have a parent reference data table.

Table A7.5 Criteria for assessing metadata for a reference data table.

No.	Question	Ans.	Go to Question / Observation
1	Does the reference data table have a definition?	Y	2
		N	Problem: A clear definition is needed.
2	Does each column in the reference data table have a clear definition?	Y	3
		N	Problem: A clear definition is needed.
3	Does the reference data table hold codes and descriptions?	Y	4.
		N	END
4	Does each code value (equivalent to each record) have a clear definition?	Y	5
		N	Possible problem: A clear definition is often needed for individual code values.
5	Is each description (i.e., the value in the description column) clear, unambiguous, and unabbreviated?	Y	6
		N	Possible problem: Users and developers may not be able to understand the meaning of the descriptions.
6	Does the reference data table hold acronyms?	Y	7
		N	END
7	For each record, does the acronym match the description?	Y	END
		N	Problem: Acronyms should correspond to descriptions.

Table A7.6 Criteria for assessing classification schemes.

No.	Question	Ans.	Go to Question / Observation
1	Is classification scheme complete?	Y	2
		N	Problem: Some transactions may not be classifiable using the classification scheme.
2	Are all categories mutually exclusive?	Y	3
		N	Problem: Some categories overlap. It will not be possible to consistently classify transactions.
3	Are there clear, readily available definitions for each category?	Y	Classification scheme is well formed.
		N	Problem: Business users/developers will not know how to consistently categorize transactions.

Table A7.7 Criteria for assessing management of reference data during a systems development project.

No.	Question	Ans.	Go to Question / Observation
A	Is there one or more persons clearly identified as responsible for the management of reference data?	Y	This will make it much easier for the rest of the project team to use reference data correctly.
		N	Problem: Project team members may start to create their own reference data independently and use it inconsistently.
B	Are production reference data values recorded when known?	Y	This will make it much easier to manage the initial production implementation.
		N	Problem: Values may be lost or reinvented independently multiple times.

No.	Question	Ans.	Go to Question / Observation
C	Is there some kind of central repository for recording production reference data values as they become known?	Y	Such a repository makes it easier to manage the initial production implementation.
		N	If the values are only recorded on paper or in some unstructured document, more work may be needed to manage the initial production implementation.
D	Are test reference data values clearly distinguished from production values?	Y	This will make it much easier to manage the initial production implementation.
		N	Problem: Errors may arise if test and production data are intermingled in the initial production load.
E	Is there a strategy for loading an initial set of production values when the system goes live?	Y	This will make it much easier to perform the initial production implementation.
		N	Potential problem: Postponing too many tasks to production implementation may make it a nightmare, particularly if it has to be repeated.

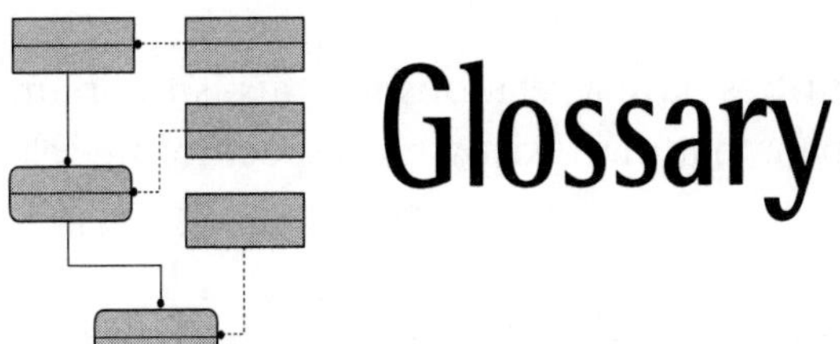

Glossary

Acronym An abbreviation formed from the first (or first few) letters of a series of words (or their syllables), such as LIBOR—**L**ondon **I**nter**b**ank **O**ffered **R**ate.

Attribute A fact about an entity. Also known as a property or characteristic of an entity. It has the same definition and representation for all instances (occurrences) of the entity.

Bucket A commonly used term to describe a column in a database whose definition is user-defined, as opposed to having been precisely defined in a data model. The attribute is typically a calculated number. This term is not generally used by data modeling professionals, although it is widely used by business users in the financial sector.

Business rule A single statement that takes data or information that an organization possesses and derives other data or information from it, or uses it to trigger an action.

Business user A person who uses information stored in computerized databases. This term is typically used to refer to those who work outside the information technology area of an organization.

Cardinality When two entities have a relationship, this is the number of each entity in the pair that may exist with respect to the relationship.

CASE Acronym for *computer-aided systems engineering,* meaning computerized applications designed to assist in the creation of computerized applications. CASE can be applied to any stage of the creation of an application, including design, implementation, and testing.

Category discriminator A single attribute of an entity supertype that determines which *entity subtype* a given instance of the supertype belongs to.

Code An attribute that uses special data to represent another attribute. This may be done for reasons such as to abbreviate long values, increase consistency of data, or encrypt data.

Code value A unique item (actual value) of data in an attribute that is a code.

Column In a physically implemented relational database, this is a specific data item belonging to a table. It is the equivalent of an attribute and is also sometimes called a *field.*

Common data Data that is utilized by many information systems of an enterprise and should ideally be shared among them. From the perspective of an individual information system, common data is any data that the system requires but is actively maintained (i.e., created, modified, and deleted) by other information system(s) in the enterprise.

Constant value A type of reference data that is specified outside the enterprise and is a non-key attribute of other reference data. It does not identify an entity, so is never part of a primary key. Examples include tax rates and fiscal year end dates.

Data The stored representation of a fact or facts.

Data analyst Someone who identifies the characteristics of data so that it can be identified, categorized, and properly documented. Relationships within the data are also identified, categorized, and documented. This person often creates data models.

Data mart A collection of data from one or a few specific areas of an enterprise. It is used by a distinct subgroup of business users to support analysis and decisions for one or a few subunits or business functions of the enterprise. It is thus more restricted in scope and utilization than a data warehouse. Like a data warehouse, the data it contains is transformed, cleaned, and reconciled. A data mart also contains software tools and metadata to facilitate the use of the data for its intended purposes.

Data model A representation of data that is found in the real world. A data model identifies data, groups it, record its characteristics, and also captures information about relationships among the data.

Data modeling The process of constructing a data model.

Data ownership The legal title to data stored in a computerized database.

Data steward A person who is responsible for the integrity and proper utilization of a particular set of data, but who does not own that data.

Data stewardship The function of a data steward.

Data warehouse A collection of data from across an enterprise that is used to support enterprise-wide analysis, forecasting, and decision making. The data is transformed, cleansed, and reconciled (particularly in terms of its relationship to time). A data warehouse also contains software tools and metadata that facilitate the use of the data for its intended purposes.

Database A collection of related data.

Database administrator A person responsible for the implementation, performance, security, maintenance, and adequate operation of one or more live databases that contain data of importance to an enterprise.

Database designer Someone who creates a logical and physical design of a database to be implemented to hold data of importance to an enterprise.

Datatype The different ways in which data can be represented in a physically implemented database. Different database products tend to have somewhat different datatypes.

DBA *See* Database administrator.

Denormalize To design a database whose normal form does not reach third normal form, in order to meet other design goals such as increased performance.

Dependent entity In IDEF1X this is a child entity that has an identifying relationship with a parent entity.

Dimension A continuum along which data values are distributed and can therefore be analyzed.

Domain of values The complete set of data values that exist for an attribute.

Enterprise A legal entity that undertakes activities.

Entity Something of importance to an enterprise, for which information exists that needs to be stored to support an enterprise's activities.

Entity subtype In IDEF1X, an entity that is a more specific type of an Entity Supertype in a hierarchy of entities that share common characteristics (attributes).

Entity supertype In IDEF1X, an entity that contains the characteristics (attributes) common to all entities in a hierarchy of entities that share common characteristics.

External data Data that is created outside the enterprise but is imported into the enterprise's information systems.

Field A data item in a record. *See also* Column.

Foreign key Key attribute from a parent entity that is migrated via a relationship into another (child) entity.

Hard-coded data Data values that are defined in program logic. These values are used to populate transaction data tables, rather than getting the values from data tables where they are defined (e.g., reference data tables).

IDEF1X An information modeling technique for designing relational databases. It has its origins in work performed for the U.S. Air Force Program for Integrated Computer Aided Manufacturing (ICAM) which created a set of techniques known as IDEF (ICAM Definition). In 1983, the U.S. Air Force Integrated Information Support System program enhanced the earlier IDEF1 information modeling technique to form IDEF1X (IDEF1 Extended).

Identifier A code used to identify an instance of an entity. It is part or all of the primary key of the entity being identified.

Identifying relationship A relationship in IDEF1X where the primary key of the parent entity becomes part of the primary key of the child entity.

Independent entity An entity in IDEF1X that has no identifying relationship with any parent entity.

Information Data communicated to an intelligence that can interpret the data and potentially alter its behavior as a result.

Information float The period of time between information coming into existence and its capture in a database.

Information quality The degree to which information can be used for the purpose for which it is intended, based on issues such as meaning, correctness, completeness, and timeliness.

Information technology Hardware and software that support the capture, storage, processing, transmission and utilization of information.

Intelligent key A term for a database column that actually consists of a concatenation of other attributes, some of which are codes. Intelligent keys violate the fundamental concept of data modeling that each distinct item of information is represented as a unique attribute.

ISO Short title for International Organization for Standardization, a major international organization responsible for creating and maintaining standards. Located in Geneva, Switzerland.

Knowledge The capacity to use information to infer other information and/or formulate actions based on information received.

Legacy system An information system created with a design that has little in common with other information systems in an enterprise. Because they are designed in a stand-alone manner, legacy systems typically have problems sharing data with other information systems in the enterprise. Legacy systems are usually built with hardware and software that is currently outdated.

Logical database design A database design that represents the data under consideration purely in terms of the data itself. The design should be in at least third normal form.

Metadata Data that helps someone to use other data.

Non-identifying relationship A relationship in IDEF1X in which the primary key of the parent entity becomes part of the non-primary key attributes of the child entity.

Normal form The correct association of attributes with entities to which they belong. In first normal form repeating groups of attributes within entities are placed in other entities. In second normal form, each non-key attribute depends on the entire primary key of the entity. In third normal form, each non-key attribute depends only on the entire primary key of the entity. There are additional higher levels of normal form.

Normalization The process of constructing a logical database design that is at least in third normal form.

Null value The absence of data in a field in a database. This is different from any kind of data value such as zero or blank.

Optionality In a relationship between two entities, the characteristic of whether or not an instance of either entity must exist.

Physical database design The design of a physically implemented database. It may differ from a logical database design for reasons such as a desire to improve performance.

Primary key The attribute or attributes of an entity that identify a unique occurrence of the entity.

Record A collection of related fields in a physically implemented computerized database.

Reference Data Any kind of data used solely to categorize other data found in a database, or solely for relating data in a database to information beyond the boundaries of the enterprise.

Referential integrity The characteristic of data within a database that satisfies the rules laid down in the database design concerning how different tables are related. There can be no inconsistency in data values, cardinality, or optionality across any relationship.

Referential integrity constraint The action(s) to be taken when data in one database table changes to ensure referential integrity with all related tables.

Relational database A computerized database in which data is contained in tables with columns, and in which relationships can exist among these tables.

Relationship The characteristic of two entities having one or more attributes in common. The primary key of the parent entity becomes a foreign key in the child entity.

Row A record in a relational database table.

Sequence number A code value that is a number that is simply incremented as a new row is added to a relational database table.

Standard A documented agreement containing technical specifications or other precise criteria to be used consistently as rules, guidelines, or definitions of characteristics, to ensure that materials, products, processes, and services are fit for their purpose. *See* [ISO00].

Status code An attribute that is a code used for describing the stages in the life cycle of an entity.

Subtype *See* Entity subtype.

Supertype *See* Entity supertype.

Surrogate key An attribute or attributes used to represent the real primary key attribute(s) of an entity. Usually used to improve database performance or ease of navigation.

Table A collection of related attributes (the representation of an entity) in a relational database.

Transaction A unit of work for an activity that an enterprise carries out.

Transaction activity data Data involved in processing a transaction.

Transaction audit data Data that records information about the steps and information content involved in processing a transaction.

Transaction structure data Data about the parties and other entities that interact in a transaction. This information must exist prior to the transaction occurring.

Type code An attribute that is a code used as a category discriminator. Sometimes also used to distinguish between different records in a poorly designed database for processing reasons.

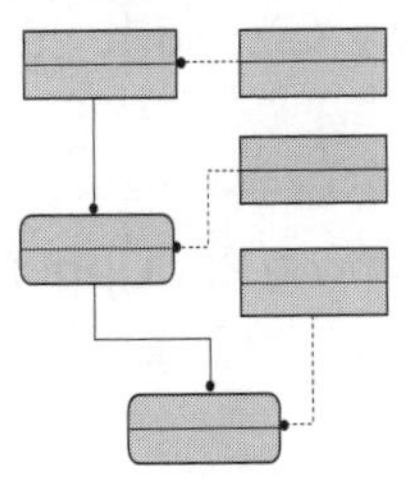

Bibliography

THE FOLLOWING ARE RECOMMENDED for further reading:

Database design: [Fl88]

Using IDEF1X: [Br92]

Data quality issues: [En99]

Building data warehouses: [Ki+98]

The role of reference data in data warehouses: [Br96]

[Br92] Bruce, T. *Designing Quality Databases with IDEF1X Information Models.* New York: Dorset House Publishing, 1992.

[Br96] Brackett, M. *The Data Warehouse Challenge: Taming Data Chaos.* New York: John Wiley & Sons, 1996.

[CA99] Computer Associates. Metadata Management, 1999. *www.cai.com/products/platinum/dw_inmm.htm.*

[Da96] Date, C. J. *An Introduction to Data Base Systems.* 6th ed. Reading: Addison-Wesley Publishing, 1996.

[DC99] DuCharme, B. *XML: The Annotated Specification.* Upper Saddle River: Prentice-Hall, 1999.

[De96] Devlin, B. *Data Warehouse from Architecture to Implementation.* Reading: Addison-Wesley Publishing, 1996.

[En99] English, L. *Improving Data Warehouse and Business Information Quality: Methods for Reducing Costs and Increasing Profits.* New York: John Wiley & Sons, 1999.

[Fl88] Fleming, C., and Von Halle, B. *Handbook of Relational Database Design.* Reading: Addison-Wesley Publishing, 1988.

[Ha99] Hay, D. *Data Model Patterns: Conventions of Thought.* New York: Dorset House Publishing, 1999.

[In96] Inmon, W. H. *Building the Data Warehouse.* New York: John Wiley & Sons, 1996.

[ISO00] International Organization for Standardization, ISO, 2000. *www.iso.ch.*

[ISOb00] ISO 3166. Maintenance Agency, 2000. *www.din.de/gremien/nas/nabd/iso3166ma/index.html.*

[Ki+98] Kimball, R., Reeves, L., et al. *The Data Warehouse Lifecycle Toolkit: Expert Methods for Designing, Developing and Deploying Data Warehouses.* New York: John Wiley & Sons, 1998.

[Li+i97] Litwin, P., Getz, K., et al. *Access 97 Developer's Handbook*, 3rd ed. San Francisco: Sybex, 1997.

[Pla99] Platinum Software. Creating the No Compromise Warehouse. White paper, 1999. *www.cai.com/products/platinum/wp/wp_dbase .htm#1.*

[Plb99] Platinum Software. Managing the Data Warehouse throughout Its Lifecycle. White paper, 1999. *www.cai.com/products/platinum /wp/wp_mngdw.htm.*

[Ro87] Ross, R. *Entity Modeling: Techniques and Application.* Boston: Database Research Group, 1987.

[Ro94] Ross, R. *The Business Rule Book: Classifying, Defining and Modeling Rules.* Boston: Database Research Group, 1994.

[Si97] Simon, A. *Data Warehousing for Dummies: A Reference for the Rest of Us.* Foster City: IDG Books Worldwide, 1997.

[SP00] Standard and Poor's Ratings Criteria, 2000. *www.standardandpoors.com /ratings/criteria/index.htm.*

[Yo+79] Yourdon, E., and Constantine, L. *Structured Design: Fundamentals of a Discipline of Computer Program and Systems Design*, 2nd ed. Englewood Cliffs: Prentice-Hall, 1979.

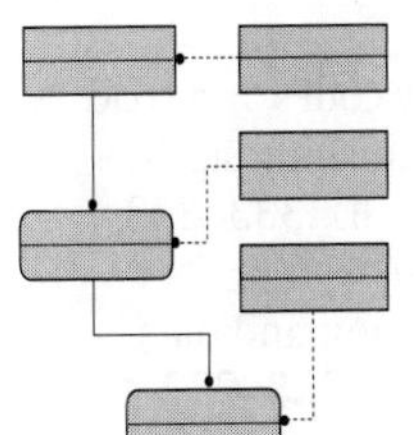

Index

F

G

H

I

About the Author

Malcolm Chisholm has over 20 years of experience in information technology in Britain, the United States, and on assignment in a number of developing countries. He has worked in a variety of enterprises in manufacturing, insurance, banking, accounting and the public sector. Most of this time has been spent in systems development and data administration, and in recent years he has worked with a number of major organizations including the United Nations Development Programme and Deloitte and Touche. A particular focus of his work has been to extract metadata from data models and use it to automate the generation of systems components.

Dr. Chisholm holds an M.A. degree from the University of Oxford, England, and a Ph.D. from the University of Bristol, England, both in zoology. In addition to his IT work, he assists his wife in running their coffee plantation in Central America.

Dr. Chisholm can be contacted at *mchisholm@refdataportal.com*